S0-AEO-789

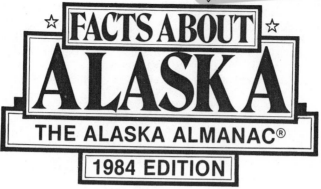

FACTS ABOUT ALASKA
THE ALASKA ALMANAC®
1984 EDITION

From the editors of ALASKA® magazine, The MILEPOST®, ALASKA GEOGRAPHIC®, and The ALASKA JOURNAL®

ALASKA NORTHWEST PUBLISHING COMPANY
Anchorage, Alaska

FACTS ABOUT ALASKA, THE ALASKA ALMANAC® is enlarged upon and updated annually. While this eighth edition contains more information than the earlier editions, we continue to seek suggestions for expanding the scope of information that is provided about Alaska.
Please send any changes, additions or suggestions to:
THE ALASKA ALMANAC®
Alaska Northwest Publishing Company
Box 4-EEE, Anchorage, Alaska 99509

We also publish:
ALASKA® magazine
ALASKA GEOGRAPHIC®
The *ALASKA JOURNAL*®
The *MILEPOST*®
and various North Country books, see pages 207-10.

Copyright© 1976, 1977, 1978, 1979, 1981, 1982, 1983 by Alaska Northwest Publishing Company. All rights reserved. No part of this book may be reproduced or transmitted in any form or by any means, electronic or mechanical, including photocopying, recording or by an information storage and retrieval system, without written permission of Alaska Northwest Publishing Company.

Eighth edition
Second printing 1984

ISBN 0-88240-241-2
ISSN 0270-5370
Key title: The Alaska Almanac

Design by Pamela Adams
Cover design and illustration by Sharon Schumacher

Alaska Northwest Publishing Company
Box 4-EEE, Anchorage, Alaska 99509
Printed in U.S.A.

General Index

FACTS ABOUT ALASKA, The ALASKA ALMANAC® has organized its subject categories alphabetically for easy reference. Following is a general index to the many topics discussed. Boldface entries signify main subject categories, and the accompanying boldface numbers the pages on which they are found.

Agriculture

Agricultural production in Alaska is still confined to a relatively small percentage of the state's total acreage. In 1982, approximately 1.5 million acres in Alaska — less than one-half of 1 percent of the state — was considered land in farms. Of that land, crops utilized only 25,000 acres; the balance was idle in pasture or uncleared land. Since 1978, state land sales have placed more than 150,000 acres of potential agricultural land into private ownership. Most of this acreage is in the Delta Junction area, where tracts of land ranging up to 3,200 acres were sold by lottery for the purpose of grain farming.

In 1982, the total value of Alaska's agricultural products was $16,488,000 ($2,228,000 higher than in 1981); crops accounted for $10.1 million of the total, livestock and poultry for $6.4 million. Broken down by region, the Matanuska Valley accounted for 58 percent of the total value; the Tanana Valley, 29.7 percent; the Kenai Peninsula, 8.8 percent; southwestern Alaska, 3.5 percent; and southeastern Alaska, 0.1 percent.

According to the state Division of Agriculture, the value and volume of principal crops in 1982 were:

Crops	Value (in sales)	Volume (in thousands)
Milk	$2,791,000	13,800.0 lbs.
Potatoes	1,425,000	102.0 cwt
Hay	1,311,000	14.3 tons
Barley (for grain)	997,000	315.0 bu.
Eggs	873,000	733.0 doz.
Vegetables (except potatoes)	737,000	29.2 cwt
Pork	625,000	604.0 lbs.
Silage	428,000	10.0 tons
Beef and Veal	309,000	801.0 lbs.
Oats	94,000	31.2 bu.

Sales of reindeer meat and by-products in 1977, the last year for which figures are available, were valued at $421,000. (Only small amounts of reindeer meat are exported to the Lower 48. Antlers are exported to the Orient, where they are sold for use in aphrodisiacs.) Most of the state's reindeer are located on the Seward Peninsula and Nunivak Island. About 30,000 reindeer roam freely across the tundra or taiga of much of western Alaska.

Alaska has experienced growth in the number of small farms through state sales of smaller tracts and the use of farming as a supplement to other income. Since 1978, 314 farm units averaging 163 acres have been sold. In 1982, there were 410 farms with annual sales of $1,000 or more.

The Matanuska Valley sells primarily to Anchorage and military markets. Dairy farming is the dominant income source, including feed crops for cows. The valley has a 120-day growing season that includes up to 19 hours of sunlight daily (occasionally producing giant-sized vegetables), warm temperatures, and moderate rainfall. During most years, supplemental irrigation is required. Residential development in the Matanuska Valley has contributed to a decline in the amount of agricultural land.

In September 1982, 13,780 acres of state land in the Point MacKenzie Agricultural Project, across Knik Arm from Anchorage, were sold by lottery. Of the 29 parcels sold, 17 are designed for development as dairy farms. Land clearing and dairy barn construction are currently in progress. It is anticipated that the remaining parcels will be used to raise crops for livestock feed.

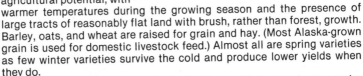

In the Tanana Valley the growing season is shorter than the Matanuska Valley, with 90 frost-free days and low precipitation levels making irrigation necessary for some crops. However, the area has the greatest agricultural potential, with warmer temperatures during the growing season and the presence of large tracts of reasonably flat land with brush, rather than forest, growth. Barley, oats, and wheat are raised for grain and hay. (Most Alaska-grown grain is used for domestic livestock feed.) Almost all are spring varieties as few winter varieties survive the cold and produce lower yields when they do.

The promotion of grain farming in the Tanana Valley has been a major effort by the state. In 1978, the Delta Agricultural Project sold 65,000 acres of land in the Delta Junction area by lottery, with 22 buyers getting roughly 3,000 acres each. By early 1982, one-fourth of the land had been cleared and planted. The primary crop is barley, which has proven to be the grain most adaptable to the valley's growing conditions. The Delta II land auction in March 1982 sold an additional 24,000 acres in 15 parcels for agricultural development. The Tanana Valley produces 90 percent of all grain grown in Alaska.

Originally scheduled for sale in the fall of 1982, 175,000 acres of farm land near Nenana are planned for disposal during the next three years.

The Kenai Peninsula produces beef, hay, eggs, and potatoes. Kodiak Island produces more beef than any other area in the state. Umnak and Unalaska islands provide graze for 3,300 sheep, the smallest number in many years, down from 3,900 in 1980 and 27,000 in 1970.

Based on Soil Conservation Service information, there are at least 20 million acres of potential farmland in Alaska suitable for raising crops, plus 118 million acres of range for livestock grazing, 100 million acres of which is suitable only for reindeer and musk ox.

More information is available from the Alaska Department of Natural Resources, Division of Agriculture, Pouch A, Wasilla, Alaska 99687.

Air Travel

Alaska is the "flyingest" state in the Union; the only practical way to reach many areas of rural Alaska is by airplane. According to the Federal Aviation Administration, Alaska Region, by December 1981 there were approximately 10,000 registered pilots — 1 out of every 40 Alaskans — and 7,450 registered aircraft — 1 for every 54 Alaskans. This figure is approximately 6 times as many pilots per capita and 12 times as many airplanes per capita as compared to the rest of the United States.

According to *Air Alaska*, Alaska has about 1,000 airports. Of these, about 195 are private-use airports, and more than 800 are available for use by the public. That puts Alaska third, behind California and Texas, in the number of airports in the state.

Lake Hood in Anchorage is one of the largest and busiest seaplane bases in the world. On a yearly basis, an average of 225 takeoffs and landings occur daily.

Merrill Field in Anchorage had 302,217 takeoffs and landings recorded in 1982 making it the 27th busiest airport in the United States for the year.

Flying in Alaska, as elsewhere, is not without its hazards. In 1982, there were 193 airplane accidents from which 58 persons lost their lives.

For pilots who wish to fly their own planes to Alaska, a booklet titled *Flight Tips for Alaskan Tourists* may be obtained from the Federal Aviation Administration, 701 C Street, P.O. Box 14, Anchorage 99513.

According to the Alaska Transportation Commission, certified air carriers with operating rights within Alaska as of June 1983 included: 224 air taxi operators; 12 contract air carriers; 7 postal contract carriers; 13 subcontract carriers; and 41 scheduled air carriers.

Scheduled passenger service is available to dozens of Alaskan communities (see Intrastate Service this section). Contact the airlines for current schedules and fares.

Air taxi operators are found in most Alaskan communities and aircraft can be chartered for transportation or for flightseeing. Planes can be chartered to fly you to a wilderness spot and pick you up later at a pre-arranged time and location. (Many charter services charge an hourly standby fee if the customer is not on time at the pickup point.) Most charter operators charge an hourly rate either per plane load or per passenger (sometimes with a minimum passenger requirement), others may charge on a per mile basis. Flightseeing trips to area attractions are often available at a fixed price per passenger. Charter fares range from $75 to $150 per person (four person minimum) for a short flightseeing trip to $350 an hour for an eight-passenger Cessna 404. Multi-engine planes are generally more expensive to charter than single-engine planes.

A wide range of aircraft is used for charter and scheduled passenger service in Alaska. The large interstate airlines — Alaska, Northwest, United, Western, and Wien — use jets (DC-10s, DC-8s, 727s, 737s, 747s); Reeve Aleutian flies Electras, YS-11s, DC-4s and DC-6s. Prop jets and single- or twin-engine prop planes on wheels, skis, and floats are used for most intrastate travel. Here are just a few of the types of aircraft flown in Alaska: DC-3s, 19-passenger Twin Otter, 10-passenger Britten-Norman Islander, 7-passenger Grumman Goose (amphibious), 5-passenger Cessna 185, 9-passenger twin engine Piper Navajo Chieftain, 5- to 8-passenger Beaver, 3- to 4-passenger Cessna 180, 5- to 6-passenger Cessna 206, and single-passenger Super Cub.

Interstate Service

U.S. carriers providing interstate passenger service: Alaska Airlines, Northwest Orient Airlines, South Pacific Island Airlines, Western Airlines, Wien Air Alaska, United Airlines, and Reeve Aleutian Airways. These carriers and Flying Tigers also provide freight service between Anchorage and Seattle. Reeve Aleutian Airways provides freight and passenger service between Cold Bay and Seattle.

International carriers servicing Alaska through the Anchorage gateway: Air France, British Airways, KLM Royal Dutch Airlines, Korean Airlines, Lufthansa German Airlines, Japan Air Lines, Northwest Orient Airlines (to and from Japan), Sabena-Belgian World Airlines, and Scandinavian Airlines.

Intrastate Service

From Anchorage

Alaska Aeronautical Industries, Box 6067, Anchorage 99502. Serves Cordova, Homer, Kenai, Valdez, and Kodiak.

Alaska Airlines, 4750 International Road, Anchorage 99502. Serves Cordova, Dutch Harbor, Fairbanks, Juneau, Kenai, Ketchikan, Kodiak, Petersburg, Sitka, Valdez, Wrangell, Yakutat, Glacier Bay, Prudhoe Bay, Nome, and Kotzebue. Additional routes are served on a contract basis by local carriers.

Inter-Valley Airlines, Box B, Chugiak 99567. Serves Palmer, Wasilla, Big Lake, Willow, Whittier, Birchwood, and Skwentna.

Reeve Aleutian Airways, 4700 West International Airport Road, Anchorage 99502. Serves the Alaska Peninsula, Aleutian Chain, and Pribilof Islands.

SEAIR, Box 6003, Anchorage 99502. Serves Bethel, Cordova, Dillingham, Kenai, King Salmon, and Kodiak Island with connections to over 60 bush communities from Akiachak to Ugashik.

Southcentral Air, P.O. Box 4324, Kenai 99611. Serves Kenai, Soldotna, Seward, and Homer.

Wien Air Alaska, 4100 International Airport Road, Anchorage 99502. Serves Aniak, Barrow, Bethel, Dillingham, Fairbanks, Fort Yukon, Galena, Iliamna, Kenai/Soldotna, King Salmon, Kodiak, Kotzebue, McGrath, Nome, Prudhoe Bay, Saint Marys, and Unalakleet.

From Barrow

Barrow Air, Box 184, Barrow 99723. Serves Atkasuk, Nuiqsut, and Wainwright.

Cape Smythe Air Service, Box 549, Barrow 99723. Serves Deadhorse, Kaktovik, Nuiqsut, Wainwright, Anaktuvuk Pass, Point Lay, Point Hope, and Kotzebue.

From Bethel

Western Yukon Air, Box 131, Saint Marys 99658. Serves Pilot Station, Saint Marys, and Emmonak.

From Cordova

Chisum Flying Service of Alaska, Box 1288, Cordova 99574. Serves Seward, Whittier, Valdez, and Icy Bay.

From Fairbanks

Air North Alaska, Box 60054, Fairbanks 99706. Serves Anaktuvuk Pass, Arctic Village, Bettles, Central, Circle, Eagle, Fort Yukon, Galena, Barter Island, Rampart, Stevens Village, Tanana, Venetie, and other points north. Also serves Juneau and Whitehorse, Yukon Territory.

Alaska Central Air, Box 60249, Fairbanks 99706. Serves Galena via Tanana, Minto, Manley Hot Springs, and Ruby.

Aurora Air Service, Box 1640, Fairbanks 99707. Serves Kobuk and intermediate points.

Frontier Flying Service, 3820 University Avenue, Fairbanks 99701. Serves Allakaket, Anaktuvuk Pass, and Bettles.

Larry's Flying Service, Box 2348, Fairbanks 99707. Serves Denali National Park (McKinley Park airstrip).

From Galena
Galena Air Service, Box 188, Galena 99741. Serves Anchorage.

From Glennallen
Gulkana Air Service, Box 31, Glennallen 99588. Serves Anchorage.

From Haines
L.A.B. Flying Service, Box 272, Haines 99827. Serves Juneau, Hoonah, and Skagway.

From Juneau
Wings of Alaska, 1873 Shell Simmons Drive, Suite 119, Juneau 99801. Serves Haines, Hoonah, Skagway and Gustavus/Glacier Bay.

From Ketchikan
Tyee Airlines, Box 8331, Ketchikan 99901. Serves Craig, Klawock, Hydaburg, Metlakatla, and other Southeast points.

From Kodiak
Kodiak Western Alaska Airlines, Box 2457, Kodiak 99615. Serves King Salmon, Dillingham, and points on Kodiak and Afognak islands.

From Kotzebue
Munz Northern Airlines, Box 727, Kotzebue 99752. Serves Noatak, Kivalina, Point Hope, Cape Lisburne, Noorvik, Kiana, Ambler, Shungnak, Kobuk, Selawik, Buckland, and Deering.

From McGrath
Hub Air Service, Box 2, McGrath 99627. Serves Nikolai, Telida, and Lime Village. Also serves Tatalina Air Force Station, Takotna, Farewell, and Flat as Alaska International Air's subcontractor.

From Nenana
Air Nor, Box 296, Nenana 99760. Serves Tanana, Hughes, Huslia, and Allakaket.

From Nome
Munz Northern Airlines, Box 790, Nome 99762. Serves more than 20 villages from Gambell and Savoonga to Shishmaref and Bethel.

From Petersburg
Alaska Island Air, Box 508, Petersburg 99833. Serves Kake.

From Tanana
Tanana Air Service, P.O. Box 36, Tanana 99777. Serves Tanana, Fairbanks, New Minto, Nenana, Rampart, and Manley Hot Springs.

From Tok
40-Mile Air, Box 539, Tok 99780. Serves Boundary, Chicken, Delta Junction, Eagle, Fairbanks, and Tetlin.

From Unalakleet
Ryan Air Service, P.O. Box 127, Unalakleet 99684. Serves Unalakleet, Nome, Kotzebue, and McGrath.

From Valdez
Valdez Airlines, Box 6714, Anchorage 99502. Serves Anchorage.

Wien Air Alaska commuter service, Box 6714, Anchorage 99502. Serves Anchorage, Kenai, Homer, and Kodiak.

Related reading: *The Alaska Airlines Story* — Aviation history of one of Alaska's major commercial airlines. 224 pages, $12.95. See page 207.

Alaska Highway

The highway runs 1,520 miles through Canada and Alaska from Milepost 0 at Dawson Creek, British Columbia, to Fairbanks, Alaska. (The highway from Milepost 1422 at Delta Junction to Milepost 1520 at Fairbanks shares a common alignment with the Richardson Highway.)

History

By agreement between the governments of Canada and the United States, the highway was built in eight months by the U.S. Army Corps of Engineers and dedicated in November 1942. Crews worked south from Delta Junction, Alaska, north and south from Whitehorse, Yukon Territory, and north from Dawson Creek, British Columbia.

Two major sections of the highway were connected on September 23, 1942, at Contact Creek, Milepost 588.1, where the Thirty-fifth Engineer Combat Regiment working west from Fort Nelson met the 340th Engineer General Service Regiment working east from Whitehorse. The last link in the highway was completed November 20, when the Ninety-seventh Engineer General Service Regiment, heading east from Tanacross, met the Eighteenth Engineer Combat Regiment at Milepost 1200.9, coming northwest from Kluane Lake. On this day a pioneer form of highway was completed. A ceremony commemorating the event was held at Soldiers Summit on Kluane Lake, and the first truck to negotiate the entire highway left that day from Soldiers Summit and arrived in Fairbanks the next day.

The highway was built to relieve Alaska from the wartime hazards of shipping and to supply a land route for wartime equipment. It was then turned over to civilian contractors for widening and graveling, replacing log bridges with steel, and rerouting at many points. Construction continues on the Alaska Highway today as more miles are paved or hard-surfaced, and stretches of road improved.

Preparation for Driving the Alaska Highway

Driving the Alaska Highway requires a few preparations such as protecting your car against gravel and carrying some spare parts. A partial list of spares includes: trailer bearings, fan belts, tires, jumper cables, siphoning hose, all-purpose plastic tape, wire, strong glue, selection of sheet-metal screws, rubber washers of various sizes, tire chains, tire pump, tire repair kit, tire breakdown tools, complete tool kit, points, condenser and spark plugs.

Preparation for gravel: Protect headlights with clear plastic covers made specifically for that purpose. In addition, you might consider a wire-mesh screen across the front of your vehicle to protect paint and radiator from flying rocks.

Substituting metal for rubber in the fuel lines underneath the car will provide longer wear. The rubber boots on axle joints of front-wheel-drive vehicles should be checked frequently. Rotating the tires every 1,000 miles or so will extend tire life.

There is practically no way to protect the windshield, although motorists have experimented with screen shields that do not seriously impair their vision. Larger towns throughout the Northland have auto-glass repair shops.

Gas tanks are often damaged. To protect them insert a rubber mat between gas tank and securing straps — old rubber floor mats and truck flaps work well.

If your car should break down on the highway and tow truck service is needed, normally you will be able to flag down a passing motorist. Travelers in the North are especially helpful in such situations and the etiquette of the country requires one to stop. If you are the only person traveling in the disabled car, be sure to leave a note on your windshield indicating when you left the car and in what direction you planned to travel. This is particularly important when traveling in winter.

Dust protection: Along the Alaska Highway dust is at its worst during dry spells, following heavy rain (which disturbs the road surface), and in construction areas. If you encounter much dust, check your air filter frequently. To help keep dust out of your vehicle, try to keep air pressure in the car by closing all windows and turning on the fan. Filtered heating and air-conditioning ducts in a vehicle bring in much less dust than open windows or vents. Mosquito netting placed over the heater/fresh air intake and flow-through ventilation will also help eliminate dust.

(See also *Highways.*)

Related reading: *The MILEPOST* ® All-the-North Travel Guide® — All travel routes in western Canada and Alaska with photos and detailed maps, including the Alaska Highway. 500 pages, $11.95. *Adventure Roads North,* from the editors of *The MILEPOST* ®. A look at the history and attractions of the roads covered in *The MILEPOST* ®. 224 pages, $14.95. See pages 207-10.

Alaska's Public Officials

Under Russia

Emperor Paul of Russia grants the Russian-American Company an exclusive trade charter in Alaska.

Chief Managers, Russian-American Company	
Alexander Andreevich Baranof	1799-1818
Leontil Andreanovich Hagemeister	January-October 1818
Semen Ivanovich Yanovski	1818-1820
Matxei I. Muravief	1820-1825
Peter Egorovich Chistiakov	1825-1830
Baron Ferdinand P. vonWrangell	1830-1835
Ivan Antonovich Kupreanof	1835-1840
Adolph Karlovich Etolin	1840-1845
Michael D. Tebenkof	1845-1850
Nikolai Y. Rosenberg	1850-1853
Alexander Ilich Rudakof	1853-1854
Stephen Vasili Voevodski	1854-1859

| Ivan V. Furuhelm | 1859-1863 |
| Prince Dmitri Maksoutoff | 1863-1867 |

Under United States

U.S. purchases Alaska from Russia in 1867; U.S. Army given jurisdiction over Department of Alaska.

Army Commanding Officers

Bvt. Maj. Gen. Jefferson C. Davis	October 18, 1867-August 31, 1870
Bvt. Lt. Col. George K. Brady	September 1, 1870-September 22, 1870
Maj. John C. Tidball	September 23, 1870-September 19, 1871
Maj. Harvey A. Allen	September 20, 1871-January 3, 1873
Maj. Joseph Stewart	January 4, 1873-April 20, 1874
Capt. George R. Rodney	April 21, 1874-August 16, 1874
Capt. Joseph B. Campbell	August 17, 1874-June 14, 1876
(Captain E. Field was in command for one month during 1875 while Captain Campbell was out of Alaska.)	
Capt. John Mendenhall	June 15, 1876-March 4, 1877
Capt. Arthur Morris	March 5, 1877-June 14, 1877

U.S. Army troops leave Alaska; the highest ranking federal official left in Alaska is the U.S. collector of customs. Department of Alaska is put under control of the U.S. Treasury Department.

U.S. Collectors of Customs

Montgomery P. Berry	June 14, 1877-August 13, 1877
H.C. DeAhna	August 14, 1877-March 26, 1878
Mottrom D. Ball	March 27, 1877-June 13, 1879

U.S. Navy is given jurisdiction over the Department of Alaska.

Navy Commanding Officers

Captain L.A. Beardslee	June 14, 1879-September 12, 1880
Comdr. Henry Glass	September 13, 1880-August 9, 1881
Comdr. Edward P. Lull	August 10, 1881-October 18, 1881
Comdr. Henry Glass	October 19, 1881-March 12, 1882
Comdr. Frederick Pearson	March 13, 1882-October 3, 1882
Comdr. Edgar C. Merriman	October 4, 1882-September 13, 1884
Lt. Comdr. Henry E. Nichols	September 14, 1884-September 15, 1884

Congress provides civil government for the new District of Alaska in 1884; on August 24, 1912, territorial status is given to Alaska.

Presidential Appointments

John H. Kinkead (President Arthur)	July 4, 1884-May 7, 1885
(He did not reach Sitka until September 15, 1884)	

Alfred P. Swineford (President Cleveland)	May 7, 1885-April 20, 1889
Lyman E. Knapp (President Harrison)	April 20, 1889-June 18, 1893
James Sheakley (President Cleveland)	June 18, 1893-June 23, 1897
John G. Brady (President McKinley)	June 23, 1897-March 2, 1906
Wilford B. Hoggatt (President Roosevelt)	March 2, 1906-May 20, 1909
Walter E. Clark (President Taft)	May 20, 1909-April 18, 1913
John F.A. Strong (President Wilson)	April 18, 1913-April 12, 1918
Thomas Riggs, Jr. (President Wilson)	April 12, 1918-June 16, 1921
Scott C. Bone (President Harding)	June 16, 1921-August 16, 1925
George A. Parks (President Coolidge)	June 16, 1925-April 19, 1933
John W. Troy (President Roosevelt)	April 19, 1933-December 6, 1939
Ernest Gruening (President Roosevelt)	December 6, 1939-April 10, 1953
B. Frank Heintzleman (President Eisenhower)	April 10, 1953-January 3, 1957
Mike Stepovich (President Eisenhower)	April 8, 1957-August 9, 1958

Alaska becomes a state January 3, 1959.

Elected Governors

William A. Egan	January 3, 1959-December 5, 1966
Walter J. Hickel*	December 5, 1966-January 29, 1969
Keith H. Miller*	January 29, 1969-December 5, 1970
William A. Egan	December 5, 1970-December 5, 1974
Jay S. Hammond	December 5, 1974-December 5, 1982
Bill Sheffield	December 5, 1982-

Hickel resigned before completing his full term as governor in order to accept the position of secretary of the interior. He was succeeded by Miller.

Delegates to Congress

In 1906, Congress authorized Alaska to send a voteless delegate to the House of Representatives.

Frank H. Waskey	1906-1907
Thomas Cale	1907-1909
James Wickersham	1909-1917
Charles A. Sulzer	1917-contested election
James Wickersham	1918-seated as delegate
Charles A. Sulzer	1919-elected; died before taking office
George Grigsby	1919-elected in a special election
James Wickersham	1921-seated as delegate, having contested election of Grigsby
Dan A. Sutherland	1921-1930

James Wickersham	1931-1933
Anthony J. Dimond	1933-1944
E. L. Bartlett	1944-1958

Unofficial delegates to Congress to promote statehood, elected under a plan first devised by Tennessee when it was seeking statehood. The Tennessee Plan Delegates were not seated by Congress but did serve as lobbyists.

Senators:	
Ernest Gruening	1956-1958
William Egan	1956-1958
Representative:	
Ralph Rivers	1956-1958

Alaska becomes 49th state in 1959 and sends two senators and one representative to U.S. Congress.

Senators:	
E. L. Bartlett	1959-1968
Ernest Gruening	1959-1968
Mike Gravel	1968-1980
Ted Stevens	1968-
Frank Murkowski	1981-
Representatives:	
Ralph Rivers	1959-1966
Howard Pollock	1966-1970
Nicholas Begich	1970-1972
Don Young	1973-

Correspondence addresses for Alaska officials:

The Honorable Bill Sheffield
Office of the Governor
Pouch A (Mail Stop 0101)
Juneau, Alaska 99811

The Honorable Stephen McAlpine
Office of the Lieutenant Governor
Pouch AA (Mail Stop 0111)
Juneau, Alaska 99811

Alaska's delegation in U.S. Congress:

The Honorable Ted Stevens
United States Senate
147 Russell Office Building
Washington, D.C. 20510

The Honorable Frank H. Murkowski
United States Senate
317 Hart Building
Washington, D.C. 20510

The Honorable Donald E. Young
House of Representatives
2331 Rayburn House Office Building
Washington, D.C. 20515

Alaska State Legislature

Members of the Thirteeth Alaska Legislature are listed below. The addresses provided should be used when the legislature is not in session. During sessions, members of the legislature receive mail at Pouch V, Juneau, Alaska 99811 (Mail Stop 3100).

House of Representatives

District 1, Ketchikan-Wrangell-Petersburg: Ron Wendte (Seat A, Democrat), 3855 Evergreen Avenue, Ketchikan 99901; Jack McBride (Seat B, Democrat), P.O. Box 7563, Ketchikan 99901.

District 2, Inside Passage-Cordova: Peter Goll (Democrat), P.O. Box 581, Haines 99827.

District 3, Baranof-Chichagof: Ben F. Grussendorf (Democrat), P.O. Box 928, Sitka 99835.

District 4, Juneau: Mike M. Miller (Seat A, Democrat), P.O. Box 1494, Juneau 99802; Jim Duncan (Seat B, Democrat), P.O. Box 690, Juneau 99802.

District 5, Kenai-Cook Inlet: Hugh Malone (Seat A, Democrat), P.O. Box 9, Kenai 99611; Milo H. Fritz (Seat B, Republican), P.O. Box 158, Anchor Point 99556.

District 6, North Kenai-South Coast: Bette M. Cato (Democrat), P.O. Box 775, Valdez 99686.

District 7, South Anchorage: Mike Szymanski (Democrat), S.R.A. Box 1304B, Anchorage 99502.

District 8, Hillside: John Cowdery (Seat A, Republican), P.O. Box 10-1623, Anchorage 99511; Sam Pestinger (Seat B, Republican), 716 West Fourth, #400, Anchorage 99501.

District 9, Sand Lake: Joe L. Hayes (Seat A, Republican), P.O. Box 1821, Anchorage 99510; Joe Flood (Seat B, Republican), 3423 West 79th, Anchorage 99502.

District 10, Mid-Town: Charlie Bussell (Seat A, Republican), P.O. Box 4-1325, Anchorage 99509; John Lindauer (Seat B, Republican), 3933 Geneva Place, Anchorage 99504.

District 11, West Side: Mitchel E. Abood, Jr. (Seat A, Republican), 4504 Spenard Road, Anchorage 99503; Mae Tischer (Seat B, Republican), 3305 Oregon Drive, Anchorage 99503.

District 12, Downtown: Rick Uehling (Seat A, Republican), 1634 Juneau Drive, Anchorage 99501; Donald E. Clocksin (Seat B, Democrat), 1527 H Street, Anchorage 99501.

District 13, Mountain View-University: Jerry Ward (Seat A, Republican), P.O. Box 2716, Anchorage 99510; Terry Martin (Seat B, Republican), 3960 Reka Drive, B-6, Anchorage 99504.

District 14, Muldoon: Ramona L. Barnes (Seat A, Republican), P.O. Box 3382, Downtown Station, Anchorage 99510; Walt Furnace (Seat B, Republican), P.O. Box 1542, Anchorage 99510.

District 15, Chugiak-Eagle Rivers-Bases: John J. Liska (Seat A, Republican), S.R. Box 421, Eagle River 99577; Randy E. Phillips (Seat B, Republican), P.O. Box 142, Eagle River 99577.

District 16, Matanuska-Susitna: Barbara Lacher (Seat A, Republican), P.O. Box 30, Wasilla 99687; Ronald L. Larson (Seat B, Democrat), Box 53, Palmer 99645.

District 17, Interior Highways: Richard Schultz (Republican), Box 355, Delta Junction 99737.

District 18, Southeast North Star Borough: Mike W. Miller (Republican), P.O. Box 55094, North Pole 99705.

District 19, Outer Fairbanks: Mike Davis (Democrat), P.O. Box 81435, College 99708.

District 20, Fairbanks City: Robert H. Bettisworth (Seat A, Republican), P.O. Box 80288, College 99708; John Ringstad (Seat B, Republican), P.O. Box 1848, Fairbanks 99707.

District 21, West Fairbanks: Niilo Koponen (Democrat), S.R. Box 10059, Fairbanks 99701.

District 22, North Slope-Kotzebue: Albert P. Adams (Democrat), P.O. Box 333, Kotzebue 99752.

District 23, Norton Sound: John G. Fuller (Democrat), P.O. Box 689, Nome 99762.

District 24, Interior Rivers: Vernon L. Hurlbert (Democrat), General Delivery, Sleetmute 99668.

District 25, Lower Kuskokwim: Anthony N. Vaska (Democrat), P.O. Box 1495, Bethel 99559.

District 26, Bristol Bay-Aleutian Islands: Adelheid Herrmann (Democrat), P.O. Box 63, Naknek 99633.

District 27, Kodiak-East Alaska Peninsula: Fred F. Zharoff (Democrat), P.O. Box 405, Kodiak 99615.

Senate

District A, Ketchikan-Wrangell-Petersburg: Robert H. Ziegler, Sr. (Democrat), 307 Bawden Street, Ketchikan 99901.

District B, Inside Passage-Cordova-Baranof: Richard I. Eliason (Republican), P.O. Box 143, Sitka 99835.

District C, Juneau: Bill Ray (Democrat), Pouch V, Juneau 99811.

District C, Kenai-Cook Inlet-North Kenai-South Coast-South Anchorage: Paul Fischer (Seat A, Republican), Box 784, Soldotna 99669; Donald E. Gilman (Seat B, Republican), P.O. Box 630, Kenai 99611.

District E, Hillside-Sand Lake: Fritz Pettyjohn (Seat A, Republican), S.R.A. 2385-M, Anchorage 99507; Jan Faiks (Seat B, Republican), S.R.A. Box 62F, Anchorage 99507.

District F, Mid-Town-West Side: Arliss Sturgulewski (Seat A, Republican), 2957 Sheldon Jackson Street, Anchorage 99504; Patrick Rodey (Seat B, Democrat), 2335 Lord Baranof, Anchorage 99503.

District G, Downtown-Mountain View-University: Joe Josephson (Seat A, Democrat), 1526 F Street, Anchorage 99501; Vic Fischer (Seat B, Democrat), 1538 Orca, Anchorage 99501.

District H, Muldoon-Chugiak-Eagle River-Bases: Rick Halford (Seat A, Republican), Box 66, Chugiak 99567; Tim Kelly (Seat B, Republican), 283 Muldoon Road, Station Box 76, Anchorage 99504.

District I, Matanuska-Susitna: Jalmar Kerttula (Democrat), Box Z, Palmer 99645.

District J, Interior Highways-Southeast North Star Borough: Pappy H. Moss (Democrat), P.O. Box 182, Delta Junction 99737.

District K, Outer Fairbanks-Fairbanks City-West Fairbanks: Don Bennett (Seat A, Republican), P.O. Box 2801, Fairbanks 99707; Bettye Fahrenkamp (Seat B, Democrat), 4016 Evergreen, Fairbanks 99701.

District L, North Slope-Kotzebue-Norton Sound: Frank R. Ferguson (Democrat), Box 131, Kotzebue 99752.

District M, Interior Rivers-Lower Kuskokwim: John C. Sackett (Republican), Box 11, Ruby 99768.

District N, Bristol Bay-Aleutian Islands-Kodiak-East Alaska Peninsula: Bob Mulcahy (Republican), P.O. Box 246, Kodiak 99615.

Related reading: *Directory of State Officials,* compiled by the Legislative Affairs Agency, Division of Public Services, Pouch Y, Juneau, Alaska 99811.

Alaska Medal of Heroism

By a law established in 1965, the Alaska governor is authorized to award, in recognition of valorous and heroic deeds, a state medal of heroism to persons who have saved a life or, at risk to their lives, have served the state or community on behalf of the health, welfare or safety of other persons. The heroism medal may be awarded posthumously. Following are recipients of the Alaska Medal of Heroism:

Randy Blake Prinzing (1969), Soldotna. Saved two lives at Scout Lake.

Nancy Davis (1971), Seattle. A stewardess who convinced an alleged highjacker to surrender to authorities.

Jeffrey Stone (1972), Fairbanks. Saved the lives of two youths from a burning apartment.

Gilbert Pelowook (1975), Savoonga. An Alaska state trooper who aided plane crash victims on Saint Lawrence Island.

Residents of Gambell (1975), Gambell. Provided aid and care for plane crash victims on Saint Lawrence Island.

George Jackinsky (1978), Kasilof. Rescued two persons from a burning aircraft.

Mike Hancock (1980), Lima, Ohio. In 1977 rescued a victim of a plane crash that brought down high-voltage lines.

John Stimson (1983), Cordova. A first sergeant in the Division of Fish and Wildlife Protection who died in a helicopter accident during an attempt to rescue others.

Robert Larson (1983), Anchorage. A Department of Public Safety employee who flew through hazardous conditions to rescue survivors of the crash that took John Stimson's life.

David Graham (1983), Kenai. Rescued a person from a burning car.

Alcoholic Beverages

At this writing, legal age of majority for possession, purchase, and consumption of alcoholic beverages is 19 years of age. Effective January 1, 1984, legal age is 21.

Any business which serves or distributes alcoholic beverages must be licensed by the state. Issuance of all types of licenses is limited to the population in a geographic area. Generally one license of each type may be issued for each 1,500 persons or fraction thereof. Licensed premises include bars, some restaurants, roadhouses, and clubs. Packaged liquor, beer, and wine are sold by licensed retailers. Recreational site licenses, caterer's permits, and special events permits allow the holder of a beverage dispensary license to sell at special (usually sporting) events, and nonprofit fraternal, civic or patriotic organizations to serve beer and wine at certain activities.

State law allows liquor outlets to operate from 8:00 A.M. to 5:00 A.M., but provides that local governments can impose tighter restrictions. Juneau and Anchorage have cut back on the number of hours liquor outlets may operate; a similar move to shorten bar hours in Fairbanks was killed by the assembly there in January 1982.

In 1982, approximately $9.2 million was generated through taxes on alcoholic beverages.

Local governments may also ban the sale of or further restrict alcoholic beverages. Barrow and Bethel have banned the sale of alcoholic beverages. Communities that have banned both the sale and importation of alcoholic beverages (prohibits knowingly bringing, sending, or transporting alcoholic beverages into the community) are:

Akolmiut	Kaltag	Quinhagak
Alakanuk	Kiana	Saint Marys
Ambler	Kipnuk	Saint Michael
Atmautluak	Kivalina	Savoonga
Brevig Mission	Kobuk	Scammon Bay
Buckland	Kongiganak	Shaktoolik
Chalkyitsik	Kotlik	Shishmaref
Chefornak	Koyuk	Shungnak
Deering	Kwethluk	Stebbins
Diomede	Kwigillingok	Teller
Eek	Mekoryuk	Tetlin
Ekwok	Minto	Togiak
Elim	Napakiak	Toksook Bay
Emmonak	Napaskiak	Tuluksak
Fortuna Ledge	Noatak	Tuntutuliak
Gambell	Noorvik	Tununak
Golovin	Old Harbor	Wainwright
Holy Cross	Platinum	Wales
Hooper Bay	Point Hope	White Mountain

On July 20, 1983, Governor Sheffield signed into law a tougher drinking driving law than existed before. Under the new law first offenders face a mandatory 72-hour jail sentence, a minimum fine of $250, and loss of driving privileges for 30 days. A second offense receives a minimum sentence of 20 days, a minimum fine of $500, and loss of license for 1 year. The third offense brings a 30-day sentence, a minimum $1,000 fine, and loss of license for 10 years.

Alyeska

Pronounced Al-ee-es-ka, this Aleut word means "the great land" and was one of the original names of Alaska. Also a 3,939-foot peak in the Chugach Mountains; Mount Alyeska is the site of the state's largest ski resort.

Amphibians

In Alaska there are three species of salamanders, two species of frogs and one species of toad. In the salamander order there are the rough-skinned newt, long-toed salamander, and northwestern salamander. In the frogs and toads order there are the boreal toad, wood frog, and spotted frog. The northern limit of each species may be the latitude at which the larvae fail to complete their development in one summer. While some species of salamander can overwinter as larvae in temperate southeastern Alaska, the shallow ponds of central Alaska freeze solid during the winter. All but the wood frog, *Rana sylvatica,* which with its shortened larval period is found widespread throughout the state and north of the Brooks Range, are found primarily in southeastern Alaska.

Related reading: *Amphibians & Reptiles in Alaska, the Yukon & Northwest Territories,* by Robert Parker Hodge. Life histories, color photos, charts and maps. 89 pages, $4.95. See page 208.

Arctic Circle

The Arctic Circle is the latitude at which the sun does not set for 1 day at summer solstice and does not rise for 1 day at winter solstice, when the sun is at its greatest distance from the celestial equator. (See also *Daylight Hours.*) The latitude, which varies slightly from year to year, is approximately 66° 33′ from the equator.

On the day of summer solstice, on June 20 or 21, the sun does not set at the Arctic Circle; because of refraction of sunlight, it appears not to set for 4 days. Farther north, at Barrow (northernmost community in the United States), the sun does not set from May 10 to August 2.

At winter solstice, December 21 or 22, the sun does not rise for 1 day at the Arctic Circle. At Barrow, it does not rise for 67 days.

Arctic Winter Games

The Arctic Winter Games, a biennial event held in mid-March for northern athletes from Alaska, Yukon Territory, and Northwest Territories, have been held since 1970, when the first games were held in Yellowknife, Northwest Territories. The last games were held in 1982 in Fairbanks. Yellowknife will host the 1984 games; Whitehorse, Yukon Territory, will be the site of the 1986 games; and the games will return to Alaska in 1988.

Basketball, gymnastics, judo, and table tennis have been dropped from the 1984 games because the AWG board felt they didn't fit the northern spirit of the games and because Canadian teams were unable to field competitive teams.

Added in 1984 will be speed skating and a speed skating-skiing-snowshoeing triathlon; and other arctic sports, such as ice hockey, indoor soccer, and the snowshoe biathlon, have been expanded by adding more athletes and splitting the competition into junior and open divisions. Other competition includes badminton, cross-country skiing, curling, figure skating, and rifle and pistol shooting.

Aurora Borealis

The Phenomena

The aurora borealis is produced by charged electrons and protons striking gas particles in the earth's upper atmosphere. The electrons and protons are released through sunspot activity on the sun and emanate into space. A few drift the one- to two-day course to Earth where they are pulled to the most northern and southern latitudes by the planet's magnetic forces.

The color of the aurora borealis varies depending on how hard the gas particles are being struck. Auroras can range from simple arcs to draperylike forms in green, red, blue and purple. The lights occur in a pattern rather than as a solid glow because electric current sheets flowing through gases create V-shaped potential double layers. Electrons near the center of the current sheet move faster, hit the atmosphere harder, and cause the different intensities of light observed in the aurora.

Displays take place as low as 40 miles above the Earth's surface, but usually begin above about 68 miles and extend hundreds of miles into space. They concentrate in two bands roughly centered above the Arctic Circle and Antarctic Circle (the latter known as aurora australis) that are about 2,500 miles in diameter. In northern latitudes the greatest occurrence of auroral displays is in the spring and fall months owing to the tilt of the planet in relationship to the sun's plane, but displays may occur on dark nights throughout the winter. If sunspot activity is particularly intense and the denser-than-usual solar wind heads to Earth, the resulting auroras can be so great they cover all but the tropical latitudes. However, the cycle of sunspot activity is such that it will be many years before the numerous, brilliant displays of the late 1950s are regularly seen again.

Some observers claim the northern lights make a noise similar to the rustle of taffeta, but scientists say the displays cannot be heard in the audible frequency range.

Photographing the Aurora Borealis

To capture the northern lights on film, you will need a sturdy tripod, a locking-type cable release (some 35mm cameras have both *time* and *bulb* settings, but most have *bulb only*, which calls for use of the locking-type cable release), and a camera with an f/3.5 lens (or faster).

It is best to photograph the lights on a night when they are not moving too rapidly. And, as a general rule, photos improve if you manage to include recognizable subjects in the foreground — trees and lighted cabins being favorites of many photographers. Set your camera up at least 75 feet back from the foreground objects to make sure that both the foreground and aurora are in sharp focus.

Normal and wide-angle lenses are best. Try to keep your exposures under a minute — 10 to 30 seconds are generally best. The following lens openings and exposure times are only a starting point, since the amount of light generated by the aurora is inconsistent. (For best results, bracket exposures widely.)

	ASA 200	ASA 400
f1.2	3 sec.	2 sec.
f1.4	5	3
f1.8	7	4
f2	20	10
f2.8	40	20
f3.5	60	30

Ektachrome 200 and 400 color films can be push-processed in the home darkroom or by some custom-color labs, allowing use of higher ASA ratings (800, 1200 or even 1600 on the 400 ASA film, for example). Kodak will push-process film if you include an ESP-1 envelope with your standard film-processing mailer. (Consult your local camera store for details.)

A few notes of caution: Protect the camera from low temperatures until you are ready to make your exposures. Some newer cameras, in particular, have electrically controlled shutters that will not function properly at low temperatures. Wind the film slowly to reduce the possibility of static electricity, which can lead to streaks on the film. Grounding the camera when rewinding can help prevent the static-electricity problem. (To ground the camera, hold it against a water pipe, drain pipe, metal fence post or other grounded object.) Follow the basic rules, experiment with exposures, and you should obtain good results.

The first photographs to show the aurora borealis in its entirety became public in early 1982. These historic photographs were taken from satellite-mounted cameras specially adapted to filter unwanted light from the sunlit portion of the earth, which is a million times brighter than the aurora. From space the aurora has the appearance of a nearly perfect circle.

Related reading: *Aurora Borealis: The Amazing Northern Lights,* by S.-I. Akasofu. A complete historical and up-to-date look at nature's amazing light show. 96 pages, $7.95. See page 208.

Baleen

Long, fringed, bonelike strips that line the mouth of baleen whales. Baleen strains out plankton, the tiny, shrimplike creatures called krill, and small fish from the water. With the consistency of fiberglass, baleen was once used for corset stays and buggy whips. Baleen is no longer of significant commercial use, although Alaska Natives still use brownish black bowhead baleen to make baskets and model ships for the tourist trade. (See also *Baskets.*)

Barabara

Pronounced *buh-rah-buh-ruh*, this traditional Aleut or Eskimo shelter is built of sod supported by driftwood or whalebone.

Baseball

The Alaska Baseball League consists of six All-Alaska amateur league teams: Anchorage Glacier Pilots (club started in 1969), Fairbanks Goldpanners (1966), Kenai Peninsula Oilers (1974), Mat-Su Miners (1980), North Pole Nicks (1980), and the Cook Inlet Bucs (1980).

The baseball season opens in June and runs through the end of July. Each team plays a round-robin schedule with the other five teams, as well as scheduling games with visiting Lower 48 teams, such as Athletes in Action. The league has a championship series the first of August, followed by a state National Baseball Congress tournament leading up to the NBC nationals at Wichita.

The caliber of play in Alaska is some of the best nationwide at the amateur level. Since 1968, Alaska teams have won eight NBC championships. (The Glacier Pilots in 1969 and 1971; the Goldpanners in 1972-74, 1976 and 1980; and the Oilers in 1981.) Major league scouts rate Alaska baseball at A to AA.

The Alaska league teams are comprised of walk-on and recruited players alike, but primarily of college players, many of whom go on to professional baseball. (Any college senior drafted by a major league team cannot play in the Alaska league.) Since its inception in 1969, the Alaska league has sent more than 100 players on to careers in major league baseball. The list is an impressive one, including such current stars as Tom Seaver, Chris Chambliss, Bruce Bochte, and Bump Wills.

Baskets

Native basketry varies greatly according to materials locally available. The Athabascan Indians of interior Alaska, for example, weave baskets from willow root gathered in late spring. The roots are steamed and roasted over a fire to loosen the outer bark; weavers then separate the bark into fine strips by pulling the roots through their teeth.

Eskimo grass baskets are made in river delta areas of southwestern Alaska from Bristol Bay north to Norton Sound and from Nunivak Island east to interior Eskimo river villages. The weavers use very fine grass harvested in fall. A coil basketry technique is followed, using coils three-fourths to one-eighth inch wide. Seal gut, traditionally dyed with berries (today with commercial dyes), is often interwoven into the baskets.

Baleen, a glossy, hard material that hangs in slats from the upper jaw of a bowhead whale, is also used for baskets. Baleen basketry originated about 1905 when Charles D. Brower, trader for a whaling company at Point Barrow, suggested, after the decline of the whalebone (baleen) industry for women's corsets, that local Eskimos make the baskets as a source of income. The baskets were not produced in any number until 1916. The weave and shape of the baskets were copied from the split-willow Athabascan baskets acquired in trade. Men, rather than women, became the basket makers. Later, baleen baskets were also made in Point Hope and Wainwright.

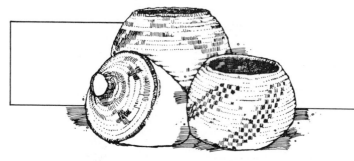

Most birch bark baskets are made by Athabascan Indians, although a few Eskimos also produce them. Commonly they are shaped as simple cylinders and are held together with root bindings. Sometimes the birch bark is cut into thin strips and woven into diamond or checkerboard patterns. Birch bark is usually collected in spring and early summer; large pieces free of knots are preferred. Birch bark baskets traditionally were used as cooking vessels; food was placed in them and hot stones added. Birch bark baby carriers also are made.

Among the finest of Alaskan baskets are the tiny, intricately woven Aleut baskets made of rye grass, which in the Aleutians is abundant, pliable and very tough. The three main styles of Aleut baskets — Attu, Atka and Unalaska — are named after the islands where the styles originated. Although the small baskets are the best known, Aleuts also traditionally made large, coarsely woven baskets for utilitarian purposes.

Tlingit, Haida and Tsimshian Indians make baskets of spruce root and cedar bark. South of Frederick Sound, basket material usually consists of strands split from the inner bark of red cedar. To the north of the sound, spruce roots are used. Maidenhair ferns are sometimes interwoven into spruce root baskets in a technique that looks like embroidery. A large spruce root basket may take months to complete.

Examples of Alaska Native basketry may be viewed in many museums within the state, including the University of Alaska Museum, Fairbanks; the Anchorage Historical and Fine Arts Museum, Anchorage; the Sheldon Jackson Museum, Sitka; and the Alaska State Museum, Juneau.

Prices for Native baskets vary greatly in the marketplace. A fine-weave grass basket may cost from $50 to $650; birch bark baskets, which look like trays, may range from $20 to $90; willow root trays may cost $500; beach grass baskets, one of the hardest to come by, may cost as much as $1,100; and baleen baskets range in price from $500 to more than $850 for medium-sized baskets. These prices are approximate and do vary greatly with the weave, material used, size, and decorations added, such as bead work or ivory.

Billiken

This pointed-head, smiling ivory figure, though long a popular Northland souvenir, is not an Eskimo invention. The billiken was patented in 1908 by Florence Pretz of Kansas City. A small, seated, Buddha-like figure, the original billikens were manufactured by the Billiken Company of Chicago and sold as good luck charms. During the 1909 Alaska-Yukon-Pacific Exposition in Seattle, thousands of these figurines were sold. Although billikens vanished soon afterward from most Lower 48 shops, someone had brought them to Nome, where King Island, Little Diomede, and Wales Eskimos began carving replicas in ivory.

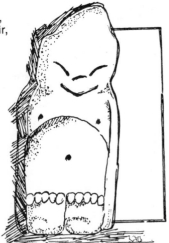

Billikens are still being made elsewhere in the world in such media as wood, concrete and glass. A popular notion contends that rubbing a billiken's tummy brings good fortune.

Birds

Authorities at the University of Alaska acknowledge 405 species of birds in Alaska. If undocumented sightings are included, the number of species increases to more than 420. Although only about half the species are water birds, they are by far the most numerous birds in the state. Thousands of ducks, geese, and swans make their way north each spring to take advantage of Alaska's lakes, tundra ponds, and river flats. In addition, millions of pelagic birds (sea birds) congregate in great nesting colonies on exposed sea cliffs along much of Alaska's coastline. Some of the best-known pelagic bird areas are in the Aleutian and Pribilof islands.

Migratory birds gather in Alaska from many corners of the world. The arctic tern travels up to 22,000 miles round trip each year from Antarctic waters to breed in Alaska. The lesser golden plover nests in Alaska and winters in Hawaii. Other species travel between Alaska and Asia.

The Copper River Delta, situated along one of the most important migration routes in the state, is relatively accessible to bird watchers via the Copper River Highway from Cordova. Each May, one of the world's largest concentrations of bird life — primarily sandpipers and dunlins—funnels by the millions through the delta region. The delta is also an important waterfowl breeding area, containing the world's only breeding population of dusky Canada geese. Approximately four-fifths of the world's population of trumpeter swans nests in Alaska. Although the swans were once thought near extinction, about 8,000 were counted in 1980.

Other important waterfowl nesting areas include the great delta between the mouths of the Yukon and Kuskokwim rivers, Yukon Flats, Innoko Flats, and Minto Lakes. Additional gathering spots during migrations include Egegik, Port Heiden, Port Moller, Izembek Bay, Chickaloon Flats, Susitna Flats, and Stikine Flats. A few species of birds — including shearwaters, albatross, and petrels — breed in Antarctic waters and winter in Alaska during the Northern Hemisphere's summer.

Four species of endangered birds are found in Alaska: the Aleutian Canada goose, the American and Arctic races of peregrine falcon, the Eskimo curlew, and the short-tailed albatross.

Alaska's top birder, Daniel Gibson, has seen more than 300 species of birds in the state.

Four chapters of the National Audubon Society are based in Alaska: the Anchorage Audubon Society, Inc. (P.O. Box 1161, Anchorage 99510), the Juneau Audubon Society (P.O. Box 1725, Juneau 99802), the Kodiak Audubon Society (Box 1756, Kodiak 99615), and the Arctic Audubon Society (P.O. Box 60524, Fairbanks 99701). In addition to trying to help people increase their knowledge of birds and their surroundings, the groups (except for Fairbanks) coordinate an annual Christmas bird count. In Fairbanks, the Fairbanks Bird Club (P.O. Box 81791, Fairbanks 99708) conducts the annual Christmas bird count.

Related reading: *Bird Sampler: A Pocket Guide to Some Alaska Birds* by Helen A. White. A handy carry-along guide. 52 pages, $1.50. Available from Alaska Northwest Publishing Company, Box 4-EEE, Anchorage, Alaska 99509. *The Alaskan Bird Sketches of Olaus Murie:* With excerpts from his field notes, compiled and edited by Margaret E. Murie. 64 pages, $11.95. *A Guide to the Birds of Alaska,* including most species found in Alaska. 320 pages. $16.95. See pages 207-10.

Blanket Toss

As effective as a trampoline, the blanket toss (or nalukataq) features a walrus hide blanket grasped by a number of people in a circle who toss a person on the blanket as high as possible for as long as that person can remain upright. Every true Eskimo festival and many non-Native occasions include the blanket toss, which was originally used to allow Eskimo hunters to spot game, such as walrus and seal, in the distance. Depending on the skill of the person being tossed and the number of tossers, a medium-weight person might typically go 20 feet in the air.

Boating

Travel by boat is an important means of transportation in Alaska, where highways cover only about one-third of the state. Until the advent of the airplane, boats were often the only way to reach many parts of Alaska. Most of Alaska's supplies still arrive by water, and in Southeast — where precipitous terrain and numerous islands make road building impossible — water travel is essential. (See also *Ferries* and *Shipping*.)

According to the U.S. Coast Guard, there are 44,488 vessels registered in Alaska. Of these, approximately 3,258 are longer than 30 feet (many are commercial fishing vessels) and 16,219 are longer than 20 feet.

To accommodate the needs of this fleet, there are approximately 8,000 slips available at public small-boat harbors in Alaska. According to the state, actual service capacity is somewhat greater because of the transient nature of many boats and certain management practices allowing "double parking." There are also harbors at various remote locations; no services other than moorage are provided at these harbors.

The Alaska Department of Transportation and Public Facilities (Pouch Z, Juneau 99811), through its regional offices, has the major responsibility for providing public floats, grids, docks, launching ramps, and associated small-boat harbor facilities throughout the coastal areas of the state. Often these facilities are leased to local governments at no cost. Moorage facilities constructed by the state are intended for boats up to a maximum of 100 feet, with a limited number of facilities for larger vessels where large boats are common. With the exception of Ketchikan, Sitka, and Juneau, there are no private marina facilities.

Recreational boating opportunities in Alaska are too numerous and varied to mention all here; Alaska has thousands of miles of lakes, rivers, and sheltered seaways. For information on boating rivers, lakes, and seaways within national forests, parks, monuments, preserves, and wildlife refuges, contact the appropriate federal agency (see related sections and *Information Sources*). For travel by boat in southeastern Alaska's sheltered seaways — or elsewhere in Alaska's coastal waters — NOAA nautical charts are available.

Canoe trails have been established on the Kenai Peninsula (contact the Kenai National Wildlife Refuge, P.O. Box 2139, Soldotna 99669); in Nancy Lake recreation area (contact the Superintendent, Mat-Su District, P.O. Box 182, Palmer 99645); and on rivers in the Fairbanks and

Anchorage areas (contact the Bureau of Land Management, P.O. Box 1150, Fairbanks 99701).

Travel by water in Alaska requires extra caution, however. Weather changes fast and is often unpredictable; it's important to be prepared for the worst. Alaska waters, even in midsummer, are cold; a person falling overboard may become immobilized by the cold water in only a few minutes. And since on many of Alaska's water routes one is so remote from civilization, help may be a long way off.

Persons inexperienced in traveling Alaska's waterways might consider employing a charter boat operator or outfitter. Guides offer local knowledge and provide all necessary equipment. The Division of Tourism (Pouch E, Juneau 99811) maintains current lists of such services. Another place to find names of guides and charter skippers is in "The Guide Post®" in ALASKA® magazine.

Related reading: *A Guide to the Queen Charlotte Islands* — Valuable information, photos, separate large map. Revised 1984 edition, 90 pages, $3.95. *Alaska National Interest Lands* — Detailed look at the flora, fauna, and recreational opportunities of Alaska's national lands. 240 pages, $14.95. *Southeast: Alaska's Panhandle* — Photos and text of Alaska's panhandle. 192 pages, $12.95. *The Stikine River* — A look at the Stikine River and its wilderness. 96 pages, $9.95. See pages 207-10.

Bore Tide

A steep, foaming wall of water formed by a flood tide surging into a constricted inlet. In Cook Inlet, where maximum tidal range approaches 40 feet, incoming tides are further compressed in Knik and Turnagain arms and tidal bores may sometimes be seen. Though one- to two-foot-high bores are more common, spring tides in Turnagain Arm may produce bore tides up to six feet high, running at speeds of up to 10 knots, and even higher bores have been reported when unusually high tides come in against a strong southeast wind. Good spots to view bore tides in Turnagain Arm are along the Seward Highway, between 26 and 37 miles south of Anchorage; they can be expected to arrive there approximately 2 hours and 15 minutes later than the tide book prediction for low tide at Anchorage. (See also *Tides*.)

Boundary, Alaska-Canada

In 1825, Russia, then owner of Alaska, and Great Britain, then owner of Canada, established the original boundary between Alaska and Canada. The demarcation was to begin at 54°40' north latitude, just north of the mouth of Portland Canal, follow the canal to 56° north latitude, then traverse the mountain summits parallel to the coast as far as 141° west longitude. From there it would conform with that meridian north to the Arctic Ocean. The boundary line along the mountain summits in southeastern Alaska was never to be farther inland than 10 leagues — about 30 miles.

After purchasing Alaska, the United States found that the wording about the boundary line was interpreted differently by the Canadians. They felt the measurements should be made inland from the mouths of bays, while Americans argued the measurements should be made from the heads of the bays. In 1903, however, an international tribunal upheld the American interpretation of the treaty providing Alaska the 1,538-mile-long border it enjoys with Canada today. If the Canadians had won their argument they would have had access to the sea, and Haines, Dyea and Skagway now would be in Canada.

The 20-foot-wide vista, a swath of land cleared 10 feet on each side of a boundary, between southeastern Alaska, British Columbia and Yukon Territory was surveyed and cleared between 1904 and 1914. Portions of the 710-mile-long boundary were again cleared in 1925, 1948, 1978 and 1982 by the International Boundary Commission. Monument and vista maintenance of 1978 and 1982 was conducted by the Canadian section of the commission.

The Alaska-Canada border along the 141st meridian was surveyed and cleared between 1904 and 1920. Astronomical observations were made to find the meridian's intersection with the Yukon River, then, under direction of the International Boundary Commission, engineers and surveyors of the U.S. Coast and Geodetic Survey and the Canadian Department of the Interior worked together north and south from the Yukon. The vista extends from Demarcation Point on the Arctic Ocean south to Mount Saint Elias in the Wrangell Mountains (from there the border cuts east to encompass southeastern Alaska). This 647-mile stretch is one of the longest straight lines on record, varying less than 50 feet its entire length. Monument and vista maintenance was carried out by the United States section of the International Boundary Commission during the summer months of 1978, 1979, 1981, 1982 and 1983.

Monuments are the actual markers of the boundary and are located so they tie in with survey networks of both the United States and Canada. Along the Alaska boundary most monuments are two-and-a-half-foot-high cones of aluminum-bronze set in concrete bases or occasionally cemented into rock. A large pair of concrete monuments with pebbled finish mark major boundary road crossings, and, because the boundary is not just a line but in fact a vertical plane dividing land and sky between the two nations, bronze plates mark tunnel and bridge crossings. One hundred ninety-one monuments stretch along the meridian, beginning 200 feet from the Arctic Ocean and ending at the south side of Logan Glacier.

Breakup

Breakup occurs when the melting snows raise the level of streams and rivers sufficiently to cause the ice to break apart and float downstream. It is one of two factors determining the open-water season for river navigation, the second being the depth of the river. Peak water conditions occur just after breakup.

The navigable season for the Kuskokwim and Yukon rivers is June 1 through September 30; Nushagak River, June 1 through August 31; and the Noatak River, late May through mid-June.

Breakup is a most spectacular experience in sight and sound. Massive pieces of ice crunch and pound against each other as they push their way downriver racing for the sea, creating noises not unlike many huge engines straining and grating. The spine-tingling sound can be heard for miles. It is a time for rejoicing, for it is the finale of winter and the herald of spring in Alaska.

Sometimes great ice jams occur causing the water to back up and flood the inhabited areas. In the spring of 1982 Fort Yukon experienced a very serious flood during the breakup.

(See also *Nenana Ice Classic*.)

Bunny Boots

Large, insulated rubber boots to protect feet from frostbite; also called vapor barrier boots. Black bunny boots are generally rated to -20°F, while the more common white bunny boots are even warmer and used in the most extreme conditions, including use on Mount McKinley. (The cumbersome boots are adequate for easy climbing but unsuitable for technical mountain climbing.) Prices range from about $50 for used boots to about $175 for new ones.

Bush

Originally considered to describe large expanses of wilderness beyond the fringes of civilization inhabited by trappers and miners, "Bush" has come to stand for any part of Alaska not accessible by road. Nowadays a community accessed by only air, water, sled or snow machine transportation is considered a bush village, and anyone living there is someone from the Bush.

The term Bush has been adapted to the small planes and their pilots who service areas lacking roads or elaborately developed airports. Bush planes are commonly equipped with floats and skis to match terrain and season. For their oftentimes courageous air service, bush pilots have become the modern frontier hero.

Related reading: *The Alaska Airlines Story,* by Archie Satterfield, 224 pages, $12.95. *Mudhole Smith: Alaska Flier,* by Lone Janson, 160 pages, $6.95. See pages 207 and 209.

Bus Lines

Scheduled bus service is available in summer to and within Alaska, although not as frequently as in the Lower 48. (Local transit service is available in some major communities.)

Alaska-Yukon Motorcoaches, 327 F Street, Anchorage 99501. Provides service between Anchorage, Haines, Skagway, Valdez, Denali National Park and Preserve, and Fairbanks, and between Fairbanks, Haines, and Valdez.

Alaskan Coachways, Ltd. (Greyhound Lines of Canada), 208 Wendell Avenue, Fairbanks 99701. Provides service between Fairbanks and Whitehorse, Yukon Territory.

Bus Alaska, P.O. Box 10138, Anchorage 99510. Service from Anchorage to Denali Park.

Kenai Peninsula Stage Lines, Box 445, Soldotna 99669. Service from Anchorage to Homer via Sterling, Cooper Landing, Soldotna and Kenai.

Norline Coaches (Yukon), Ltd., 3211-A Third Avenue, Whitehorse, Yukon Territory. Provides service between Whitehorse and Tok via Dawson City.

Valdez/Anchorage Bus Lines, P.O. Box 867, Valdez 99686. Service from Valdez to Anchorage via Glennallen.

White Pass and Yukon Motorcoaches, 300 Elliott Avenue West, Seattle, Washington 98119. Provides service between Skagway and Whitehorse.

Cabin Fever

A state of mind blamed on cold, dark winter weather when people are often housebound; characterized by depression, preoccupation, discontent, and occasionally violence. Has been described as "a 12-foot stare in a 10-foot room." Commonly thought to afflict miners and trappers spending a lonely winter in the wilderness, but, in truth, these people remain active and outdoors enough to remain content. It is more likely to strike the snowbound or disabled. The arrival of spring or a change of scene usually relieves the symptoms.

Cache

Pronounced *cash*, this small storage unit is built to be inaccessible to marauding animals. In appearance it is not unlike a miniature log cabin mounted on stilts and reached by a ladder that bears, dogs, foxes and other hungry or curious animals can't climb. Extra precautions include wrapping tin around the poles to prevent climbing by clawed animals and extending the floor a few feet in all directions from the top of the poles for those clever enough to get that high anyway.

Squirrels are the most notorious of Alaska's cache-marauding critters. To be truly animal-proof, a cache should be built in a clearing well beyond the 30-foot leaping distance a squirrel can manage from treetop.

Trappers, homesteaders, and others who live in remote areas use the cache as a primitive food freezer in winter. A cache may also contain extra fuel and bedding. Size is determined by need. Sometimes a cache will be built between three or four straight trees growing close together.

Calendar of Events

JANUARY

Aniak — Kuskokwim 300 Sled Dog Race. **Haines** — Alcan 200 and Snow Machine Events. **Soldotna** — Clark Memorial Sled Dog Race; Peninsula Winter Games.

FEBRUARY

Anchorage — Fur Rendezvous. **Cordova** — Annual Iceworm Festival. **Fairbanks** — Arctic Wildlife Photography and Invitational Alaska Native Sculpture, both at University of Alaska Museum. **Girdwood-Mount Alyeska** — Mid-Winter Carnival. **Homer** — Winter Carnival. **Juneau-Eaglecrest** — Nordic Weekend. **Kenai** — Winter Carnival and Snowmachine Race. **Nenana** — Tripod Raising Festival. **Seldovia** — Annual Fuzzball Carnival. **Soldotna** — Alaska State Championship Sled Dog Race and Weight Pulling Contest. **Valdez** — Winter Carnival. **Wrangell** —Tent City Festival.

MARCH

Anchorage — Iditarod Trail Sled Dog Race to Nome. **Aniak** —Winter Carnival. **Dillingham** — Beaver Round-Up. **Fairbanks** — Junior North American Sled Dog Race; Limited Class North American Sled Dog Race; Festival of Native Arts, University of Alaska; Open North American Championship Sled Dog Race and Winter Carnival; Jeff Studdert Invitational Sled Dog Race; Dance Festival; International Curling Bonspiel. **Juneau-Eaglecrest** — Winter Carnival. **Ketchikan** — Boat, Recreation, and Travel Show. **Kotzebue** — Goodwin-Ferguson 248-Mile Inter-Village Snowmachine Race. **Nome** — Month of Iditarod (finish line for race). **North Pole** — Winter Carnival. **Sitka** — Second Annual Southeast Alaska Eight-Ball Pool Tournament. **Wasilla** — Iditarod Winter Carnival.

APRIL

Haines — Alaska State Community Theater Drama Festival; Northwest Region Drama Festival. **Girdwood-Mount Alyeska** — Spring Carnival. **Juneau-Eaglecrest** — Ski-to-Ski Relay; Southeast Alaska Championships, final USA slalom and giant slalom races. **Ketchikan** — Home Show. **Whittier** — Alaskan Crab Festival.

MAY

Delta — Buffalo Wallow, Square Dancing. **Fairbanks** — Dance Festival, University of Alaska. **Haines** — Salmon Derby. **Homer** — Annual Spring Arts Festival. **Ketchikan** — Little League Salmon Derby and King Salmon

Derby. **Kodiak** — Crab Festival. **Nome** — Annual Polar Bear Swim in the Bering Sea. **Petersburg** — Little Norway Festival. **Savoonga** — Walrus Festival. **Seward** — Spring into Summer Fun Time. **Sitka** — Salmon Derby. **Wrangell** — 32d Annual King Salmon Derby.

JUNE

Anchorage — Mayor's Midnight Sun Marathon; Pleasure Faire. **Barrow** — Nalukatuk Whaling Festival (dependent on whaling season). **Fairbanks** — Tanana Raft Classic; Yukon 800 Marathon Riverboat Race; Midnight Sun Baseball Game; KIAK Road Rally to Nenana. **Kodiak** — Buskin River Raft Race. **Nenana** — River Daze. **Nome** — Midnight Sun Festival. **Petersburg** — Salmon Derby. **Sitka** — All-Alaska Logging Championships; Southeast Folk Dance Festival; BACA Art Show. **Tanana** — Nuchalawoya Festival. **Wrangell** — Annual Salmon Bake.

JULY

Fourth of July celebrations in most towns and villages. **Fairbanks** — Golden Days; KCFB Bike Race to Nenana; Summer Arts Festival, University of Alaska; World Eskimo-Indian Olympics, University of Alaska. **Haines** — Fort Seward Days. **Homer** — Halibut Derby. **Ketchikan** — Loggers' Carnival. **Kotzebue** — Northwest Native Trade Fair. **Seward** — Mount Marathon Race. **Sitka** — Alaska Arts Southeast Fine Arts Camp. **Soldotna** — Progress Days. **Sterling** — Annual Moose River Raft Race. **Talkeetna** —Moose Dropping Festival. **Wasilla** —Water Festival.

AUGUST

Aniak — Mid-Kuskokwim Agricultural Fair. **Delta** — Deltana Fair. **Fairbanks** — Boreal-Arctic Vegetation Conference, University of Alaska; Tanana Valley Silver Salute. **Haines** — Southeast Alaska State Fair. **Juneau** — Golden North Salmon Derby. **Ketchikan** — Seafest; Blueberry Festival. **Kodiak** — State Fair and Rodeo; *Cry of the Wild Ram,* historical outdoor drama. **Metlakatla** — Founders Day Celebration. **Ninilchik** — Biggest Little Fair in Alaska. **Palmer** — Alaska State Fair. **Seward** — Silver Salmon Festival. **Skagway** — Annual Hugs and Kisses Road Run. **Valdez** — Silver Salmon Derby; Gold Rush Days. **Wrangell** — Annual Silver Salmon Derby.

SEPTEMBER

Anchorage — Alaska Festival of Music. **Fairbanks** — Equinox Marathon, University of Alaska. **Whittier** — Celebration/Salmon Derby.

OCTOBER

Fairbanks — Oktoberfest. **Seward** — Anniversary Fall Festival. **Sitka** — Alaska Day Celebration.

NOVEMBER

Fairbanks — Northern Invitational Mixed Curling Spiel; 10th Annual Christmas Crafts Bazaar. **Kenai** — Christmas Tree Lighting Ceremony. **Ketchikan** — Spring in the Rain Festival; Holiday Fashion Show.

DECEMBER

Anchorage — Christmas Tree Lighting Ceremony. **Barrow** — Christmas Festival. **North Pole** — Candle Lighting and Awards Ceremony.

Camping

Numerous public and privately operated campgrounds are found along Alaska's highways. Electrical hookups and dump stations are scarce. Alaska's back country offers virtually limitless possibilities for wilderness camping. Get permission before camping on private land. If the land is publicly owned, it's worthwhile to contact the agency that manages the land regarding regulations and hiking/camping conditions. Additional details about camping are found in *The MILEPOST®* (available from Alaska Northwest Publishing Company; see page 209).

The U.S. Forest Service maintains campgrounds in the Tongass (southeastern Alaska) and Chugach (southcentral Alaska) national forests, most with tent and trailer sites and minimum facilities. All campgrounds are available first-come, first-served; campground fees vary, from three dollars per night (Tongass National Forest) to five and six dollars per night (Chugach National Forest) depending upon facilities, which in the Chugach can include firegates, pit toilets, garbage pickup, picnic tables and water depending upon the campground. Chugach campgrounds are open from Memorial Day through Labor Day, or until snow conditions cause closing. More information is available in *Community Opportunity Guide,* published by the Regional Forester's Office, Tongass National Forest, P.O. Box 1628, Juneau 99802 or from the Forest Supervisor, Chugach National Forest, 2221 East Northern Lights Boulevard, Suite 238, Anchorage 99508.

The National Park Service (Alaska Regional Office: 2525 Gambell Street, Anchorage 99503) at Denali National Park offers one walk-in and six campgrounds accessible by road; all are available on a first-come, first-served basis. Situated near the park entrance and open year-round are Riley Creek, for tents and trailers, and Morino, for walk-in tent campers. The others are open between May and September, depending on weather. Brochures may be obtained from Denali National Park, P.O. Box 9, Denali Park 99755.

Glacier Bay National Park and Katmai National Park each offer one campground for walk-in campers. Back-country camping is permitted in Denali, Glacier Bay, Katmai and Klondike Gold Rush parks, as well as the other national parks and monuments in Alaska.

Alaska Division of Parks (619 Warehouse Drive, Suite 210, Anchorage 99501) maintains the most extensive system of roadside campgrounds and waysides in Alaska. All are on a first-come, first-served basis. There are no fees.

U.S. Fish and Wildlife Service (state office: 1011 East Tudor, Anchorage 99503) has several wildlife refuges open to campers, although most are not accessible by highway. The Kenai National Wildlife Refuge, however, has several campgrounds accessible from the Sterling Highway linking Homer and Anchorage.

The Bureau of Land Management maintains 27 campgrounds in interior Alaska. BLM campgrounds are free. The BLM has three public-use cabins: the Borealis-LeFevre, the Fred Blixt, and the Cripple Creek. A user fee of two dollars per party per night is required for permits which may be obtained at the BLM Fairbanks District Office, Box 1150, Fairbanks 99701. Brochures describing BLM campgrounds are also available.

(See also *State Park System; National Wildlife Refuges; Hiking; Forest Service Cabins; National Parks, Preserves and Monuments;* and *National Forests.*)

Chambers of Commerce

(Area code throughout Alaska: 907. See also Convention and Visitor Bureaus.)

Alaska State Chamber, 310 Second Street, Juneau 99801, 586-2323
Anchorage Chamber, 415 F Street, Anchorage 99501, 272-2401
Arctic Chamber, P.O. Box 284, Kotzebue 99752, 442-3401
Chugiak-Eagle River Chamber, Box 249, Eagle River 99599
Greater Copper Valley Chamber, P.O. Box 113, Copper Center 99573
Cordova Chamber, P.O. Box 99, Cordova 99574, 424-7260
Delta Junction Chamber, P.O. Box 978, Delta Junction 99737, 895-4439/9641
Dillingham Chamber, P.O. Box 236, Dillingham 99576
Greater Fairbanks Chamber, Box 7446, Fairbanks 99701, 452-1105
Haines Chamber, P.O. Box 518, Haines 99827, 766-2202
Homer Chamber, P.O. Box 541, Homer 99603, 235-7740
Greater Juneau Chamber, 1711 Glacier Avenue, Suite 207, Juneau 99801, 586-6420
Kenai Chamber, P.O. Box 497, Kenai 99611
Greater Ketchikan Chamber, P.O. Box 5957, Ketchikan 99901
Kodiak Area Chamber, P.O. Box 1485, Kodiak 99615, 486-5557
Mid Valley Chamber, Box 193, Houston 99694, 892-6540
Mountain View Chamber, 4231 Mountain View Drive, Mountain View 99504
Nenana Valley Chamber, P.O. Box 268, Nenana 99760
Nome Chamber, P.O. Box 11, Nome 99762, 443-2201
North Pole Community Chamber, P.O. Box 5071, North Pole 99705
Greater Palmer Chamber, P.O. Box 45, Palmer 99645, 745-2880
Petersburg Chamber, P.O. Box 529, Petersburg 99833, 772-3646
Prince of Wales Chamber, Box 227, Craig 99921, 828-3377
Seldovia Chamber, Drawer F, Seldovia 99663
Seward Chamber, P.O. Box 756, Seward 99664, 224-3046
Greater Sitka Chamber, P.O. Box 638, Sitka 99835, 747-8604
Skagway Chamber, P.O. Box 194, Skagway 99840, 983-2264
Soldotna Chamber, P.O. Box 236, Soldotna 99669, 262-9814
Talkeetna Chamber, P.O. Box 334, Talkeetna 99676
Tok Chamber, P.O. Box 389, Tok 99780, 883-4221
Valdez Chamber, P.O. Box 512, Valdez 99686, 835-2330
Greater Wasilla Chamber, P.O. Box 1300, Wasilla 99687, 376-2121
Whittier Chamber, P.O. Box 703, Whittier 99693, 472-2352
Wrangell Chamber, P.O. Box 49, Wrangell 99929

Cheechako

Pronounced *chee-chak-ko,* or *chee-chak-er* by some old-time Alaskans, the word means tenderfoot or greenhorn. According to *The Chinook Jargon,* a dictionary of the old trading language used by traders from the Hudson's Bay Company from the early 1800s, the word cheechako comes from combining the Chinook Indian word *chee,* meaning new, fresh, or just now, with the Nootka Indian word *chako,* which means to come, to approach, or to become. *The Chinook Jargon, A Complete and Exhaustive Lexicon of the Oldest Trade Language of the American Continent,* which was compiled by George C. Shaw and published in 1909, is made up of words from English, French, and at least six different western Indian languages. It was not much used in Alaska except where there were Hudson's Bay Company posts, such as at Wrangell and Fort Yukon.

Chilkoot Trail

The Chilkoot Trail, from Skagway over Chilkoot Pass to Lake Bennett, British Columbia, was one of the established routes to Yukon Territory gold fields during the Klondike gold rush of 1897-98. Thousands of gold stampeders climbed the tortuous trail over Chilkoot Pass that winter. Those who reached Lake Bennett built boats to float down the Yukon River to Dawson City.

Today, the 33-mile Chilkoot Trail is part of Klondike Gold Rush National Historical Park and is climbed each year by hundreds of backpackers. The Chilkoot Trail begins about 8 miles from Skagway on Dyea Road. There are a dozen campgrounds along the trail and ranger stations on both the Alaska and British Columbia portions of the trail (the trail crosses the international border at 3,739-foot Chilkoot Pass, 16.5 miles from the trail head). The trail ends at Bennett, site of a White Pass and Yukon Route railway station, but since the railway suspended service, hikers must walk another 7 miles along the tracks to the Skagway-Carcross Highway, where they can catch a bus to either Skagway or

Carcross. For more information, contact Klondike Gold Rush National Historical Park, Box 517, Skagway 99840.

Related reading: *Chilkoot Pass: The Most Famous Trail in the North.* Revised and expanded second edition by Archie Satterfield. History and a hiking guide. 214 pages, $7.95. See page 208.

Chill Factor

Wind chill can lower the effective temperature many degrees. While Alaska's regions of lowest temperatures also generally have little wind, activity such as riding a snowmobile or even walking can produce the same effect on exposed skin.

Temperature (Fahrenheit)	Wind Chill Temperature at			
	10 mph	20 mph	30 mph	45 mph
40	28	18	13	10
30	16	4	-2	-6
20	4	-10	-18	-22
10	-9	-25	-33	-38
0	-21	-39	-48	-54
-10	-33	-53	-63	-70
-20	-46	-67	-79	-85
-30	-58	-82	-94	-102
-40	-70	-96	-109	-117

The wind's chill factor, when severe, can lead to frostnip (the body's early-warning signal of potential damage from cold — noticeable by a "nipping" feeling in the extremities), frostbite (the forming of small ice crystals in the body tissues), or hypothermia (the dangerous lowering of the body's general temperature). Other factors that combine with wind chill to bring on these potentially damaging or fatal effects are exposure to wet, exhaustion and lack of adequate clothing.

Chitons

World famous as edible delicacies are two of Alaska's marine invertebrates, the king and tanner crabs. However, other shallow-water invertebrates are also favorites of many Alaskans. Two are the gumboot and Chinese slipper chitons. Chitons are oval-shaped creatures whose shells are made up of eight overlapping plates. They fasten themselves tightly to rocks and must be pried loose. The gumboot, largest chiton in the world, is named for its tough, leathery, reddish brown covering which hides its plates. It has long been traditional food for southeastern Alaska Indians.

Related reading: *Cooking Alaskan,* by the editors of *ALASKA®* magazine. Over 1,500 recipes explain everything about the art of cooking the Alaska way. 500 pages, $14.95. *Under Alaskan Seas, The Shallow Water Marine Invertebrates*, by Lou and Nancy Barr. The complete guidebook and reference work to more than 240 varied and fascinating species of Alaska marine invertebrates. Color photographs. 208 pages, $14.95. See pages 207-10.

Climate

According to the Alaska state climatologist, Alaska's climate zones are maritime, transition, continental, and arctic. With the exception of the transition zone along western Alaska, the zones are divided by mountain ranges that form barriers to shallow air masses and modify those deep enough to cross the ranges. The Brooks Range inhibits the southward movement of air from the Arctic Ocean, thus separating the arctic climate zone from the Interior. The Chugach, Wrangell, Aleutian and Alaska mountain ranges limit northward air movement or at least dry the air before it reaches the Interior's continental zone.

Other meteorologic/oceanographic factors affecting Alaska's climate zones are air temperature, water temperature, cloud coverage, and wind

and air pressure. The amount of moisture that air can hold in a gaseous state is highly dependent on its temperature. Warm air can contain more water vapor than cold air. Therefore, precipitation, as rain or snow or other forms, is likely to be heavier from warm than from cold air. Water temperatures change more slowly and much less than land temperatures. For this reason, coastal areas have temperatures more stabilized from summer to winter than do inland areas, which incur wide temperature ranges.

Clouds act as insulation for the earth's surface, reflecting away solar radiation, yet preventing heat which is present from escaping into space.

Wind results from air pressure differences and the tendency of the atmosphere to equalize these differences. If the only influence on the wind were atmospheric pressures, air would flow directly from high to low pressure. However, since the earth is rotating, wind tends to blow around a low pressure center in a counterclockwise direction and around a high pressure center in a clockwise direction. The more the pressure difference between two points, the stronger the wind.

Climate Zones

The maritime climate zone includes Southeast, the northern gulf coast, and the Aleutian Chain. Temperatures are mild — relatively warm in the winter and cool in summer. Precipitation is heavy, 50 to 200 inches annually along the coast and up to 400 inches on mountain slopes. Storms are frequently from the west and southwest resulting in strong winds along the Aleutian Islands and the Alaska Peninsula. Amchitka Island's weather station has recorded the windiest weather in the state, followed by Cold bay. Frequent storms with accompanying high winds account for rough seas with occasional waves up to 50 feet in the Gulf of Alaska, particularly in fall and winter.

The transition zone is, in effect, two separate zones. One is the area between the Coast Mountains and the Alaska Range, which includes Anchorage and the Matanuska Valley. Summer temperatures are higher than those of the maritime climate zone, with colder winter temperatures and less precipitation. Temperatures, however, are not as extreme as in the continental zone. Another transition zone includes the west coast of the state from Bristol Bay to Point Hope. This area has cool summer temperatures that are somewhat colder than those of the maritime zone and cold winter temperatures similar to the continental zone. Cold winter temperatures are partly due to the sea ice in the Chukchi and Bering seas.

The continental climate zone covers the majority of the body of Alaska except the coastal fringes and the arctic slope. It has extreme high and low temperatures and low precipitation. There are fewer clouds in the continental zone than elsewhere so there is more warming by the sun during the long days of summer and more cooling during the long nights of winter. Precipitation is light because air masses affecting the area lose most of their moisture crossing the mountains to the south.

Arctic, north of the Brooks Range, has cold winters, cool summers, and desertlike precipitation. Prevailing winds are from the northeast off the arctic ice pack, which never gets far offshore. Summers are generally cloudy and winters are clear and cold. The cold air allows little precipitation and inhibits evaporation, and because continuous permafrost prevents the percolation of water into the soil, the area is generally marshy with numerous lakes. (See also *Permafrost*.)

The chart below shows normal monthly temperatures and precipitation for 14 communities in Alaska. Included are maximum monthly snowfall for December and annual precipitation. The chart is based on data from NOAA and the Alaska state climatologist.

Average Temperatures (Fahrenheit) and Precipitation (inches)

	Anchorage	Barrow	Bethel	Cold Bay	Fairbanks	Homer	Juneau	Ketchikan	King Salmon	Kodiak	McGrath	Nome	Petersburg	Valdez
January														
Temperature	13.0	-14.4	4.9	28.3	-12.8	20.8	21.8	32.9	12.5	31.9	-10.2	5.8	25.8	25.1
Precipitation	0.80	0.21	0.78	.53	1.65	3.69	13.73	13.73	1.04	8.29	0.81	0.81	8.65	5.05
February														
Temperature	17.9	-14.4	4.9	28.3	-12.8	20.8	21.8	32.9	12.5	31.9	-10.2	5.8	25.8	25.1
Precipitation	0.93	0.17	0.68	2.27	0.42	1.93	3.74	13.57	0.88	6.29	0.63	0.52	8.27	4.1
March														
Temperature	23.7	-15.9	10.7	28.6	8.5	26.9	31.2	38.2	19.2	32.7	8.2	6.6	34.0	30.2
Precipitation	0.69	0.17	0.8	2.31	0.4	1.28	3.34	11.75	1.13	4.06	0.72	0.57	7.17	3.46
April														
Temperature	35.4	-1.7	23.4	33.0	30.2	35.5	39.1	43.2	31.1	38.0	26.7	17.9	40.1	37.7
Precipitation	0.66	0.21	0.71	1.95	0.27	1.31	2.92	12.36	1.05	4.84	0.79	0.64	6.84	3.13
May														
Temperature	46.3	18.8	40.3	39.5	48.2	42.2	46.5	49.1	42.3	43.2	44.6	35.7	46.6	44.7
Precipitation	0.57	0.16	0.8	2.47	0.57	1.07	3.41	9.62	1.18	7.73	0.72	0.54	5.89	2.44
June														
Temperature	54.4	33.3	50.6	45.4	59.3	48.8	52.7	54.4	50.1	49.7	55.2	45.4	52.5	51.0
Precipitation	1.08	0.37	1.34	2.16	1.32	1.05	2.98	7.49	1.5	3.37	1.44	1.19	5.23	2.13
July														
Temperature	58.1	38.9	54.7	50.3	61.5	52.8	55.7	58.2	54.6	53.7	58.2	50.5	55.9	55.0
Precipitation	1.97	0.86	2.11	2.5	1.77	1.47	4.13	7.65	2.08	3.91	2.06	2.2	5.26	3.95
August														
Temperature	56.2	38.0	52.8	51.2	56.6	52.8	54.6	58.6	54.0	54.8	54.4	49.9	55.0	54.1
Precipitation	2.11	.98	3.46	3.7	1.86	2.36	5.02	11.31	3.13	5.21	2.74	3.11	7.08	3.72
September														
Temperature	48.2	30.6	45.0	47.5	44.9	47.3	49.2	54.1	47.1	49.9	44.0	42.3	50.1	47.7
Precipitation	2.45	0.59	2.22	3.77	1.09	2.86	6.4	13.52	2.78	7.6	2.04	2.34	10.4	8.26
October														
Temperature	34.6	14.2	29.7	39.5	25.0	37.3	41.8	46.7	33.2	41.2	25.0	28.0	43.3	38.9
Precipitation	1.73	0.55	1.29	4.29	0.74	3.28	7.71	24.71	1.92	9.99	1.14	1.26	16.97	9.12
November														
Temperature	21.7	-1.0	17.5	34.3	3.9	28.9	32.7	39.8	23.0	34.7	5.5	16.2	35.3	29.7
Precipitation	1.11	0.3	0.96	4.04	0.67	2.91	5.15	16.93	1.4	6.67	1.16	0.94	11.46	6.0
December														
Temperature	13.8	-12.9	4.8	29.5	-10.1	21.8	26.8	35.8	12.0	29.6	-9.4	4.4	29.9	21.0
Precipitation	1.1	0.18	0.98	2.85	0.73	2.58	4.66	16.7	1.24	6.28	1.05	0.65	10.92	5.34
Snowfall (mean)	14.9	2.5	5.1	9.8	12.3	14.0	25.2	16.9	8.9	13.3	17.1	8.3	24.5	70.1
Annual														
Temperature	35.3	9.0	28.3	37.9	25.9	36.6	40.0	45.7	32.8	40.7	25.0	25.5	41.6	38.3
Precipitation	15.2	4.75	16.13	35.01	10.37	23.75	53.15	159.34	19.33	74.24	15.3	14.77	104.14	56.7

Climate Records
Highest temperature: 100°F, at Fort Yukon, June 27, 1915.

Lowest temperature: -80°F, at Prospect Creek Camp, January 23, 1971.

Most annual average precipitation: 332.29 inches, at MacLeod Harbor (Montague Island), 1976.

Most precipitation in 24 hours: 15.2 inches, in Angoon, October 12, 1982.

Least precipitation in a year: 1.61 inches, at Barrow, 1935.

Most monthly precipitation: 70.99 inches, at MacLeod Harbor, November 1976.

Most snowfall in a season: 974.5 inches, at Thompson Pass, 1952-53.

Most snowfall in 24 hours: 62 inches, at Thompson Pass, December 1955.

Most monthly snowfall: 297.9 inches, at Thompson Pass, February 1953.

Least snowfall in a season: 3 inches, at Barrow, 1935-36.

Highest recorded snow depth in one season (also highest ever recorded in North America): 356 inches on Wolverine Glacier, Kenai Peninsula, after winter of 1976-77.

Highest recorded wind speed: 139 mph, at Shemya Island, December 1959.

Coal

About half of the coal resource of the United States is believed to be in Alaska. The demonstrated coal reserve base of the state is over 6 billion short tons, identified coal resources are about 160 billion short tons, and hypothetical and speculative resource estimates range upward to 6 trillion short tons. The three largest coal provinces of the state are northwestern Alaska, Cook Inlet-Susitna Lowland, and the Nenana Trend. Geologists estimate that perhaps 80 percent of Alaska's coal underlies the 23-million-acre National Petroleum Reserve on the North Slope. Although the majority of the coals are of bituminous and subbituminous ranks, anthracite coal does occur in the Bering River and Matanuska fields. In addition to the vast resource base and wide distribution, the extremely low sulfur contents and near proximity to coastal access in certain areas and to the Far East in general are important selling points for Alaska coal.

Exploration, technology, and economics will ultimately determine the marketability of Alaska's coal resources. Large-scale exploration programs have been conducted in most of Alaska's coal fields by private industry and state and federal governments. Diamond Shamrock Corporation and Placer Amex Company are developing the Beluga coal field west of Anchorage on Cook Inlet with hope of initial production for export in 1985. Exploration is under way in the Bering River, Nenana, Yentna and Beluga Lake areas for possible later utilization.

The state's domestic coals can be substituted for expensive and uncertain supplies of fuel oil in many Alaska towns and villages. Mine-mouth power plants and the generation of synthetic fuels (as methanol) are other options. Pacific Rim countries are potential markets for large-scale coal exports. Test shipments of Alaska coal to Korean markets have been made in hopes of establishing long-term contracts. Production of 800,000 short tons per year at the Usibelli Coal Mine near Healy, the only active coal operation in the state, is slated to double in the next three years to meet the terms of the first Asian contract for Alaska coal. Shipments of coal from the mine near Healy will travel via rail cars to Seward and by cargo ships to Korea.

Constitution of Alaska

NOTE: Boxed sections have been amended, see pages 50-52.

Preamble

We the people of Alaska, grateful to God and to those who founded our nation and pioneered this great land, in order to secure and transmit to succeeding generations our heritage of political, civil, and religious liberty within the Union of States, do ordain and establish this constitution for the State of Alaska.

Article I
Declaration of Rights
SECTION 1. This constitution is dedicated to the principles that all persons have a natural right to life, liberty, the pursuit of happiness, and the enjoyment of the rewards of their own industry; that all persons are equal and entitled to equal rights, opportunities, and protection under the law; and that all persons have corresponding obligations to the people and to the State.

SECTION 2. All political power is inherent in the people. All government originates with the people, is founded upon their will only, and is instituted solely for the good of the people as a whole.

SECTION 3. No person is to be denied the enjoyment of any civil or political right because of race, color, creed, or national origin. The legislature shall implement this section.

SECTION 4. No law shall be made respecting an establishment of religion, or prohibiting the free exercise thereof.

SECTION 5. Every person may freely speak, write, and publish on all subjects, being responsible for the abuse of that right.

SECTION 6. The right of the people peaceably to assemble, and to petition the government shall never be abridged.

SECTION 7. No person shall be deprived of life, liberty, or property, without due process of law. The right of all persons to fair and just treatment in the course of the legislative and executive investigations shall not be infringed.

SECTION 8. No person shall be held to answer for a capital, or otherwise infamous crime, unless on a presentment or indictment of a grand jury, except in cases arising in the armed forces in time of war or public danger. Indictment may be waived by the accused. In that case the prosecution shall be by information. The Grand Jury shall consist of at least twelve citizens, a majority of whom concurring may return an indictment. The power of grand juries to investigate and make recommendations concerning the public welfare or safety shall never be suspended.

SECTION 9. No person shall be put in jeopardy twice for the same offense. No person shall be compelled in any criminal proceeding to be a witness against himself.

SECTION 10. Treason against the state consists only in levying war against it, or in adhering to its enemies, giving them aid and comfort. No person shall be convicted of treason, unless on the testimony of two witnesses to the same overt act, or on confession in open court.

SECTION 11. In all criminal prosecutions, the accused shall have the right to a speedy and public trial, by an impartial jury of twelve; except that the legislature may provide for a jury of not more than twelve nor less than six in courts not of record. The accused is entitled to be informed of the nature and cause of the accusation; to be released on bail, except for capital offenses when the proof is evident or the presumption great; to be confronted with the witnesses against him; to have compulsory process for obtaining witnesses in his favor, and to have the assistance of counsel for his defense.

SECTION 12. Excessive bail shall not be required, nor excessive fines imposed nor cruel and unusual punishments inflicted. Penal administration shall be based on the principle of reformation and upon the need for protecting the public.

SECTION 13. The privilege of the writ of habeas corpus shall not be suspended, unless when in cases of rebellion or actual or imminent invasion, the public safety requires it.

SECTION 14. The right of the people to be secure in their persons, houses and other property, papers, and effects, against unreasonable searches and seizures, shall not be violated. No warrants shall issue, but upon probable cause supported by oath or affirmation, and particularly describing the place to be searched, and the persons or things to be seized.

SECTION 15. No bill of attainder or ex post facto law shall be passed. No law impairing the obligation of contracts, and no law making any irrevocable grant of special privileges or immunities shall be passed. No conviction shall work corruption of blood or forfeiture of estate.

SECTION 16. In civil cases where the amount in controversy exceeds two hundred fifty dollars, the right of trial by a jury of twelve is preserved to the same extent as it existed at common law. The legislature may make provision for a verdict by not less than three-fourths of the jury and, in courts not of record, may provide for a jury of not less than six or more than twelve.

SECTION 17. There shall be no imprisonment for debt. This section does not prohibit civil arrest of absconding debtors.

SECTION 18. Private property shall not be taken or damaged for public use without just compensation.

SECTION 19. A well-regulated militia being necessary to the security of a free state, the right of the people to keep and bear arms shall not be infringed.

SECTION 20. No member of the armed forces shall in time of peace be quartered in any house without the consent of the owner or occupant, or in time of war except as prescribed by law. The military shall be in strict subordination to the civil power.

SECTION 21. The enumeration of rights in this constitution shall not impair or deny others retained by the people.

AMENDMENT: SECTION 22
SEE PAGE 51.

Article II
The Legislature

SECTION 1. The legislature power of the State is vested in the legislature consisting of a senate with a membership of twenty and a house of representatives with a membership of forty.

SECTION 2. A member of the legislature shall be a qualified voter who has been a resident of Alaska for at least three years and of the district from which elected for at least one year, immediately preceding his filing for office. A senator shall be at least twenty-five years of age and a representative at least twenty-one years of age.

SECTION 3. Legislators shall be elected at general elections. Their terms begin on the fourth Monday of the January following election unless otherwise provided by law. The term of representatives shall be two years, and the term of senators, four years. One-half of the senators shall be elected every two years. (*Exercising its authority under this section the legislature has provided that legislative terms begin on the second Monday in January; See AS 24.05.080.*)

SECTION 4. A vacancy in the legislature shall be filled for the unexpired term as provided by law. If no provision is made, the governor shall fill the vacancy by appointment.

SECTION 5. No legislator may hold any other office or position of profit under the United States or the State. During the term for which elected and for one year thereafter, no legislator may be nominated, elected, or appointed to any other office or position of profit which has been created, or the salary or emoluments of which have been increased, while he was a member. This section shall not prevent any person from seeking or holding the office of governor, lieutenant governor, or member of Congress. This section shall not apply to employment by or election to a constitutional convention. (The above Constitutional Amendment was approved by the voters of the State August 25, 1970. The words secretary of state were changed to lieutenant governor.)

SECTION 6. Legislators may not be held to answer before any other tribunal for any statement made in the exercise of their legislative duties while the legislature is in session. Members attending, going to, or returning from legislative sessions are not subject to civil process and are privileged from arrest except for felony or breach of the peace.

SECTION 7. Legislators shall receive annual salaries. They may receive a per diem allowance for expenses while in session and are entitled to travel expenses going to and from sessions. Presiding officers may receive additional compensation.

SECTION 8. The legislature shall convene each year on the fourth Monday in January, but the month and day may be changed by law. (Exercising its authority under this section, the legislature has provided that it shall convene on the second Monday in January; See AS 24.05.090.)

SECTION 9. Special sessions may be called by the governor or by vote of two-thirds of the legislators. The vote may be conducted by the legislative council or as prescribed by law. At special sessions called by the governor, legislation shall be limited to subjects designated in his proclamation calling the session or to subjects presented by him. Special sessions are limited to thirty days.

SECTION 10. Neither house may adjourn or recess for longer than three days unless the other concurs. If the two houses cannot agree on the time of adjournment and either house certifies the disagreement to the governor, he may adjourn the legislature.

SECTION 11. There shall be a legislative council, and the legislature may establish other interim committees. The council and other interim committees may meet between legislative sessions. They may perform duties and employ personnel as provided by the legislature. Their members may receive an allowance for expenses while performing their duties.

SECTION 12. The houses of each legislature shall adopt uniform rules of procedure. Each house may choose its officers and employees. Each is the judge of the election and qualifications of its members and may expel a member with the concurrence of two-thirds of its members. Each shall keep a journal of its proceedings. A majority of the membership of each house constitutes a quorum to do business, but a smaller number may adjourn from day to day and may compel attendance of absent members. The legislature shall regulate lobbying.

SECTION 13. Every bill shall be confined to one subject unless it is an appropriation bill or one codifying, revising, or rearranging existing laws. Bills for appropriations shall be confined to appropriations. The subject of each bill shall be expressed in the title. The enacting clause shall be: "Be it enacted by the Legislature of the State of Alaska."

SECTION 14. The legislature shall estab-lish the procedure for enactment of bills into law. No bill may become law unless it has passed three readings in each house on three separate days, except that any bill may be advanced from second to third reading on the same day by concurrence of three-fourths of the house considering it. No bill may become law without an affirmative vote of a majority of the membership of each house. The yeas and nays on final passage shall be entered in the journal.

SECTION 15. The governor may veto bills passed by the legislature. He may, by veto, strike or reduce items in appropriations bills. He shall return any vetoed bill, with a statement of his objections, to the house of origin.

SECTION 16. Upon receipt of a veto message, the legislature shall meet immedi-ately in joint session and reconsider passage of the vetoed bill or item. Bills to raise revenue and appropriation bills or items, although vetoed, become law by affirmative vote of three-fourths of the membership of the legislature. Other vetoed bills become law by affirmative vote of two-thirds of the membership of the legislature. The vote on reconsideration of a vetoed bill shall be entered on the journals of both houses.

SECTION 17. A bill becomes law if, while the legislature is in session, the governor neither signs nor vetoes it within fifteen days, Sundays excepted, after its delivery to him. If the legislature is not in session and the governor neither signs nor vetoes a bill within twenty days, Sundays excepted, after its delivery to him, the bill becomes law.

SECTION 18. Laws passed by the legislature become effective ninety days after enactment. The legislature may, by concurrence of two-thirds of the member-ship of each house, provide for another effective date.

SECTION 19. The legislature shall pass no local or special act if a general act can be made applicable. Whether a general act can be made applicable shall be subject to judicial determination. Local acts necessi-tating appropriations by a political sub-division may not become effective unless approved by a majority of the qualified voters voting thereon in the subdivision affected.

SECTION 20. All civil officers of the State are subject to impeachment by the legislature. Impeachment shall originate in the senate and must be approved by a two-thirds vote of its members. The motion for impeachment shall list fully the basis for the proceeding. Trial on impeachment shall be conducted by the house of representa-tives. A supreme court justice designated by the court shall preside at the trial. Concurrence of two-thirds of the members of the house is required for a judgment of impeachment. The judgment may not extend beyond removal from office, but shall not prevent proceedings in the courts on the same or related charges.

SECTION 21. The legislature shall estab-lish procedures for suits against the State.

Article III
The Executive
SECTION 1. The executive power of the State is vested in the governor.

SECTION 2. The governor shall be at least thirty years of age and a qualified voter of the State. He shall have been a resident of Alaska at least seven years immediately preceding his filing for office, and he shall have been a citizen of the United States for at least seven years.

SECTION 3. The governor shall be chosen by the qualified voters of the State at a general election. The candidate receiving the greatest number of votes shall be governor.

SECTION 4. The term of office of the governor is four years, beginning at noon on the first Monday in December following his election and ending at noon on the first Monday in December four years later.

SECTION 5. No person who has been elected governor for two full successive terms shall be again eligible to hold that office until one full term has intervened.

SECTION 6. The governor shall not hold any other office or position of profit under the United States, the State, or its political subdivisions.

SECTION 7. There shall be a lieutenant governor. He shall have the same qualifications as the governor and serve for the same term. He shall perform such duties as may be prescribed by law and as may be delegated to him by the governor. (*The above Constitutional Amendment was approved by the voters of the State August 25, 1970. The words secretary of state were changed to lieutenant governor.*)

SECTION 8. The lieutenant governor shall be nominated in the manner provided by law for nominating candidates for other elective offices. In the general election the votes cast for a candidate for governor shall be considered as cast also for the candidate for lieutenant governor running jointly with him. The candidate whose name appears on the ballot jointly with that of the successful candidate for governor shall be elected lieutenant governor. (*The above Constitutional Amendment was approved by the voters of the State August 25, 1970. The words secretary of state were changed to lieutenant governor.*)

SECTION 9. In case of the temporary absence of the governor from office, the lieutenant governor shall serve as acting governor. (*The above Constitutional Amendment was approved by the voters of the State August 25, 1970. The words secretary of state were changed to lieutenant governor.*)

SECTION 10. If the governor-elect dies, resigns, or is disqualified, the lieutenant governor elected with him shall succeed to the office of governor for the full term. If the governor-elect fails to assume office for any other reason, the lieutenant governor elected with him shall serve as acting governor, and shall succeed to the office if the governor-elect does not assume his office within six months of the beginning of the term. (*The above Constitutional Amendment was approved by the voters of the State August 25, 1970. The words secretary of state were changed to lieutenant governor.*)

SECTION 11. In case of a vacancy in the office of governor for any reason, the lieutenant governor shall succeed to the office for the remainder of the term. (*The above Constitutional Amendment was approved by the voters of the State August 25, 1970. The words secretary of state were changed to lieutenant governor.*)

SECTION 12. Whenever for a period of six months, a governor has been continuously absent from office or has been unable to discharge the duties of his office by reason of mental or physical disability, the office shall be deemed vacant. The procedure for determining absence and disability shall be prescribed by law.

SECTION 13. Provisions shall be made by law for succession to the office of governor and for an acting governor in the event that the lieutenant governor is unable to succeed to the office or act as governor. No election of a lieutenant governor shall be held except at the time of electing a governor. (*The above Constitutional Amendment was approved by the voters of the State August 25, 1970. The words secretary of state were changed to lieutenant governor.*)

SECTION 14. When the lieutenant governor succeeds to the office of governor, he shall have the title, power, duties and emoluments of that office. (*The above Constitutional Amendment was approved by the voters of the State August 25, 1970. The words secretary of state were changed to lieutenant governor.*)

SECTION 15. The compensation of the governor and the lieutenant governor shall be prescribed by law and shall not be diminished during their term of office, unless by general law applying to all salaried officers of the State. (*The above Constitutional Amendment was approved by the voters of the State August 25, 1970. The words secretary of state were changed to lieutenant governor.*)

SECTION 16. The governor shall be responsible for the faithful execution of the laws. He may, by appropriate court action or proceeding brought in the name of the State, enforce compliance with any constitutional or legislative mandate, or restrain violation of any constitutional or legislative power, duty, or right by any officer, department, or agency of the State or any of its political subdivisions. This authority shall not be construed to authorize any action or proceeding against the legislature.

SECTION 17. Whenever the governor considers it in the public interest, he may convene the legislature, either house, or the two houses in joint session.

SECTION 18. The governor shall, at the beginning of each session, and may at other times, give the legislature information concerning the affairs of the State and recommend the measures he considers necessary.

SECTION 19. The governor is commander-in-chief of the armed forces of the State. He may call out these forces to execute the laws, suppress or prevent insurrection or lawless violence, or repel invasion. The governor, as provided by law, shall appoint all general and flag officers of the armed forces of the State, subject to confirmation by a majority of the members of the legislature in joint session. He shall appoint and commission all other officers.

SECTION 20. The governor may proclaim martial law when the public safety requires it in case of rebellion or actual or imminent invasion. Martial law shall not continue for longer than twenty days without the approval of a majority of the members of the legislature in joint session.

SECTION 21. Subject to procedures prescribed by law, the governor may grant pardons, commutations, and reprieves, and may suspend and remit fines and forfeitures. This power shall not extend to impeachment. A parole system shall be provided by law.

SECTION 22. All executive and administrative offices, departments, and agencies of the state government and their respective functions, powers, and duties shall be allocated by law among and within not more than twenty principal departments, so as to group them as far as practicable according to major purposes. Regulatory quasijudicial, and temporary agencies may be established by law and need not be allocated within a principal department.

SECTION 23. The governor may make changes in the organization of the executive branch or in the assignment of functions among its units which he considers necessary for efficient administration. Where these changes require the force of law, they shall be set forth in executive orders. The legislature shall have sixty days of a regular session, or a full session if of shorter duration, to disapprove these executive orders. Unless disapproved by resolution concurred in by a majority of the members in joint session, these orders become effective at a date thereafter to be designated by the governor.

SECTION 24. Each principal department shall be under the supervision of the governor.

SECTION 25. The head of each principal department shall be a single executive unless otherwise provided by law. He shall be appointed by the governor, subject to confirmation by a majority of the members of the legislature in joint session, and shall serve at the pleasure of the governor, except as otherwise provided in this article with respect to the lieutenant governor. The heads of all principal departments shall be citizens of the United States. (*The above Constitutional Amendment was approved by the voters of the State August 25, 1970. The words secretary of state were changed to lieutenant governor.*)

SECTION 26. When a board or commission is at the head of a principal department or a regulatory or quasi-judicial agency, its members shall be appointed by the governor, subject to confirmation by a majority of the members of the legislature in joint session, and may be removed as provided by law. They shall be citizens of the United States. The board or commission may appoint a principal executive officer when authorized by law, but the appointment shall be subject to the approval of the governor.

SECTION 27. The governor may make appointments to fill vacancies occurring during a recess of the legislature, in offices requiring confirmation by the legislature.

The duration of such appointments shall be prescribed by law.

Article IV
The Judiciary

SECTION 1. The judicial power of the State is vested in a supreme court, a superior court and the courts established by the legislature. The jurisdiction of courts shall be prescribed by law. The courts shall constitute a unified judicial system for operation and administration. Judicial districts shall be established by law.

SECTION 2. (a) The supreme court shall be the highest court of the State, with final appellate jurisdiction. It shall consist of three justices, one of whom is chief justice. The number of justices may be increased by law upon the request of the supreme court.

(b) The chief justice shall be selected from among the justices of the supreme court by a majority vote of the justices. His term of office is three years. A justice may serve more than one term as chief justice but he may not serve consecutive terms in that office. (*The above Constitutional Amendment was approved by the voters of the State August 25, 1970. Subsection (b) was added.*)

SECTION 3. The superior court shall be the trial court of general jurisdiction and shall consist of five judges. The number of judges may be changed by law.

SECTION 4. Supreme court justices and superior court judges shall be citizens of the United States and of the State, licensed to practice law in the State, and possessing any additional qualifications prescribed by law. Judges of other courts shall be selected in a manner, for terms, and with qualifications prescribed by law.

SECTION 5. The governor shall fill any vacancy in an office of supreme court justice or superior court judge by appointing one of two or more persons nominated by the judicial council.

SECTION 6. Each supreme court justice and superior court judge shall, in the manner provided by law, be subject to approval or rejection on a non-partisan ballot at the first general election held more than three years after his appointment. Thereafter, each supreme court justice shall be subject to approval or rejection in a like manner every tenth year, and each superior court judge, every sixth year.

SECTION 7. The office of any supreme court justice or superior court judge becomes vacant ninety days after the election at which he is rejected by a majority of those voting on the question, or for which he fails to file his declaration of candidacy to succeed himself.

SECTION 8. The judicial council shall consist of seven members. Three attorney members shall be appointed for six-year terms by the governing body of the organized state bar. Three non-attorney members shall be appointed by the governor subject to confirmation by a majority of the members of the legislature in joint session. Vacancies shall be filled for the unexpired term in like manner. Appointments shall be made with due consideration to area representation and without regard to political affiliation. The chief justice of the supreme court shall be ex officio the seventh member and. chairman of the judicial council. No member of the judicial council, except the chief justice, may hold any other office or position of profit under the United States or the State. The judicial council shall act by concurrence of four or more members and according to rules which it adopts.

SECTION 9. The judicial council shall conduct studies for improvement of the administration of justice, and make reports and recommendations to the supreme court and to the legislature at intervals of not more than two years. The judicial council shall perform other duties assigned by law.

SECTION 10. The. commission or judicial qualifications shall consist of nine members, as follows: one justice of the supreme court, elected by the justices of the supreme court; three judges of the superior court, elected by the judges of the superior court; one judge of the district court, elected by the judges of the district court; two members who have practiced law in this state for ten years, appointed by the governing body of the organized bar; and two persons who are not judges, retired judges, or members of the state bar, appointed by the governor and subject to confirmation by a majority of the members of the legislature in joint session. In addition to being subject to impeachment under Section 12 of this article, a justice or judge may be disqualified from acting as such and may be suspended, removed from office, retired, or censured by the supreme court upon the recommendation of the commission. The powers and duties of the commission and the bases for judicial disqualification shall be established by law. (*The above Constitutional Amendment was approved by the voters of the State August 27, 1968. Section 10, Article IV, pertaining to Incapacity of Judges was repealed.*)

SECTION 11. Justices and judges shall be retired at the age of seventy except as provided in this article. The basis and amount of retirement pay shall be prescribed by law. Retired judges shall render no further service on the bench except for special assignments as provided by court rule.

SECTION 12. Impeachment of any justice or judge for malfeasance or misfeasance in the performance of his official duties shall be according to procedure prescribed for civil officers.

SECTION 13. Justices, judges, and members of the judicial council and the commission on judicial qualifications shall receive compensation as prescribed by law. Compensation of justices and judges shall not be diminished during their terms of office, unless by general law applying to all salaried officers of the State. (*The above Constitutional Amendment was approved by the voters of the State August 27, 1968. The words "and the commission on judicial qualifications" were incorporated in this Section.*)

SECTION 14. Supreme court justices and superior court judges while holding office may not practice law, hold office in a political party, or hold any other office or position of profit under the United States,

the State, or its political subdivisions. Any supreme court justice or superior court judge filing for another elective public office forfeits his judicial position.

SECTION 15. The supreme court shall make and promulgate rules governing the administration of all courts. It shall make and promulgate rules governing practice and procedure in civil and criminal cases in all courts. These rules may be changed by the legislature by two-thirds vote of the members elected to each house.

SECTION 16. The chief justice of the supreme court shall be the administrative head of all courts. He may assign judges from one court or division thereof to another for temporary service. The chief justice shall, with the approval of the supreme court, appoint an administrative director to serve at the pleasure of the supreme court and to supervise the administrative operations of the judicial system. (*The above Constitutional Amendment was approved by the voters of the State August 25, 1970. The amendment substituted "the pleasure of the supreme court" for "his pleasure" in the last sentence.*)

Article V
Suffrage and Elections

SECTION 1. Every citizen of the United States who is at least eighteen years of age, who meets registration requirements which may be prescribed by law, and who is qualified to vote under this article, may vote in any state or local election. A voter shall have been, immediately preceding the election, for one year a resident of Alaska and for thirty days a resident of the election district in which he seeks to vote, except that for purposes of voting for President and Vice President of the United States other residency requirements may be prescribed by law. Additional voting qualifications may be prescribed by law for bond issue elections of political subdivisions. (*The above Constitutional Amendment was approved by the voters of the State August 25, 1970. It changed the voting age from nineteen years to eighteen years and deleted the sentence: "A voter shall be able to read or speak the English language as prescribed by law, unless prevented by physical disability."*)

SECTION 2. No person may vote who has been convicted of a felony involving moral turpitude unless his civil rights have been restored. No person may vote who has been judicially determined to be of unsound mind unless the disability has been removed.

SECTION 3. Methods of voting, including absentee voting, shall be prescribed by law. Secrecy of voting shall be preserved. The procedure for determining election contests, with right of appeal to the courts, shall be prescribed by law.

SECTION 4. The legislature may provide a system of permanent registration of voters, and may establish voting precincts within election districts.

SECTION 5. General elections shall be held on the second Tuesday in October of every even-numbered year, but the month and day may be changed by law.

(Exercising its authority under this section, the legislature has provided that the date of general election is the Tuesday after the first Monday in November in every even-numbered year; See AS 15.15.020.)

Article VI
Legislative Apportionment

SECTION 1. Members of the house of representatives shall be elected by the qualified voters of the respective election districts. Until reapportionment, election districts and the number of representatives to be elected from each district shall be as set forth in Section 1 of Article XIV.

SECTION 2. Members of the senate shall be elected by the qualified voters of the respective senate districts. Senate districts shall be as set forth in Section 2 of Article XIV, subject to changes authorized in this article.

SECTION 3. The governor shall reapportion the house of representatives immediately following the official reporting of each decennial census of the United States. Reapportionment shall be based upon civilian population within each election district as reported by the census.

SECTION 4. Reapportionment shall be by the methods of equal proportions, except that each election district having the major fraction of the quotient obtained by dividing total civilian population by forty shall have one representative.

SECTION 5. Should the total civilian population within any election district fall below one-half of the quotient, the district shall be attached to an election district within its senate district, and the reapportionment for the new district shall be determined as provided in Section 4 of this article.

SECTION 6. The governor may further redistrict by changing the size and area of election districts, subject to the limitations of this article. Each new district so created shall be formed of contiguous and compact territory containing as nearly as practicable a relatively integrated socio-economic area. Each shall contain a population at least equal to the quotient obtained by dividing the total civilian population by forty. Consideration may be given to local government boundaries. Drainage and other geographic features shall be used in describing boundaries whenever possible.

SECTION 7. The senate districts, described in Section 2 of Article XIV, may be modified to reflect changes in election districts. A district, although modified, shall retain its total number of senators and its approximate perimeter.

SECTION 8. The governor shall appoint a reapportionment board to act in an advisory capacity to him. It shall consist of five members, none of whom may be public employees or officials. At least one member each shall be appointed from the Southeastern, Southcentral, Central and Northwestern Senate Districts. Appointments shall be made without regards to political affiliation. Board members shall be compensated.

SECTION 9. The board shall elect one of its members chairman and may employ temporary assistants. Concurrence of three members is required for a ruling or determination, but a lesser number may conduct hearings or otherwise act for the board.

SECTION 10. Within ninety days following the official reporting of each decennial census, the board shall submit to the governor a plan for reapportionment and redistricting as provided in this article. Within ninety days after receipt of the plan, the governor shall issue a proclamation of reapportionment and redistricting as provided in this article. Within ninety days after receipt of the plan, the governor shall issue a proclamation of reapportionment and redistricting. An accompanying statement shall explain any change from the plan of the board. The reapportionment and redistricting shall be effective for the election of members of the legislature until after the official reporting of the next decennial census.

SECTION 11. Any qualified voter may apply to the superior court to compel the governor, by mandamus or otherwise to perform his reapportionment duties or to correct any error in redistricting or reapportionment. Application to compel the governor to perform his reapportionment duties must be filed within thirty days of the expiration of either of the two ninety-day periods specified in this article. Application to compel correction of any error in redistricting or reapportionment must be filed within thirty days following the proclamation. Original jurisdiction in these matters is hereby vested in the superior court. On appeal, the cause shall be reviewed by the supreme court upon the law and the facts.

Article VII
Health, Education, and Welfare

SECTION 1. The legislature shall by general law establish and maintain a system of public schools open to all children of the State, and may provide for other public educational institutions. Schools and institutions so established shall be free from sectarian control. No money shall be paid from public funds for the direct benefit of any religious or other private educational institution.

SECTION 2. The University of Alaska is hereby established as the state university and constituted a body corporate. It shall have title to all real and personal property now or hereafter set aside for or conveyed to it. Its property shall be administered and disposed of according to law.

SECTION 3. The University of Alaska shall be governed by a board of regents. The regents shall be appointed by the governor, subject to confirmation by a majority of the members of the legislature in joint session. The board shall, in accordance with law, formulate policy and appoint the president of the university. He shall be the executive officer of the board.

SECTION 4. The legislature shall provide for the promotion and protection of public health.

SECTION 5. The legislature shall provide for public welfare.

Article VIII
Natural Resources

SECTION 1. It is the policy of the State to encourage the settlement of its land and the

43

development of its resources by making them available for maximum use consistent with the public interest.

SECTION 2. The legislature shall provide for the utilization, development, and conservation of all natural resources belonging to the State, including land and waters, for the maximum benefit of its people.

SECTION 3. Wherever occurring in the natural state, fish, wildlife, and waters are reserved to the people for common use.

SECTION 4. Fish, forests, wildlife, grasslands, and all other replenishable resources belonging to the State shall be utilized, developed, and maintained on the sustained yield principle, subject to preferences among beneficial uses.

SECTION 5. The legislature may provide for facilities, improvements, and services to assure greater utilization, development, reclamation, and settlement of lands, and to assure fuller utilization and development of the fisheries, wildlife, and waters.

SECTION 6. Lands and interests therein, including submerged and tidal lands, possessed or acquired by the State, and not used or intended exclusively for governmental purposes, constitute the state public domain. The legislature shall provide for the selection of lands granted to the State by the United States, and for the administration of the state public domain.

SECTION 7. The legislature may provide for the acquisition of sites, objects, and areas of natural beauty or of historic, cultural, recreational, or scientific value. It may reserve them from the public domain and provide for their administration and preservation for the use, enjoyment, and welfare of the people.

SECTION 8. The legislature may provide for the leasing of, and the issuance of permits for exploration of, any part of the public domain or interest therein, subject to reasonable concurrent uses. Leases and permits shall provide, among other conditions, for payment by the party at fault for damage or injury arising from noncompliance with terms governing concurrent use, and for forfeiture in the event of breach of conditions.

SECTION 9. Subject to the provisions of this section, the legislature may provide for the sale or grant of state lands, or interests therein, and establish sales procedures. All sales or grants shall contain such reservations to the State of all resources as may be required by Congress or the State and shall provide for access to these resources. Reservation of access shall not unnecessarily impair the owners' use, prevent the control of trespass, or preclude compensation for damages.

SECTION 10. No disposals or leases of state lands, or interests therein, shall be made without prior public notice and other safeguards of the public interest as may be prescribed by law.

SECTION 11. Discovery and appropriation shall be the basis for establishing a right in those minerals reserved to the State which, upon the date of ratification of this constitution by the people of Alaska, were subject to location under the federal mining laws. Prior discovery, location, and filing, as prescribed by law, shall establish a prior right to these minerals and also a prior right to permits, leases, and transferable licenses for their extraction. Continuation of these rights shall depend upon the performance of annual labor, or the payment of fees, rents, or royalties, or upon other requirements as may be prescribed by law. Surface uses of land by a mineral claimant shall be limited to those necessary for the extraction or basic processing of the mineral deposits, or for both. Discovery and appropriation shall initiate a right, subject to further requirements of law, to patent of mineral lands if authorized by the State and not prohibited by Congress. The provisions of this section shall apply to all other minerals reserved to the State which by law are declared subject to appropriation.

SECTION 12. The legislature shall provide for the issuance, types and terms of leases for coal, oil, gas, oil shale, sodium, phosphate, potash, sulfur, pumice, and other minerals as may be prescribed by law. Leases and permits giving the exclusive right of exploration for these minerals for specific periods and areas, subject to reasonable concurrent exploration as to different classes of minerals, may be authorized by law. Like leases and permits giving the exclusive right of prospecting by geophysical, geochemical, and similar methods for all minerals may also be authorized by law.

SECTION 13. All surface and subsurface waters reserved to the people for common use, except mineral and medicinal waters, are subject to appropriation. Priority of appropriation shall give prior right. Except for public water supply, an appropriation of water shall be limited to stated purposes and subject to preferences among beneficial uses, concurrent or otherwise, as prescribed by law, and to the general reservation of fish and wildlife.

SECTION 14. Free access to the navigable or public waters of the State, as defined by the legislature, shall not be denied any citizen of the United States or resident of the State, except that the legislature may by general law regulate and limit such access for other beneficial uses or public purposes.

SECTION 15. No exclusive right or special privilege of fishery shall be created or authorized in the natural waters of the State.

SECTION 16. No person shall be involuntarily divested of his right to the use of waters, his interests in lands, or improvements affecting either, except for a superior beneficial use or public purpose and then only with just compensation and by operation of law.

SECTION 17. Laws and regulations governing the use or disposal of natural resources shall apply equally to all persons similarly situated with reference to the subject matter and purpose to be served by the law or regulation.

SECTION 18. Proceeding in eminent domain may be undertaken for private ways of necessity to permit essential access for extraction or utilization of resources. Just compensation shall be made for property taken or for resultant damages to other property rights.

Article IX
Finance and Taxation

SECTION 1. The power of taxation shall never be surrendered. This power shall not be suspended or contracted away, except as provided in this article.

SECTION 2. The lands and other property belonging to the citizens of the United States residing without the State shall never be taxed at a higher rate than the lands and other property belonging to the residents of the State.

SECTION 3. Standards for appraisal of all property assessed by the State or its political subdivisions shall be prescribed by law.

SECTION 4. The real and personal property of the State or its political subdivisions shall be exempt from taxation under conditions and exceptions which may be provided by law. All, or any portion of, property used exclusively for nonprofit religious, charitable, cemetery, or educational purposes, as defined by law, shall be exempt from taxation. Other exemptions of like or different kind may be granted by general law. All valid existing exemption shall be retained until otherwise provided by law.

SECTION 5. Private leaseholds, contracts, or interests in land or property owned or held by the United States, the State, or its political subdivisions, shall be taxable to the extent of the interests.

SECTION 6. No tax shall be levied, or appropriation of public money made, or public property transferred, nor shall the public credit be used, except for a public purpose.

SECTION 7. The proceeds of any state tax or license shall not be dedicated to any special purpose, except when required by the federal government for state participation in federal programs. This provision shall not prohibit the continuance of any dedication for special purposes existing upon the date of ratification of this constitution by the people of Alaska.

SECTION 8. No state debt shall be contracted unless authorized by law for capital improvements and ratified by the majority of the qualified voters of the State who vote on the question. The State may, as provided by law and without ratification, contract debt for the purpose of repelling invasion, suppressing insurrection, defending the State in war, meeting natural disasters, or redeeming indebtedness outstanding at the time this constitution becomes effective.

SECTION 9. No debt shall be contracted by any political subdivision of the State, unless authorized for capital improvements by its governing body and ratified by a majority vote of those qualified to vote and voting on the question.

SECTION 10. The State and its political subdivisions may borrow money to meet appropriations for any fiscal year in anticipation of the collection of the revenues for that year, but all debt so contracted shall be paid before the end of the next fiscal year.

SECTION 11. The restrictions on contracting debt do not apply to debt incurred through the issuance of revenue bonds by a public enterprise or public corporation of the State or a political subdivision, when the only security is the revenues of the enterprise or corporation. The restrictions do not apply to indebtedness to be paid from special assessments on the benefited property, nor do they apply to refunding indebtedness of the State or its political subdivisions.

SECTION 12. The governor shall submit to the legislature, at a time fixed by law, a budget for the next fiscal year setting forth all proposed expenditures and anticipated income of all departments, offices, and agencies of the state. The governor, at the same time, shall submit a general appropriation bill to authorize the proposed expenditures, and a bill or bills covering recommendations in the budget for new or additional revenues.

SECTION 13. No money shall be withdrawn from the treasury except in accordance with appropriations made by law. No obligation for the payment of money shall be incurred except as authorized by law. Unobligated appropriations outstanding at the end of the period of time specified by law shall be void.

SECTION 14. The legislature shall appoint an auditor to serve at its pleasure. The auditor shall conduct post-audits as prescribed by law and shall report to the legislature and to the governor.

AMENDMENT: SECTION 15
SEE PAGE 51.

AMENDMENT: SECTION 16
SEE PAGE 52.

Article X
Local Government

SECTION 1. The purpose of this article is to provide for maximum local self-government with a minimum of local government units, and to prevent duplication of tax-levying jurisdictions. A liberal construction shall be given to the powers of local government units.

SECTION 2. All local government powers shall be vested in boroughs and cities. The State may delegate taxing powers to organized boroughs and cities only.

SECTION 3. The entire State shall be divided into boroughs, organized or unorganized. They shall be established in a manner and according to standards provided by law. The standards shall include population, geography, economy, transportation, and other factors. Each borough shall embrace an area and population with common interests to the maximum degree possible. The legislature shall classify boroughs and prescribe their powers and functions. Methods by which boroughs may be organized, incorporated, merged, consolidated, reclassified, or dissolved shall be prescribed by law.

SECTION 4. The governing body of the organized borough shall be the assembly, and its composition shall be established by law or charter. Each city of the first class, and each city of any other class designated by law, shall be represented on the assembly by one or more members of its council. The other members of the assembly shall be elected from and by the qualified voters resident outside such cities.

SECTION 5. Service areas to provide special services within an organized borough may be established, altered, or abolished by the assembly, subject to the provisions of law or charter. A new service area shall not be established if, consistent with the purposes of this article, the new service can be provided by an existing service area, by incorporation as a city, or by annexation to a city. The assembly may authorize the levying of taxes, charges, or assessments within a service area to finance the special services.

SECTION 6. The legislature shall provide for the performance of services it deems necessary or advisable in unorganized boroughs, allowing for maximum local participation and responsibility. It may exercise any power or function in an unorganized borough which the assembly may exercise in an organized borough.

SECTION 7. Cities shall be incorporated in a manner prescribed by law, and shall be a part of the borough in which they are located. Cities shall have the powers and functions conferred by law or charter. They may be merged, consolidated, classified, reclassified, or dissolved in the manner provided by law.

SECTION 8. The governing body of a city shall be the council.

SECTION 9. The qualified voters of any borough of the first class or city of the first class may adopt, amend, or repeal a home rule charter in a manner provided by law. In the absence of such legislation, the governing body of a borough or city of the first class shall provide the procedure for the preparation and adoption or rejection of the charter. All charters, or parts or amendments of charters, shall be submitted to the qualified voters of the borough or city, and shall become effective if approved by a majority of those who vote on the specific question.

SECTION 10. The legislature may extend home rule to other boroughs and cities.

SECTION 11. A home rule borough or city may exercise all legislative powers not prohibited by law or by charter.

SECTION 12. A local boundary commission or board shall be established by law in the executive branch of the state government. The commission or board may consider any proposed local government boundary change. It may present proposed changes to the legislature during the first ten days of any regular session. The change shall become effective forty-five days after presentation or at the end of the session, whichever is earlier, unless disapproved by a resolution concurred in by a majority of the members of each house. The commission or board, subject to law, may establish procedures whereby boundaries may be adjusted by local action.

SECTION 13. Agreements, including those for cooperative or joint administration of any functions or powers, may be made by any local government with any other local government, with the State, or with the United States, unless otherwise provided by law or charter. A city may transfer to the borough in which it is located any of its powers or functions unless prohibited by law or charter, and may in like manner revoke the transfer.

SECTION 14. An agency shall be established by law in the executive branch of the state government to advise and assist local governments. It shall review their activities, collect and publish local government information, and perform other duties prescribed by law.

SECTION 15. Special service districts existing at the time a borough is organized shall be integrated with the government of the borough as provided by law.

Article XI
Initiative, Referendum, and Recall

SECTION 1. The people may propose and enact laws by the initiative, and approve or reject acts of the legislature by the referendum.

SECTION 2. An initiative or referendum is proposed by an application containing the bill to be initiated or the act to be referred. The application shall be signed by not less than one hundred qualified voters as sponsors, and shall be filed with the lieutenant governor. If he finds it in proper form he shall so certify. Denial of certification shall be subject to judicial review. (*The above Constitutional Amendment was approved by the voters of the State August 25, 1970. The words secretary of state were changed to lieutenant governor.*)

SECTION 3. After certification of the application, a petition containing a summary of the subject matter shall be prepared by the lieutenant governor for circulation by the sponsors. If signed by qualified voters, equal in number to ten per cent of those who voted in the preceding general election and resident in at least two-thirds of the election districts of the State, it may be filed with the lieutenant governor. (*The above Constitutional Amendment was approved by the voters of the State August 25, 1970. The words secretary of state were changed to lieutenant governor.*)

SECTION 4. An initiative petition may be filed at any time. The lieutenant governor shall prepare a ballot title and proposition summarizing the proposed law, and shall place them on the ballot for the first statewide election held more than one hundred twenty days after adjournment of the legislative session following the filing. If, before the election, substantially the same measure has been enacted, the petition is void. (*The above Constitutional Amendment was approved by the voters of the State August 25, 1970. The words Secretary of state were changed to lieutenant governor.*)

SECTION 5. A referendum petition may be filed only within ninety days after adjournment of the legislative session at which the act was passed. The lieutenant governor shall prepare a ballot title and proposition summarizing the act and shall place them on the ballot for the first statewide election held more than one hundred eighty days after adjournment of that session. (*The above Constitutional Amendment was approved by the voters of the State August 25, 1970. The words secretary of state were changed to lieutenant governor.*)

SECTION 6. If a majority of the votes cast on the proposition favor its adoption, the initiated measure is enacted. If a majority of the votes cast on the proposition favor the rejection of an act referred, it is rejected. The lieutenant governor shall certify the election returns. An initiated law becomes effective ninety days after certification, is not subject to veto, and may not be repealed by the legislature within two years of its effective date. It may be amended at any time. An act rejected by referendum is void thirty days after certification. Additional procedures for the initiative and referendum may be prescribed by law. (*The above Constitutional Amendment was approved by the voters of the State August 25, 1970. The words secretary of state were changed to lieutenant governor.*)

SECTION 7. The initiative shall not be used to dedicate revenues, make or repeal appropriations, create courts, define the jurisdiction of courts or prescribe their rules, or enact local or special legislation. The referendum shall not be applied to dedications of revenue, to appropriations, to local or special legislation, or to laws necessary for the immediate preservation of the public peace, health, or safety.

SECTION 8. All elected public officials, in the State except judicial officers, are subject to recall by the voters of the State or political subdivision from which elected. Procedures and grounds for recall shall be prescribed by the legislature.

Article XII
General Provisions

SECTION 1. The State of Alaska shall consist of all the territory, together with the territorial waters appurtenant thereto, included in the Territory of Alaska upon the date of ratification of this constitution by the people of Alaska.

SECTION 2. The State and its political subdivisions may cooperate with the United States and its territories, and with other states and their political subdivisions on matters of common interest. The respective legislative bodies may make appropriations for this purpose.

SECTION 3. Service in the armed forces of the United States or of the State is not an office or position of profit as the term is used in this constitution.

SECTION 4. No person who advocated, or who aids or belongs to any party or organization or association which advocates, the overthrow by force or violence of the government of the United States or of the State shall be qualified to hold any public office of trust or profit under this constitution.

SECTION 5. All public officers, before entering upon the duties of their offices, shall take and subscribe to the following oath or affirmation: "I do solemnly swear (or affirm) that I will support and defend the Constitution of the United States and the Constitution of the State of Alaska, and

that I will faithfully discharge my duties as ⌐̲ ̲ ̲ . to the best of my ability." The legislature may prescribe further oaths or affirmations.

SECTION 6. The legislature shall establish a system under which the merit principle will govern the employment of persons by the State.

SECTION 7. Membership in employee retirement systems of the State or its political subdivisions shall constitute a contractual relationship. Accrued benefits of these systems shall not be diminished or impaired.

SECTION 8. The enumeration of specified powers in this constitution shall not be construed as limiting the powers of the State.

SECTION 9. The provisions of this constitution shall be construed to be self-executing whenever possible.

SECTION 10. Titles and subtitles shall not be used in construing this constitution. Personal pronouns used in this constitution shall be construed as including either sex.

SECTION 11. As used in this constitution, the terms "by law" and "by the legislature," or variations of these terms, are used interchangeably when related to law-making powers. Unless clearly inapplicable, the law-making powers assigned to the legislature may be exercised by the people through the initiative, subject to the limitations of Article XI.

SECTION 12. The State of Alaska and its people forever disclaim all right and title in or to any property belonging to the United States or subject to its disposition, and not granted or confirmed to the State or its political subdivisions, by or under the act admitting Alaska to the Union. The State and its people further disclaim all right or title in or to any property, including fishing rights, the right or title to which may be held by for any Indian, Eskimo, or Aleut, or community thereof, as that right or title is defined in the act of admission. The State and its people agree that, unless otherwise provided by Congress, the property, as described in this section, shall remain subject to the absolute disposition of the United States. They further agree that no taxes will be imposed upon any such property, until otherwise provided by the Congress. This tax exemption shall not apply to property held by individuals in fee without restrictions on alienation.

SECTION 13. All provisions of the act admitting Alaska to the Union which reserve rights or powers to the United States, as well as those prescribing the terms or conditions of the grants of lands or other property, are consented to fully by the State and its people.

Article XIII
Amendment and Revision

SECTION 1. Amendments to this constitution may be proposed by a two-thirds vote of each house of the legislature. The lieutenant governor shall prepare a ballot title and proposition summarizing each proposed amendment, and shall place them on the ballot for the next statewide election. If a majority of the votes cast on the proposition favor the amendment, it shall be adopted. Unless otherwise provided in the amendment, it becomes effective thirty days after the certification of the election returns by the lieutenant governor. (*The above Constitutional Amendment was approved by the voters of the State August 25, 1970. The words secretary of state were changed to lieutenant governor.*)

SECTION 2. The legislature may call constitutional conventions at any time.

SECTION 3. If during any ten-year period a constitutional convention has not been held, the lieutenant governor shall place on the ballot for the next general election the question: "Shall there be a Constitutional Convention?" If a majority of the votes cast on the question are in the negative, the question need not be placed on the ballot until the end of the next ten-year period. If a majority of the votes cast on the question are in the affirmative delegates to the convention shall be chosen at the next regular statewide election, unless the legislature provides for the election of the delegates at a special election. The lieutenant governor shall issue the call for the convention. Unless other provisions have been made by law, the call shall conform as nearly as possible to the act calling the Alaska Constitutional Convention of 1955, including, but not limited to, number of members, districts, election and certification of delegates, and submission and ratification of revisions and ordinances. The appropriation provisions of the call shall be self-executing and shall constitute a first claim on the state treasury. (*The above Constitutional Amendment was approved by the voters of the State August 25, 1970. The words secretary of state were changed to lieutenant governor.*)

SECTION 4. Constitutional Conventions shall have plenary power to amend or revise the constitution, subject only to ratification by the people. No call for a constitutional convention shall limit these powers of the convention.

Article XIV
Apportionment Schedule

SECTION 1. Members of the House of Representatives shall, according to the reapportionment schedule of the governor, dated July 24, 1981, be elected from the election districts and in the numbers shown below:

House District	Name of District	Number of Representatives
1	Ketchikan-Wrangell-Petersburg	2 (A-B)
2	Inside Passage-Cordova	1
3	Baranof-Chichagof	1
4	Juneau	2 (A-B)
5	Kenai-Cook Inlet	2 (A-B)
6	North Kenai-South Coast	1
7	South Anchorage	1
8	Hillside	2 (A-B)
9	Sand Lake	2 (A-B)
10	Mid-Town	2 (A-B)
11	West Side	2 (A-B)
12	Downtown	2 (A-B)
13	Mountain View-University	2 (A-B)
14	Muldoon	2 (A-B)
15	Chugiak-Eagle Rivers-Bases	2 (A-B)
16	Matanuska-Susitna	2 (A-B)
17	Interior Highways	1
18	Southeast North Star Borough	1
19	Outer Fairbanks	1
20	Fairbanks City	2 (A-B)
21	West Fairbanks	1
22	North Slope-Kotzebue	1
23	Norton Sound	1
24	Interior Rivers	1
25	Lower Kuskokwim	1
26	Bristol Bay-Aleutian Islands	1
27	Kodiak-East Alaska Peninsula	1

In all two member house districts candidates will run for designated seats indicated by Seat A and Seat B. Candidates will file for one of the available seats. Each qualified voter in the district may cast one vote for their choice among the candidates for each seat. The candidate receiving the greatest number of votes cast for each seat is elected.

SECTION 2. Members of the senate shall be elected in 1982 from the following senate districts except those seats where an asterisk (*) indicates the existing senator's term will continue until January 1985;

Senate District	Composed of Election Districts	Length of Term
A.	Ketchikan-Wrangell-Petersburg	4 years
B.	Inside Passage-Cordova-Baranof-Chichagof	2 years*
C.	Juneau	4 years
D.	Kenai-Cook Inlet-North Kenai-South Coast-South Anchorage	Seat A—2 years Seat B—4 years
E.	Hillside-Sand Lake	Seat A—2 years Seat B—4 years
F.	Mid-Town-West Side	Seat A—2 years Seat B—4 years
G.	Downtown-Mountain View-University	Seat A—2 years Seat B—4 years
H.	Muldoon-Chugiak-Eagle River-Bases	Seat A—2 years Seat B—4 years
I.	Matanuska-Susitna	2 years*
J.	Interior Highways-Southeast North Star Borough	2 years*
K.	Outer Fairbanks-Fairbanks City-West Fairbanks	Seat A—2 years Seat B—4 years
L.	North Slope-Kotzebue-Norton Sound	4 years
M.	Interior Rivers-Lower Kuskokwim	4 years
N.	Bristol Bay-Aleutian Islands-Kodiak-East Alaska Peninsula	2 years

In all two member senate districts candidates will run for designated seats indicated by Seat A and Seat B. Candidate will file for one of the available seats. Each qualified voter may cast one vote for their choice among the candidates for each seat. The candidate receiving the greatest number of votes cast for each seat is elected.

SECTION 3. The election districts set forth in Section 1 shall include the following territory:

1. *Ketchikan-Wrangell-Petersburg* — District 1 is an area within a line proceeding from Dixon Entrance in a northerly direction up Clarence Strait, passing west of Zarembo Island, northerly up Duncan Canal, across Frederick Sound to a point just north and west of Cape Fanshaw, then northeasterly to the Canadian border and southerly along the Canadian border to the point of beginning at Dixon Entrance. The district includes the Ketchikan Gateway Borough, Wrangell, Petersburg, Metlakatla, Hyder, Saxman, Meyers Chuck and Kupreanof.

2. *Inside Passage-Cordova* — District 2 is composed of that portion of Southeast Alaska between Dixon Entrance and Port Gravina on Prince William Sound that is not contained in Districts 1, 3 and 4. Included within its boundaries are the communities of Cordova, Yakutat, Haines, Skagway, Klukwan, Gustavus, Angoon, Kake, Thorne Bay, Klawock, Craig and Hydaburg.

3. *Baranof-Chichagof* — District 3 consists of Baranof Island and Chichagof Island. The communities on the islands include Sitka, Pelican, Hoonah, Tenakee Springs and Port Alexander.

4. *Juneau* — District 4 boundaries coincide with those of the City and Borough of Juneau.

5. *Kenai-Cook Inlet* — District 5 includes all of the coastal areas of the east and west sides of Cook Inlet that lie south and west of Nikishka. Sterling is also with the district.

6. *North Kenai-South Coast* — District 6 includes the northern quarter of the Kenai Peninsula, Nikishka, Hope, Cooper Landing, Moose Pass, Seward, Whittier and Valdez.

7. *South Anchorage* — District 7 contains the suburban southern and southeastern reaches of the Municipality of Anchorage, including the community council areas of Eldon, Old Seward/Oceanview, Rabbit Creek, Turnagain Arm and Girdwood Valley. Its northern boundary proceeds east from the inlet on Klatt Road to the New Seward Highway, southerly on the New Seward Highway to DeArmoun Road, east on DeArmoun Road to Morgaard Road, easterly on Morgaard Road to DeArmoun Road, easterly and southerly on Rabbit Creek.

8. *Hillside* — District 8 is bounded on the south by Rabbit Creek, Morgaard Road and DeArmoun Road and on the west by the Seward Highway. At Tudor Road the boundary proceeds east to Bragaw Road where it turns south. This district includes the neighborhood council areas of Campbell Park, Abbott Loop, Huffman-O'Malley, Mid-Hillside, Hillside East and Glen Alps.

9. *Sand Lake* — District 9 is bounded by a line beginning at the inlet and proceeding east on Klatt Road. The line proceeds north on the New Seward Highway to Dimond Boulevard where it turns west. At Minnesota Drive the line turns north and proceeds to International Airport Road where it turns west and extends to the inlet. The district includes the community council areas of Sand Lake and Klatt Road.

10. *Mid-Town* — District 10 is bounded by a line beginning at the intersection of the

Seward Highway and Dimond Boulevard. The line proceeds west to Minnesota Drive, north to International Airport Road, east to the Alaska Railroad, north by northwest along the railroad right of way to Tudor Road, east to Arctic Boulevard, north to 36th Avenue, east on 36th Avenue to C Street, north to Northern Lights Boulevard, west to Spenard Road, north to W. 25th Street, west to Minnesota Drive, north to Chester Creek, easterly to Lake Otis Road, south to Tudor Road, west to the New Seward Highway and south to the point of beginning. The district includes the community council areas of North Star, Rogers Park, Tudor, and parts of Spenard and Taku-Campbell.

11. *West Side* — District 11 is bounded by the boundary of District 10 on the east, International Airport Road on the south, and the inlet and Chester Creek on the north. It includes the community council area of Turnagain and the major part of the Spenard area.

12. *Downtown* — District 12 is bounded by Chester Creek on the south, Bragaw Road on the east, Commercial Drive and the Elmendorf reservation boundary on the north and the inlet on the west. Included are the community council areas of Government Hill, Downtown, Penland Park and South Addition, and parts of the areas of Fairview, North Mountain View and Airport Heights.

13. *Mountain View-University* — District 13 is bounded by a line beginning at the intersection of Tudor Road and Lake Otis Road proceeding east to Baxter Road, north to Northern Lights Boulevard, west to Boniface Road, north to the Glenn Highway, west on the Glenn Highway, northerly and westerly around North Mountain View along the Elmendorf military reservation boundary, south to the Glenn Highway, east to Bragaw Road, south to Chester Creek, westerly to Lake Otis Road and south to the point of beginning. The district includes the community council areas of Russian Jack Park and University, and parts of the North Mountain View and Airport Heights areas.

14. *Muldoon* — District 14 includes Stuckagain Heights and the community council areas of Northeast and Scenic Park. That part of the Northeast area bounded by Boniface Road, DeBarr Road, Turpin Street and the Glenn Highway is included in District 15.

15. *Chugiak-Eagle River-Bases* — District 15 includes the community council areas of Eklutna Valley, Chugiak, Birchwood, and Eagle River Valley. Also included are Fort Richardson, Elmendorf Air Force Base and that area of the Northeast community council area bounded by Boniface Road, DeBarr Road, Turpin Street and the Glenn Highway.

16. *Matanuska-Susitna* — District 16 is comprised of the Matanuska-Susitna Borough, including the communities of Talkeetna, Willow, Houston, Big Lake, Wasilla, Bodenburg Butte, Palmer, Sutton, Peter's Creek, Montana and Chickaloon.

17. *Interior Highways* — District 17 is made up of those areas outside of the Matanuska-

Susitna Borough and the Fairbanks North Star Borough which are along the Glenn, Parks, Richardson and Alaska Highways. Included are Paxson, Gulkana, Glennallen, Copper Center, Tonsina, Tazlina, McCarthy, Eagle, Delta, Fort Greely, Tanacross, Tok, Tetlin, Northway, Nenana, Anderson, Healy and Cantwell.

18. *Southeast North Star Borough* — District 18 encompasses the southeast section of the Fairbanks North Star Borough. It includes North Pole, Eielson Air Force Base, Salcha and Harding Lake.

19. *Fort Wainwright-Outer Fairbanks* — District 19 includes Livengood, Ester, Goldstream Road, the Steese Highway, the eastern half of the Farmers Loop Road, Fort Wainwright, Chena Hot Springs Road, Circle, Central and Circle Hot Springs.

20. *Fairbanks City* — District 20 is bounded by the Noyes Slough and University Avenue on the west, the Fairbanks International Airport on the Southwest, the Tanana River on the south and Fort Wainwright on the east. The Creamers Field area is included as the northern edge of the district.

21. *West Fairbanks* — District 21 includes the western half of Farmers Loop Road and the area west of the Noyes Slough and University Avenue to, but not including, the Ester area.

22. *North Slope-Kotzebue* — District 22 includes the areas of the North Slope Borough/Arctic Slope Regional Corporation and the Northwest Alaska Native Association.

23. *Norton Sound* — District 23 includes the area of the Bering Straits Regional Corporation; Shishmaref, Diomede, Teller, Nome, Koyuk and Saint Michael, and the coastal communities as far south as Hooper Bay and Paimiut. Chevak is also included along with Yukon River villages down river from Mountain Village.

24. *Interior Rivers* — District 24 includes the community on or near the great interior rivers, the Yukon, the Koyukuk and the Kuskokwim, as far down river as Mountain Village on the Yukon and Tuluksak on the Kuskokwim. Minto and Manley Hot Springs are included; Eagle and Circle are not included.

25. *Lower Kuskokwim* — District 25 includes the Kuskokwim River communities down river from Akiak and the coastal communities from Newtok to Platinum.

26. *Bristol Bay-Aleutian Islands* — District 26 includes all of the Bristol Bay Native Corporation area except Ivanof Bay, Perryville, Chignik Lake, Chignik Lagoon and the Lake Clark-Lake Iliamna communities. Included are the remainder of the Alaska Peninsula communities, the Aleutian communities, the Bristol Bay communities as far west as Twin Hills, communities as far up river as Aleknagik and Koliganek and the Lake Clark and Lake Iliamna communities. The Bristol Bay Borough is also included.

27. *Kodiak-East Alaska Peninsula* — District 27 covers the Kodiak Island Borough and the Alaska Peninsula communities of Ivanof Bay, Perryville, Chignik Lake, Chignik and Chignik Lagoon.

Amendments

The following constitutional amendments were approved by the voters of Alaska on August 22, 1972:

ARTICLE I, SECTION 3

Section 3: No person is to be denied the enjoyment of any civil or political right because of race, color, creed, sex, or national origin. The legislature shall implement this section. (*The amendment added the word "sex" to this section.*)

ARTICLE I, SECTION 22

Section 22: The right of the people to privacy is recognized and shall not be infringed. The legislature shall implement this section. (*The entire section was added as a new amendment.*)

ARTICLE II, SECTION 8

The legislature has further provided that it shall convene on the second Monday in January except in the year immediately following a gubernatorial election when it shall convene on the third Monday in January.

ARTICLE V, SECTION 1

Section 1: Every citizen of the United States who is at least eighteen years of age, who meets registration residency requirements which may be prescribed by law, and who is qualified to vote under this article, may vote in any state or local election. A voter shall have been, immediately preceding the election, a thirty day resident of the election district in which he seeks to vote, except that for purposes of voting for President and Vice President of the United States other residency requirements may be prescribed by law. Additional voting qualifications may be prescribed by law for bond issue elections of political subdivisions. (*This amendment gave the legislature authority to prescribe registration residency requirements and changed the residency requirements from one year in the state and thirty days in the election district to thirty days in the election district.*)

ARTICLE VIII, SECTION 15

Section 15: No exclusive right or special privilege of fishery shall be created or authorized in the natural waters of the State. This section does not restrict the power of the State to limit entry into any fishery for purposes of resource conservation, to prevent economic distress among fishermen and those dependent upon them for a livelihood and to promote the efficient development of the aquaculture in the State. (*This amendment would permit the State to limit entry into any fishery for the purposes of resource conservation, to prevent economic distress among fishermen and to promote the efficient development of aquaculture in the State.*)

ARTICLE X, SECTION 4

Section 4: The governing body of the organized borough shall be the assembly, and its composition shall be established by law or charter. (*This amendment would establish that assembly representation is to be based on law or charter.*)

The following constitutional amendments were approved by the voters of Alaska on November 2, 1976:

ARTICLE II, SECTION 9
SPECIAL SESSIONS

Special sessions may be called by the governor or by vote of two-thirds of the legislators. The vote may be conducted by the legislative council or as prescribed by law. At special sessions called by the governor, legislation shall be limited to subjects designated in his proclamation calling the session, to subjects presented by him, and the reconsideration of bills vetoed by him after adjournment of the last regular session. Special sessions are limited to thirty days.

ARTICLE II, SECTION 16
ACTION UPON VETO

Upon receipt of a veto message during a regular session of the legislature, the legislature shall meet immediately in joint session and reconsider passage of the vetoed bill or item. Bills to raise revenue and appropriation bills or items, although vetoed, become law by affirmative vote of three-fourths of the membership of the legislature. Other vetoed bills become law by affirmative vote of two-thirds of the membership of the legislature. Bills vetoed after adjournment of the first regular session of the legislature shall be reconsidered by the legislature sitting as one body no later than the fifth day of the next regular or special session of that legislature. Bills vetoed after adjournment of the second regular session shall be reconsidered by the legislature sitting as one body no later than the fifth day of a special session of that legislature, if one is called. The vote on reconsideration of a vetoed bill shall be entered on the journals of both houses.

ARTICLE IX, SECTION 7
DEDICATED FUNDS

The proceeds of any state tax or license shall not be dedicated to any special purpose, except as provided in section 15 of this article or when required by the federal government for state participation in federal programs. This provision shall not prohibit the continuance of any dedication for special purposes existing upon the date of ratification of this section by the people of Alaska.

ARTICLE IX, SECTION 15
ALASKA PERMANENT FUND

At least twenty-five percent of all mineral lease rentals, royalties, royalty sale proceeds, federal mineral revenue sharing payments and bonuses received by the State shall be placed in a permanent fund, the principal of which shall be used only for those income-producing investments specifically designated by law as eligible for permanent fund investments. All income from the permanent fund shall be deposited in the general fund unless otherwise provided by law.

The following constitutional amendments were approved by the voters of Alaska on November 2, 1982:

ARTICLE IV, SECTION 10

Section 10: The Commission on Judicial Conduct shall consist of nine members, as follows: three persons who are justices or judges of state courts, elected by the justices and judges of state courts; three members who have practiced law in this state for ten years, appointed by the governor from nominations made by the governing body of the organized bar and subject to confirmation by a majority of the members of the legislature in joint session; and three persons who are not judges, retired judges, or members of the state bar, appointed by the governor and subject to confirmation by a majority of the members of the legislature in joint session. In addition to being subject to impeachment under Section 12 of this article, a justice or judge may be disqualified from acting as such and may be suspended, removed from office, retired, or censured by the supreme court upon the recommendation of the commission. The powers and duties of the commission and the bases for judicial disqualification shall be established by law.

ARTICLE IX, SECTION 8

Section 8: No state debt shall be contracted unless authorized by law for capital improvements or unless authorized by law for housing loans for veterans, and ratified by a majority of the qualified voters of the State who vote on the question. The State may, as provided by law and without ratification, contract debt for the purpose of repelling invasion, suppressing insurrection, defending the State in war, meeting natural disasters, or redeeming indebtedness outstanding at the time this constitution becomes effective.

ARTICLE IX, SECTION 16

Section 16: Except for appropriations for Alaska permanent fund dividends, appropriations of revenue bond proceeds, appropriations required to pay the principal and interest on general obligation bonds, and appropriations of money received from a non-State source in trust for a specific purpose, including revenues of a public enterprise or public corporation of the State that issues revenue bonds, appropriations from the treasury made for a fiscal year shall not exceed $2,500,000,000 by more than a cumulative change, derived from federal indices as prescribed by law, in population and inflation since July 1, 1981. Within this limit, at least one-third shall be received for capital projects and loan appropriations. The legislature may exceed this limit in bills for appropriations to the Alaska permanent fund and in bills for appropriations for capital projects, whether of bond proceeds or otherwise, if each bill is approved by the governor, or passed by affirmative vote of three-fourths of the membership of the legislature over a veto or item veto, or becomes law without signature, and is also approved by the voters as prescribed by law. Each bill for appropriations for capital projects in excess of the limit shall be confined to capital projects of the same type, and the voters shall, as provided by law, be informed of the cost of operations and maintenance of the capital projects. No other appropriation in excess of this limit may be made except to meet a state of disaster declared by the governor as prescribed by law. The governor shall cause any unexpended and unappropriated balance to be invested so as to yield competitive market rates to the treasury.

Continental Divide

The Continental Divide extends into Alaska, but unlike its portions in the Lower 48, which divide the country into east-west watersheds, the Continental Divide in Alaska trends through the Brooks Range, separating watersheds that drain north into the Arctic Ocean and west and south into the Bering Sea.

According to *Alaska Science Nuggets,* until recently geologists thought the Brooks Range a structural extension of the Rocky Mountains, but recent thinking now assumes the range to be 35 to 200 million years older than the Rockies. The Alaska Range, on the other hand, is comparatively young, only about 5 million years. (See also *Mountains.*)

Convention and Visitor Bureaus

Anchorage Convention and Visitors Bureau, 201 East Third Avenue, Anchorage 99501. Phone (907) 276-4118.

Fairbanks Visitor and Convention Bureau, 550 First Avenue, Fairbanks 99701. Phone (907) 456-5774.

Homer Convention and Visitor Bureau, Box 2706, Homer 99603. Phone (907) 235-7875.

Juneau Convention and Visitor Bureau, 101 Egan Drive, Juneau 99801. Phone (907) 586-2284.

Kenai Peninsula Convention and Visitor Bureau, Box 497, Kenai 99611. Phone (907) 283-7989.

Ketchikan Visitors Bureau, Box 7055, Ketchikan 99901. Phone (907) 225-6166.

Nome Convention and Visitors Bureau, P.O. Box 251, Nome 99762.

Sitka Visitor Bureau, Box 1226, Sitka 99835. Phone (907) 747-5940.

Skagway Convention and Visitors Bureau, P.O. Box 415, Skagway 99840.

Cost of Living

Food — average cost for one week at home for a family of four with elementary schoolchildren (compiled March 1983; U.S. average $75.20):

Juneau	$ 95.55
Anchorage	$ 80.96
Fairbanks	$ 92.98
Nome	$143.93
Kotzebue	$128.59

Housing — average cost of single family residence with three bedrooms, including land (compiled July 1983):

Juneau	$128,910 (buy); $1,081/mo. (rent)
Anchorage	$128,887 (buy); $1,170/mo. (rent)
Fairbanks	$119,800 (buy); $1,017/mo. (rent)
Nome	$129,950 (buy); rental figure n/a
Kotzebue	$140,000 (buy); rental figure n/a

Gasoline — average cost for 55-gallon drum (compiled March 1983):

Juneau	$75.90
Anchorage	$63.25
Fairbanks	$70.12
Nome	$99.00
Kotzebue	not available

Heating Oil — average cost for 55-gallon drum (compiled March 1983):

Juneau	$81.03
Anchorage	$58.02
Fairbanks	$68.75
Nome	$95.15
Kotzebue	not available

Taxes — city and borough (Alaska has no state income tax), as of December 1982:

Juneau	3 percent sales
Anchorage	none
Fairbanks	5 percent sales
Nome	3 percent sales
Kotzebue	3 percent sales

Annual family income for families of four: Alaska, with $31,037, had the highest estimated median income in fiscal year 1982, 39 percent higher than the U.S. average.

Courts

The Alaska court system operates at four levels: the supreme court, the court of appeals, superior court, and district court. The Alaska judiciary is funded by the state and administered by the supreme court.

The five-member supreme court, established by the Alaska Constitution in 1959, has final appellate jurisdiction of all actions and proceedings in lower courts.

The three-member court of appeals was established in 1980 to relieve the supreme court of some of its ever-increasing caseload. The supreme court retained its ultimate authority in all cases, but concentrated its attention on civil appellate matters, giving authority in criminal and quasi-criminal matters to the court of appeals. The court of appeals has appellate jurisdiction in certain superior court proceedings and jurisdiction to review district court decisions.

In fiscal year 1981-82, 257 civil cases and 33 criminal cases were filed with the supreme court. The criminal cases were all handled by the court of appeals. The supreme court received 1 sentence appeal. The court of appeals received 245 merit filings and 120 sentence filings.

The superior court is the trial court with original jurisdiction in all civil and criminal matters and appellate jurisdiction over all matters appealed by the district court. The superior court has exclusive jurisdiction in probate and in cases concerning minors under 18 years of age. There are 26 superior court judges.

The district court has jurisdiction over misdemeanor violations and violations of ordinances of political subdivisions. In civil matters, the district court may hear cases for recovery of money, damages, or specific personal property if the amount does not exceed $10,000 or $15,000 in cases involving automobile accidents. The district court may also establish death and issue marriage licenses, summons, writs of habeas corpus, and search and arrest warrants. District court criminal decisions may be appealed directly to the court of appeals, by-passing the superior court. There are 15 district court judges.

Administration of the superior and district courts is divided by region into four judicial districts: First Judicial District, Southeast; Second Judicial District, Nome-Kotzebue; Third Judicial District, Anchorage-Kodiak-Kenai; and Fourth Judicial District, Fairbanks.

District magistrates serve rural areas and help ease the work load of district courts in metropolitan areas. In criminal matters, magistrates may give judgment of conviction upon a plea of guilty to any state misdemeanor, and may try state misdemeanor cases if the defendant waives his right to a district court judge. Magistrates may also hear municipal ordinance violations and state traffic infractions without the consent of the accused. In civil matters, magistrates may hear cases for recovery of money, damages, or specific personal property if the amount does not exceed $1,000.

Supreme court justices and judges of the court of appeals, superior court, and district court are appointed by the governor from candidates submitted by the Alaska Judicial Council. All justices and judges must be citizens of the United States and have been residents of Alaska for at least five years. A justice must be licensed to practice law in Alaska at the time of appointment and have engaged in active law practice for eight years. A court of appeals judge must be a state resident for five years immediately preceding appointment, have been engaged in the active practice of law not less than eight years immediately preceding appointment, and be licensed to practice law in Alaska. Qualifications of a superior court judge are the same as for supreme court justices, except that only five years of active practice are necessary. A district court judge must be 21 years of age, a resident for at least five years immediately preceding appointment, a graduate of an accredited law school, and have served for seven years as a magistrate in the state.

Each supreme court justice and each judge of the court of appeals is subject to approval or rejection by a majority of the voters of the state on a nonpartisan ballot at the first general election held more than three years after appointment. Thereafter, each justice must participate in a retention election every 10 years. A court of appeals judge must participate every eight years.

Superior court judges are subject to approval or rejection by voters of their judicial district at the first general election held more than three years after appointment. Thereafter, it is every sixth year. District court judges must run for retention in their judicial districts in the first general election held more than one year after appointment and every fourth year thereafter.

The Alaska State Supreme Court, 1959-1983

Justice		Tenure
John H. Dimond		1959-1971
Walter H. Hodge		1959-1960
Buell A. Nesbett		1959
Chief Justice		1959-1970
Harry O. Arend		1960-1965
Jay A. Rabinowitz		1965-
Chief Justice	1972-1975	1978-1981

George F. Boney	1968-1972
Chief Justice	1970-1972
Roger G. Connor	1968-1983
Robert C. Erwin	1970-1978
Robert Boochever	1972-1980
Chief Justice	1975-1978
James M. Fitzgerald	1972-1975
Edmond W. Burke	1975-
Chief Justice	1981-
Warren M. Mathews	1978-
Allen T. Compton	1980-
Daniel A. Moore	1983-

Cruises

There are many opportunities for cruising Alaska waters, either aboard charter boats, scheduled boat excursions, or luxury cruise ships. (See also *Ferries*.)

Charter boats are readily available in southeastern and southcentral Alaska. Charter boat trips range from day-long fishing and sightseeing trips to overnight and longer customized trips or package tours. There is a wide range of charter boats, from simple fishing boats to sailboats, yachts, and mini-class cruise ships.

In summer, scheduled boat excursions — from all-day trips to overnight cruises — are available at the following locations: Ketchikan (Misty Fiords); Sitka (harbor and area tours); Bartlett Cove and Gustavus (Glacier Bay); Valdez and Whittier (Columbia Glacier, Prince William Sound); Seward (Resurrection Bay, Kenai Fjords); Homer (Kachemak Bay); and Fairbanks (Chena and Tanana rivers).

For details and additional information on charter boat operators and scheduled boat excursions, contact the Alaska Division of Tourism, Pouch E-101, Juneau 99811.

From May through September, more than a dozen luxury cruise ships carry visitors to Alaska via the Inside Passage. Cruise ships depart from San Francisco, California, Seattle, Washington, and Vancouver, British Columbia; one line sails out of Ketchikan and Juneau. Cruises last from five days to two weeks and include port calls at southeastern Alaska towns, cruising Tracy Arm, Glacier Bay, and other waters in the Inside Passage. Three cruise lines include the Gulf of Alaska. The following 9 cruise ship companies and 15 ships cruise to Alaska:

Canadian Cruise Lines, Ltd., 401-1208 Wharf Street, Victoria, British Columbia V8W 2B9; *Prince George,* offering 7-day round trips from Vancouver.

Costa Cruises, One Biscayne Tower, Miami, Florida; *Daphne,* providing 7-day round trips from Vancouver.

Cunard Lines, 555 Fifth Avenue, New York, New York 10017; *Cunard Princess* and *Sagafjord,* with voyages to Gulf of Alaska.

Exploration Cruise Lines, 1500 Metropolitan Park Building, Seattle, Washington 98101; *Majestic Alaska Explorer* and *Great Rivers Explorer,* providing 7-day cruises from Ketchikan; *Glacier Bay Explorer,* providing 2-and 3-night cruises to Glacier Bay from Juneau.

Princess Cruises, 2121 Fourth Avenue, Suite 1800, Seattle, Washington 98121; *Sun Princess* and *Island Princess,* with 7-day round trips from Vancouver; *Pacific Princess,* offering 12-day round trips from San Francisco.

Royal Viking Line, One Embarcadero Center, San Francisco, California 94111; *Royal Viking Sea,* offering 12-day round trips from San Francisco.

Sitmar Cruises, 10100 Santa Monica Boulevard, Los Angeles, California 90067; *Fair Sky,* providing 14-day round trips to southeastern Alaska, two cruises also including the Gulf of Alaska.

Westours, 300 Elliott Avenue West, Seattle, Washington 98119; *Noordam, Rotterdam,* and *Nieuw Amsterdam* with 8-day round trips from Seattle.

World Explorer Cruises, Three Embarcadero Center, Suite 2500, San Francisco, California 94111; *Universe,* offering 14-day round trips to the Gulf of Alaska from San Francisco.

Cultural and Historical Organizations

Cultural Resources in Alaska: A Guide to People and Organizations, published by Heritage Conservation and Recreation Service, U.S. Department of the Interior, May 1981, lists the following cultural and historical organizations:

Alaska Association for the Arts, P.O. Box 2786, Fairbanks 99707

Alaska Historical Aircraft Society, 6610 Teshlar Drive, Anchorage 99507

Alaska Historical Commission, 3211 Providence Drive, Anchorage 99504

Alaska Historical Society, Box 10355, Anchorage 99502

Alaska Humanities Forum, 429 D Street, Anchorage 99501

Alaska State Council on the Arts, 619 Warehouse Drive, Suite 220, Anchorage 99501

Alaskan Anthropological Association, c/o Karen Workman, 3310 East 41st Avenue, Anchorage 99504

Anchorage Arts Council, 402 West Third Avenue, #7, Anchorage 99501

Association for Historic Preservation, c/o Wilda Marston, 2001 Turnagain Parkway, Anchorage 99503

Bristol Bay Historical Society, Naknek 99633

Chilkat Valley Historical Society, Box 623, Haines 99827

Circle District Historical Society, Central 99730

Cook Inlet Historical Society, 121 West Seventh Avenue, Anchorage 99501

Copper River Basin Historical Society, Box 282, Glennallen 99588

Copper Valley Historical Society, Copper Center 99573

Cordova Historical Society, Box 391, Cordova 99574

Council for Alaskan Archeology, SRA Box 455-B, Anchorage 99507

Cultural Facilities Development Committee, 127 South Franklin Street, Juneau 99801
Delta Historical Society, Box 255, Delta Junction 99737
Eagle Historical Society, Eagle 99738
Gambell Historical Society, Gambell 99742
Greater Juneau Arts and Humanities Council, Box 562, Juneau 99802
Heritage North, 2911 West 33rd, Anchorage 99503
Homer Society of Natural History/Pratt Museum, P.O. Box 682, Homer 99603
Hope and Sunrise Historical Society, Hope 99605
Institute of Alaska Native Arts, Inc., P.O. Box 80583, Fairbanks 99708
Kasilof Area Historical Society, Box 134, Kasilof 99610
Kenai Arts and Humanities Council, Box 59, Kenai 99611
Kenai Historical Society, Box 1348, Kenai 99611
Kenai Peninsula Historical Society, Box 56, Soldotna 99925
Ketchikan Arts Council, P.O. Box 8321, Ketchikan 99901
Klawock Historical Society, Klawock 99925
Kodiak Historical Society and Baranof Museum/Erskine House, Box 61, Kodiak 99615
Matanuska Valley Historical Society and Museum, Greater Palmer Chamber of Commerce, Palmer 99645
Ninilchik Historical Society, Ninilchik 99639
Resurrection Bay Historical Society, Seward 99664
Saint Herman's Theological Seminary, Box 728, Kodiak 99615
Sitka Historical Society and Museum, P.O. Box 2414, Sitka 99835
Skagway/Dyea Historical Society, Box 86, Skagway 99840
Southeast Alaska Regional Arts Council, P.O. Box 2133, Sitka 99835
Talkeetna Historical Society, Talkeetna 99676
Tanana/Yukon Historical Society, P.O. Box 1794, Fairbanks 99707
Tok Historical Society, Tok 99780
Tongass Historical Society, 629 Dock Street, Ketchikan 99901
Unalaska Arts and Historical Society, Unalaska 99695
Upper Tanana/Fortymile Historical Society, Box 222, Tok 99780
Valdez Historical Society, Box 6, Valdez 99686
Wasilla-Knik-Willow Creek Historical Society, Box 874, Wasilla 99687
Wrangell Historical Society, Box 1050, Wrangell 99929
Yakutat Historical Society, Box 245, Yakutat 99689

Dalton Highway

An all-weather gravel road that bridges the Yukon River, climbs the Brooks Range, and crosses the tundra plains before reaching the Prudhoe Bay oil fields on the coast of the Arctic Ocean. Commonly called the North Slope Haul Road, the Dalton Highway has been partially opened by the state for summer public use.

Named for James Dalton, a post-World War II explorer who played a large role in the development of North Slope oil and gas industries, the 416-mile road was built to provide access to the northern half of the 800-mile trans-Alaska oil pipeline during construction. In 1982, the average number of monthly one-way trips was: heavy trucks, 3,498; light vehicles, 852; and tourist (summer months only), 243. Total number of vehicles in 1982 was 55,185. Road repairs made year-round at a cost of $5.5 million.

The public may drive the road's first 215.4 miles to Disaster Creek at Dietrich. North of Dietrich, the highway is closed to the public without a permit obtained from the Alaska Department of Transportation and Public Facilities, 2301 Peger Road, Fairbanks 99701.

Fuel, limited food services, and tire repairs, as well as wrecker service at five dollars per mile, are available — in exchange for cash — at the Yukon Bridge and at Coldfoot. Travelers are advised that dust clouds, soft shoulders, large trucks traveling fast, and sometimes narrow, rough road surfaces may make stopping along the roadway dangerous. Also, since safe drinking water is not available along the road, travelers should carry their own.

The Dalton Highway begins at Milepost 73.5 on the Elliott Highway, just about five miles north of Livengood.

Daylight Hours

(See also *Arctic Circle*)

Maximum (At Summer Solstice, June 20 or 21)

	Sunrise/continuous	Sunset	Hours of daylight
Barrow	May 10	August 2	84 days continuous
Fairbanks	12:59 A.M.	10:48 P.M.	21:49 hours
Anchorage	2:21 A.M.	9:42 P.M.	19:21 hours
Juneau	3:51 A.M.	10:09 P.M.	18:18 hours
Ketchikan	4:04 A.M.	9:33 P.M.	17:29 hours
Adak	5:27 A.M.	10:10 P.M.	16:43 hours

Minimum (At Winter Solstice, December 21 or 22)

	Sunrise	Sunset	Hours of daylight
Barrow	*	*	0:00 hours
Fairbanks	9:59 A.M.	1:41 P.M.	3:42 hours
Anchorage	9:14 A.M.	2:42 P.M.	5:28 hours
Juneau	9:46 A.M.	4:07 P.M.	6:21 hours
Ketchikan	9:12 A.M.	4:18 P.M.	7:06 hours
Adak	9:52 A.M.	5:38 P.M.	7:46 hours

*For the period November 18 through January 24 — 67 days — there is no daylight in Barrow.

Diamond Willow

Fungi, particularly *Valsa sordida Nitschke,* is generally thought to be the cause of diamond-shaped patterns in the wood of some willow trees. There are 33 varieties of willow in Alaska, of which at least 5 can develop diamonds. They are found throughout the state, but are most plentiful in river valleys. Diamond willow, stripped of bark, is used to make lamps, walking sticks, and novelty items.

Dog Mushing

(See also *Iditarod Trail Sled Dog Race*)

In many areas of the state where snow machines had just about replaced the working dog team, the sled dog has made a comeback due in part to the resurgence of race interest and a rekindled appreciation for the reliability of nonmechanical transportation. In addition to working and racing dog teams, many people keep 2 to 10 sled dogs for recreational mushing.

Sled dog racing is Alaska's official state sport. Races ranging from world championship class to local club meets are held throughout the winter.

The sprint or championship races are usually run over two or three days with the cumulative time for the heats deciding the winner. Distances for the heats vary from about 12 miles to 30 miles. The size of dog teams also varies, with mushers using anywhere from 7 to 16 dogs in their teams. Since racers are not allowed to replace dogs in the team, most finish with fewer than they started with (attrition may be caused by anything from tender feet to sore muscles).

Purses range from trophies for the club races to $25,000, including heat money, for the championships. The purse is split between the finishers.

Statistics for two of the biggest races (see pages 92-93 for the Iditarod records) follow.

World Championship Sled Dog Race, Anchorage

Held in February. Best elapsed time in three heats over three days, 24 miles each day.

		Elapsed Time (minutes:seconds)				
		Day 1	Day 2	Day 3	Total	Purse
1973	Carl Huntington	106:53	106:54	107:10	310:57	$10,000
1974	Roland Lombard	105:32	208:34	101:36	310:10	10,000
1975	George Attla	98:09	107:01	104:18	309:28	12,000
1976	George Attla	98:39	102:64	102:32	303:35	12,000
1977	Carl Huntington	97:42	105:29	*	201:11	12,000
1978	George Attla	102:59	108:38	107:11	318:48	15,000
1979	George Attla	99:51	97:23	99:07	296:21	15,000
1980	Dick Brunk	83:25	82:35	*	166:00	15,000
1981	George Attla	90:04	85:43	91:34	267:21	20,000

1982 George Attla	73:19	75:36	76:56	225:51	20,000
1983 Harris Dunlap	82:29	88:58	89:05	260:32	25,000

*Trail conditions shortened race

Open North American Sled Dog Championship, Fairbanks

Held in March. Best elapsed time in three heats over three days; 20 miles on Days 1 and 2, 30 miles on Day 3.

	Elapsed Time (minutes:seconds)				
	Day 1	Day 2	Day 3	Total	Purse
1973 Harold Greenway	69:05	75:42	112:72	257:19	$ 8,500
1974 Alfred Attla	72:00	74:25	108:29	254:54	9,000
1975 George Attla	69:56	70:16	104:05	244:17	9,000
1976 Harvey Drake	72:00	73:43	116:00	261:43	10,000
1977 Carl Huntington	71:20	71:40	109:00	252:00	12,000
1978 George Attla	71:07	68:05	106:53	246:05	15,000
1979 George Attla	68:41	70:07	104:44	243:32	15,000
1980 Harvey Drake	63:48	66:49	94:30	225:07	15,000
1981 Peter Norberg	73:01	70:55	109:07	253:03	15,000
1982 Harris Dunlap	69:17	72:14	105:43	247:14	15,000
1983 Gareth Wright*	65:43	68:31	99:36	233:50	15,000

*This was Gareth's second win of this race. He took his first championship in 1950.

Other major races around the state are:

Alaska State Championship Race, Kenai-Soldotna. Two heats in two days, 15.4 miles each day. Held in February.

All-Alaska Sweepstakes. Last run in 1916, the Nome Kennel Club sponsors this 408-mile Nome to Candle and back race. Held in March.

Clark Memorial Sled Dog Race, Soldotna to Hope, 100 miles. Held in January.

Iditarod Trail Sled Dog Race (See *Iditarod Trail Sled Dog Race.*)

Kusko 300, Bethel to Aniak. Held in January.

Tok Race of Champions, Tok. Two heats in two days, 20.5 miles a day. Held in March.

Willow Winter Carnival Race, Willow. Two heats in two days, 18 miles each day. Held in January.

Women's World Championship Race, Anchorage. Three heats in three days, 12 miles each day. Held in February.

Related reading: *Racing Alaskan Sled Dogs,* by Bill Vaudrin. Expert mushers, racers and breeders give inside advice. Includes 30 years of racing records. 133 pages, $7.95. See page 210.

Earthquakes

Between 1899 and 1982 nine Alaska earthquakes occurred that equaled or exceeded a magnitude of 8 on the Richter scale. During the same period, more than 70 earthquakes took place that were of magnitude 7 or greater.

For 1982 there were three Alaska earthquakes larger than magnitude 6 — all of them happened in the Aleutian Islands. The largest with Richter magnitude of 6.5 occurred on January 25 in the Fox Islands. The other two occurred on the 1st and the 31st of July in the Andreanof and Rat islands, respectively, and had magnitudes of 6.3 and 6.2.

According to the University of Alaska's Geophysical Institute, earthquake activity in Alaska typically follows the same pattern from month to month, interspersed with sporadic swarms, or groups of small earthquakes, and punctuated every decade or so by a great earthquake and its aftershocks. The most active part of the state seismically is the Aleutian Islands arc system. Seismicity related to this system extends into the Gulf of Alaska and northward into interior Alaska to a point near Mount McKinley. These earthquakes are largely the result of underthrusting of the North Pacific plate and are characteristically deeper in the earth than most earthquakes. Many earthquakes resulting from this underthrusting occur in Cook Inlet — particularly near Mount Iliamna and Mount Redoubt — and near Mount McKinley. North of the Alaska Range, in the central Interior, most earthquakes are of shallow origin.

An earthquake created the highest seiche, or splash wave, ever recorded when, on the evening of July 9, 1958, a quake with a magnitude of 8 on the Richter scale rocked the Yakutat area. A landslide containing approximately 40 million cubic yards of rock plunged into Gilbert Inlet at the head of Lituya Bay. The gigantic splash resulting from the slide sent a wave 1,740 feet up the opposite mountain side, denuding it of trees and soil down to bedrock. It then fell back and swept through the length of the bay and out to sea. One fishing boat anchored in Lituya Bay at the time was lost with its crew of two; another was carried over a spit of land by the wave and soon after foundered, but its crew was saved. A third boat anchored in the bay miraculously survived intact. A total of four square miles of coniferous forest was destroyed.

The most destructive earthquake to strike Alaska occurred at 5:36 P.M. on Good Friday, March 27, 1964 — a day now referred to as Black Friday. Registering between 8.4 and 8.6 on the Richter scale in use at the time, its equivalent Richter magnitude has since been revised upward to 9.2, making it the strongest earthquake ever recorded in North America. With its primary epicenter deep beneath Miners Lake in northern Prince William Sound, the earthquake spread shock waves that were felt 700 miles away. The earthquake and seismic waves that followed killed 131 persons, 114 of them Alaskans. The death tally was: Anchorage, 9; Chenega, 23; Kodiak, 19; Point Nowell, 1; Point Whitshed, 1; Port Ashton, 1; Port Nellie Juan, 3; Seward, 13; Valdez, 31; Whittier, 13.

The 1964 earthquake released 80 times the energy of the San Francisco earthquake of 1906 and moved more earth farther, both horizontally and vertically, than any other earthquake ever recorded, save the 1960 Chilean earthquake. In the 69-day period after the main quake, there were 12,000 jolts of 3.5 magnitude or greater.

The highest sea wave caused by the 1964 earthquake occurred when an undersea slide near Shoup Glacier in Port Valdez triggered a wave that toppled trees 100 feet above tidewater and deposited silt and sand 170 feet above salt water.

Education

Education in Alaska is provided largely by the state, with a small percentage of federal, private and denominational schools. According to the 1983 *Alaska Education Directory,* Alaska has approximately 550 public schools, over 50 private and denominational schools, and 20 Bureau of Indian Affairs day schools.

The 20 Bureau of Indian Affairs schools are located in remote villages, with enrollment ranging from 17 to 158 students in kindergarten through the eighth grade. Each BIA school has a principal and from 1 to 8 teachers. In mid-1983, negotiations were under way to transfer all BIA operations to the state. In July 1983, Congress passed a measure transferring Mount Edgecumbe Boarding High School, which the federal government closed after the 1982-83 school year, to the state. Earlier reports estimated the cost of refurbishing the boarding school to safety codes at $20 million.

The state Board of Education has seven members appointed by the governor. (In addition, two nonvoting members are appointed by the board to represent the military and public school students.) The board is responsible for setting policy for education in Alaska schools and appoints a commissioner of education to carry out its decisions. The 550 public schools are controlled by 53 school districts, and each school district elects its own school board. There are 21 Regional Education Attendance Areas which oversee education in rural areas outside the 32 city and borough school districts.

In addition, any student in grades K-12 may choose to study at home through the unique state-operated Centralized Correspondence Study program, which also serves traveling students, GED students, and students living in remote areas. During the 1982-83 school year, 968 K-12 students and 188 adult GED students were enrolled in this program. Home study has been an option for Alaskan students since 1939 when the first program was initiated.

The state Department of Education also operates the Alaska Vocational Technical Center at Seward and a number of other education programs ranging from adult basic education to literacy skills.

Alaskans aged 7 through 16 are required to attend school. According to state regulations a student must earn a minimum of 19 high school credits to receive a high school diploma (many school districts require more than 19 credits). The state Board of Education has stipulated that 1 credit must be earned in each of the following: language arts, social studies, math, science, and physical education. Local school boards set the remainder of the required credits.

Since 1976, the state has provided secondary school programs to any community in which an elementary school is operated and one or more children of high school age who wish to attend high school. This mandate was the result of a suit initiated on behalf of Molly Hootch, a high school age student from Emmonak. Prior to the so-called Molly Hootch Decree, high school age students in villages without a secondary school attended high school outside their village. Of the 127 villages originally eligible for high school programs under the Molly Hootch Decree, only a few remain without any.

There are approximately 6,500 teachers and administrators in the public schools and 91,000 students enrolled in public schools in 1982-83. The Anchorage School District accounts for almost 40 percent of the state's student enrollment. The size of schools in Alaska varies greatly, from 3,000-student high schools in Anchorage to 24-student one-room schools in remote rural areas.

Approximately 75 percent of the department's operating funds is provided by the state, 20 percent by local governments, and 5 percent by the federal government.

(See also *School Districts* and *Universities and Colleges*.)

Employment

The average number of people employed in the state during 1982 was 194,400. The average unemployment rate was 9.9 percent, with a high of 11.3 percent in January and February 1982. Only twice during 1976-82 did Alaska's unemployment rate dip below the national average.

Alaska's unemployment is traditionally highest in winter, when construction and cannery work slow down. Jobless rates in the winter of 1983 were 12.5 percent in January and 12.3 percent in February.

Unemployment figures vary depending on area and economy. The depressed lumber industry, for instance, accounted for high unemployment in Ketchikan, where logging is a major industry. Unemployment figures for February 1983 by selected areas were as follows: Anchorage, 8.7 percent; Cordova, 14.4 percent; Seward, 21.1 percent; Fairbanks, 16.5 percent; Nome, 9.2 percent; and Juneau, 11.5 percent.

Alaska law requires that for state-funded projects, 95 percent of the employees be state residents.

If you're seriously considering a move to Alaska to seek a job, first make a visit and see it for yourself. Jobs are scarce in Alaska and housing is expensive — there are now, and will be in the foreseeable future, plenty of Alaska residents out of work and anxious to find jobs. For additional information, write: Alaska Department of Labor, Alaska State Employment Service, P.O. Box 3-7000, Juneau 99811. Employment offices are located in most major communities.

Energy and Power

For the purposes of classifying power usage, the state of Alaska can be divided into three major regions, each having similar energy patterns, problems, and resources: the Extended Railbelt region; the Southeast region; and the Bush region.

The Extended Railbelt region consists of major urban areas linked by the Alaska Railroad (Seward, Anchorage, and Fairbanks). The south-central area of this region uses relatively inexpensive natural gas in Cook Inlet and small hydroelectrical power plants for electrical production and heating. The Fairbanks-Tanana Valley area uses primarily coal and also oil to meet its electrical needs. Future electrical demand for the Railbelt region will be met by a combination of hydropower and coal- and gas-fired generators. Currently in the planning stages are several major

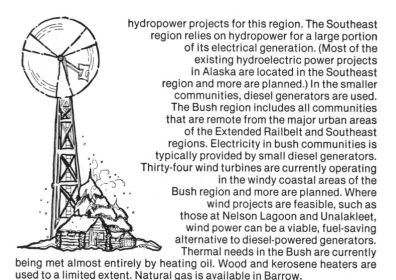

hydropower projects for this region. The Southeast region relies on hydropower for a large portion of its electrical generation. (Most of the existing hydroelectric power projects in Alaska are located in the Southeast region and more are planned.) In the smaller communities, diesel generators are used. The Bush region includes all communities that are remote from the major urban areas of the Extended Railbelt and Southeast regions. Electricity in bush communities is typically provided by small diesel generators. Thirty-four wind turbines are currently operating in the windy coastal areas of the Bush region and more are planned. Where wind projects are feasible, such as those at Nelson Lagoon and Unalakleet, wind power can be a viable, fuel-saving alternative to diesel-powered generators. Thermal needs in the Bush are currently being met almost entirely by heating oil. Wood and kerosene heaters are used to a limited extent. Natural gas is available in Barrow.

Eskimo Ice Cream

Also called *akutak* (Yup'ik Eskimo word for Eskimo ice cream), this classic Native delicacy, popular throughout Alaska, is traditionally made of whipped berries, seal oil and snow. Sometimes shortening, raisins and sugar are added. In different regions, different variations will be found. One favored variation uses the soopalallie berry, *Shepherdia canadensis,* a bitter species which forms a frothy mass like soapsuds when beaten. Another name for the soopalallie berry is soapberry.

Related reading: *Alaska Wild Berry Guide and Cookbook,* by the editors of *ALASKA®* magazine. How to find, identify and prepare Alaska's wild berries. 216 pages, $13.95. From the same people, *Cooking Alaskan.* More than 1,500 recipes for cooking Alaska style. 500 pages, $14.95. See pages 207 and 208.

Ferries

The state Department of Transportation and Public Facilities, Division of Marine Highway Systems, provides year-round scheduled ferry service for passengers and vehicles to communities in southeastern and southwestern Alaska. (The southeastern and southwestern Alaska state ferry systems do not connect with each other.)

A fleet of seven ferries on the southeastern system connects the ports of Ketchikan, Metlakatla, Hollis, Wrangell, Petersburg, Kake, Sitka, Angoon, Pelican, Hoonah, Tenakee Springs, Juneau (downtown and Auke Bay ports), Haines, and Skagway. These southeastern communities — with the exception of Haines and Skagway — are accessible only by ferry or by airplane. The southeastern ferry system also provides regularly scheduled service from Prince Rupert, British Columbia, and Seattle, Washington, to southeastern Alaska. The seven vessels of the southeastern system are the *Aurora, Columbia, Chilkat, LeConte, Malaspina, Matanuska* and *Taku.*

Southwestern Alaska is served by two ferries. The *Tustumena* serves Seward, Port Lions, Kodiak, Homer, Seldovia, Cordova, and Valdez, with limited summer service to Chignik, Sand Point, King Cove, Cold Bay, and Dutch Harbor. In summer, the *Bartlett* provides service between Valdez, Cordova, and Whittier.

Scheduled state ferry service to southeastern Alaska began in 1963; ferry service to Kodiak Island began in 1964. The first three ferries of the Alaska ferry fleet were the *Malaspina, Matanuska,* and *Taku,* built at an approximate cost of $4.5 million each. The names were selected by then governor William A. Egan.

Reservations are required for vehicles and staterooms on all sailings. Passenger reservations are required on some sailings. The address of the main office of the Alaska Marine Highway Systems is Pouch R, Juneau 99811; phone (907) 465-3941 or 465-3940 (recorded message).

Embarking Passenger and Vehicle Totals (in thousands) on Alaskan Mainline† Ferries

| | Southeastern System | | Southwestern System | |
	Vehicles	Passengers	Vehicles	Passengers
1982	51.0	220.0	15.5	57.0
1981	44.1*	181.5*	15.1	55.8
1980	44.3	189.5	14.0	49.4
1979	42.9	169.4	13.8	48.9
1978	38.6	161.9	13.2	46.6
1977	40.0	148.5	12.5	38.8
1976	46.3	181.7	11.7	44.4
1975	45.9	184.5	12.8	45.0
1974	41.4	174.7	12.4	44.6
1973	39.4	162.7	11.3	40.7
1972	39.4	162.7	9.9	35.9
1970	28.5	137.2	7.7	25.8
1965	25.8	123.7	3.2	6.9

†Mainline ports for Southeast are: Seattle, Vancouver (1970 to 1973 only), Prince Rupert, Ketchikan, Wrangell, Petersburg, Sitka, Juneau, Haines, and Skagway. Mainline ports for southwestern Alaska are: Anchorage (1970 to 1973 only), Cordova, Valdez, Whittier, Homer, Seldovia, Kodiak, Seward, and Port Lions.
*Does not include totals of passengers (9.5) and vehicles (2.9) on the MV *Aurora.*

Alaska State Ferry Data

Vessel	Began Service	Length (feet)	Speed (knots)	Passengers	Vehicles	Cabins
Aurora	1977	235	14	250	47	0
Bartlett	1969	193	14	170	38	0
Chilkat	1959	99	10	75	15	0
Columbia	1973	418	19	1,000	180	96
LeConte	1974	235	14	250	47	0
Malaspina	1963*	408	16.5	750	120	86
Matanuska	1963	408	16.5	750	120	112

Taku	1963	352	16	500	105	30
Tustumena	1964	296	14	220	50	27

*Lengthened and renovated 1972.

Nautical miles between ports

Southeastern System

Seattle-Ketchikan	650	Tenakee-Hoonah	47
Seattle-Prince Rupert	573	Angoon-Hoonah	60
Prince Rupert-Ketchikan	91	Hoonah-Juneau (AB)*	45
Ketchikan-Metlakatla	16	Sitka-Hoonah	115
Ketchikan-Hollis	40	Hoonah-Pelican	
Hollis-Petersburg	122	via South Pass	58
Hollis-Wrangell	95	Hoonah-Juneau	68
Ketchikan-Wrangell	89	Juneau-Haines	91
Wrangell-Petersburg	41	Haines-Skagway	13
Petersburg-Juneau	108	Juneau (AB)-Haines	68
Petersburg-Kake	59	Petersburg-Juneau (AB)	120
Kake-Sitka	110	Petersburg-Sitka	156
Sitka-Angoon	66	Juneau (AB)-Sitka	136
Angoon-Tenakee	33	*AB = Auke Bay	

Southwestern System

Seward-Cordova	146	Kodiak-Port Lions	27
Seward-Valdez	143	Kodiak-Homer	126
Cordova-Valdez	73	Homer-Seldovia	16
Valdez-Whittier	84	Kodiak-Sand Point via	
Seward-Kodiak	175	Sitkinak Strait	353

Fish Wheel

Widely used for subsistence salmon fishing, the fish wheel, fastened to a river shore, is a current-propelled machine that scoops fish heading upstream to spawn, providing an easy and inexpensive way of catching salmon without injuring them. Contrary to popular belief, Alaska Natives did not invent the fish wheel. Caucasians apparently first introduced the fish wheel on the Tanana River in 1904. Soon after, it appeared on the Yukon River, where it was used by both whites and Natives. It first appeared on the Kuskokwim in 1914, when prospectors introduced it for catching salmon near Georgetown.

Today subsistence fishing with the use of a fish wheel is allowed on the Copper River as well as the Yukon River and its tributaries. Currently, there are 166 limited-entry permits for the use of fish wheels by commercial salmon fishermen on the Yukon River system — the only district where they may be used commercially. Individuals may be both commercial and subsistence fishermen using the same gear. Commercial and subsistence fishing times with wheels are regulated.

Prior to its appearance in Alaska, the fish wheel was used on the East Coast, on the Sacramento River in California and the Columbia River.

Fishing
Commercial
Alaska's commercial fish production is greater in value than that of any other state in the country and second in terms of volume, according to the National Marine Fisheries Service.

Value and Volume of Alaska Fish and Shellfish Landings

Year	Value	Volume (in pounds)
1976	$219,071,000	600,203,000
1977	333,844,000	658,754,000
1978	482,207,000	767,167,000
1979	622,284,000	854,247,000
1980	561,751,000	983,664,000
1981	639,797,000	975,245,000
1982	575,569,000	878,935,000

Source: *Fisheries of the United States 1982*, Department of Commerce

Value of Alaska's commercial fish landings in 1982 of $575.6 million was followed by: California, second in value at $241.2 million; Louisiana, $239.9 million; Massachusetts, $204.2 million; and Texas, $186.2 million.

Volume of Alaska's commercial fish landings in 1982 of 878.9 million pounds was second only to Louisiana, which recorded a volume of 1,718.7 million pounds in 1982. (In 1981, the United States was fourth in world commercial fishery landings as it has placed the last several years; Japan was first with 14 percent of the total 74.8 million metric tons, the USSR was second with 13 percent, and China was third with 6 percent and the U.S. had 5 percent.) Alaska's record year for landing volume was 1980 with 1,053.9 million pounds.

Kodiak was the second leading U.S. port in terms of value in 1982, claiming $90.1 million in commercial fish landings. Los Angeles, California, was first with $92.9 million, and New Bedford, Massachusetts, was third with $85 million. Three other Alaska ports were ranked with the top 50 ports in the United States: Dutch Harbor was seventh with $47.8 million; Petersburg was eighteenth with $19.6 million; and Akutan was twenty-eighth with $15.6 million. Kodiak holds the U.S. port value record with its 1981 landings worth $132.9 million.

In 1982, Alaska trawl fish landings by U.S. fishermen were 61 million pounds, up 33 million pounds from the year before. The landings were valued at $18 million, an increase of $10.6 million from 1981. These substantial increases were due to heavy fishing on Pacific cod for salt cod and frozen fillets. Additionally, U.S. fishermen participated in 10 joint ventures delivering 404 million pounds of trawl fish valued at $25 million to foreign processors. These figures, too, represent significant increases over 1981 landings (210 million pounds worth $14.4 million).

Foreign fishing in Alaska waters, as in other U.S. waters, is governed by the Magnuson Fishery Conservation and Management Act of 1976. This act provides for the conservation and exclusive management by the U.S. of all fishery resources within the U.S. fishery conservation zone (except for highly migratory species of tuna). The U.S. fishery conservation zone established by the act extends from 3 nautical miles from shore to 200 nautical miles from shore. In addition, the act provides for exclusive management authority over continental shelf fishery resources and anadromous species (those that mature in the ocean then ascend streams to spawn in fresh water) beyond the 200-mile limit, except when they are within any recognized foreign nation's territorial sea. Foreign countries fishing within the U.S. zone do so under agreement with the U.S. and are subject to various fees. The 200-mile limit went into effect in 1977.

Foreign catch within the United States fishery conservation zone was 3.1 billion pounds in 1982, with Alaska supplying the largest share (95 percent) of the foreign catch, according to the National Marine Fisheries Service. The total foreign catch of trawl fish in Alaska waters was 2.9 billion pounds, down 4 million pounds from 1981. About 90 percent of the foreign catch (2.6 billion pounds) came from the Bering Sea and Aleutian Islands area; the remaining 339 million pounds came from the Gulf of Alaska.

Alaska's 1982 king crab fishery was a bust for the industry. The NMFS reported a total catch of 32.8 million pounds, down tremendously from the 1981 catch of 88.1 million pounds (not an exceedingly good year) and the five-year (1977-81) average of 131.6 million pounds. Select fisheries were closed after NMFS surveys showed a drastic decline in the numbers of female king crabs, from 53.8 million in the summer to 14 million at year's end. Tests to discover the reasons for the decline were inconclusive; however, speculation includes parasites, disease, an increase in the numbers of predators such as cod and halibut which feed on young crab, overfishing, warmer water temperatures (which may directly affect the crab or indirectly affect another species in the food chain that is important to crab development and reproduction), the cold spring and rainy summer of 1982, and a combination of some or all of these possiblities.

The Bering Sea-Aleutian Islands tanner crab industry also encountered a drop in pounds landed. *Chionoecetes bairdi* came in at 12.6 million pounds worth $13.5 million, down from 30.4 million pounds worth $17.7 million. While dropping in the amount of poundage landed (28.3 million pounds from 50.5 million), 1982 landings of *C. opilio* were valued at $20.8 million, up from $13.1 million in 1981.

Statewide totals for other shellfish landed in 1982 include the following: tanner crab, 68.8 million pounds; Dungeness, 15.5 million pounds; scallops, 835,000 pounds; and octopus, 111,000 pounds. Alaska landings of all shrimp were 16.9 million pounds, valued at $6.6 million.

Halibut landings off Alaska totaled 31 million pounds in 1982, up from 1980's 26.4 million pounds. The Alaska catch of halibut accounted for 93 percent of U.S. landings. The average price for domestic halibut was 81¢ per pound round weight.

According to the Alaska Department of Fish and Game, salmon was the most important commercial species in value in 1982 and was followed by shellfish (a reversal from 1981). Following are ADF&G ex-vessel value figures:

Value of Alaska's Commercial Fisheries to Fishermen
(in millions of dollars)

Species	1976	1977	1978	1979	1980	1981	1982
Salmon	118.0	170.8	243.9	344.6	281.3	484.9	305.5
Shellfish	97.5	158.7	227.8	238.7	215.2	245.5	213.5
Halibut	20.5	17.6	23.4	32.9	13.5	19.3	21.4
Herring	2.5	2.7	7.2	32.7	12.2	18.6	20.2
Groundfish	1.1	1.6	3.3	6.3	8.9	24.0	40.9

Preliminary Commercial Salmon Harvest 1982 Calendar
Year (in thousands of fish)

Region	King	Red	Silver	Pink	Chum	Total
Southeast	300	1,496	2,135	24,230	1,359	29,520
Central (Prince William Sound, Cook Inlet, Kodiak, Chignik, and Bristol Bay)	330	21,423	2,070	23,141	3,323	50,287
Arctic-Yukon-Kuskokwim	208	96	699	243	1,608	2,854
Westward (Alaska Peninsula, and Aleutian Islands)	46	6,510	1,142	17,158	4,262	29,118
Total	884	29,525	6,046	64,772	10,552	111,779

Related reading: *Alaska Blues: A Fisherman's Journal,* by Joe Upton. Award-winning saga of salmon fishing in southeastern Alaska. 236 pages, 198 black-and-white photos, $14.95. *Fisheries of the North Pacific,* by Robert J. Browning; 1980 revision of the earlier classic. 424 pages, $24.95. *Pacific Troller: Life on the Northwest Fishing Grounds,* by Francis E. Caldwell. 144 pages, $5.95. *The Pacific Halibut: The Resource and the Fishery,* by F. Heward Bell. Soft-cover, $19.95 and hardbound, $24.95. Includes nearly 300 pages of history on the fishery; with more than 300 photos, maps, and illustrations. See pages 207-10.

Sport
There are 11 sport fishing management areas in Alaska, each with its own bag and possession limits and possible special provisions. Current copies of *Alaska Sport Fishing Regulations Summary* are available from the Department of Fish and Game, Box 3-2000, Juneau 99802. Also available from the department are the free booklets *Sport Fishing Predictions* and the *Alaska Sport Fishing Guide.*

Regulations
A sport fishing license is required for residents and nonresidents 16 years of age or older. (Alaskan residents 60 years of age or more who have resided in the state for 30 or more consecutive years do not need a sport fishing license; a special identification card is issued for this exemption.)

Resident sport fishing licenses cost $10, valid for the calendar year issued (nonresident, $36; 3-day nonresident, $10; 14-day nonresident, $20). A resident is a person who has maintained a permanent place of abode within the state for 12 consecutive months and has continuously maintained his voting residence in the state. Military personnel on active duty permanently stationed in the state and their dependents can purchase a nonresident military sport fishing license ($10).

Nearly all sporting goods stores in Alaska sell fishing licenses. They are also available by mail from the Licensing Section, Alaska Department of Revenue, Fish and Game License Division, 1111 West Eighth Street, Juneau 99801.

Alaska's 11 Sport Fishing Management Areas

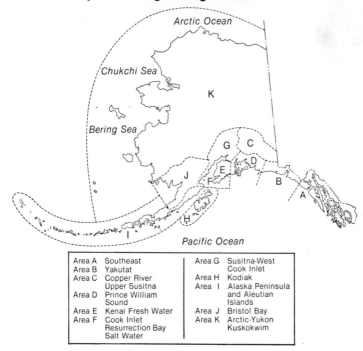

Area A	Southeast	Area G	Susitna-West Cook Inlet
Area B	Yakutat	Area H	Kodiak
Area C	Copper River Upper Susitna	Area I	Alaska Peninsula and Aleutian Islands
Area D	Prince William Sound	Area J	Bristol Bay
Area E	Kenai Fresh Water	Area K	Arctic-Yukon Kuskokwim
Area F	Cook Inlet Resurrection Bay Salt Water		

Sport Fish Species	Best Bait, Lure	State Record (lbs./oz.)
Arctic char	spoon, eggs	17.8
Arctic grayling	flies	4.13
Burbot	bait	24.12
Chum salmon	spoon	27.3
Cutthroat trout	bait, spin, flies	8.6
Dolly Varden	bait, spin, flies	17.8
Halibut	octopus, herring	440
King salmon	herring	93
Kokanee	spin, eggs	2
Lake trout	spoon, plug	47
Northern pike	spoon, spin	38
Pink salmon	small spoon	12.9
Rainbow trout	flies, lures, bait	42.2
Red salmon	flies	16
Sheefish	spoon	52.8
Silver salmon	herring, spoon	26
Steelhead trout	spoon, eggs	42.2
Whitefish	flies, eggs	7.2

Related reading: *The Freshwater Fishes of Alaska* by James E. Morrow, illustrated by Marion J. Dalen. A complete species-by-species index of the fish found in Alaska's rivers and lakes. With drawings and color plates. 248 pages, $24.95. See page 208.

Forest Service Cabins

There are 178 U.S. Forest Service public-use recreational cabins available for $10 per party (no limit) per night in Alaska. Tongass National Forest in southeastern Alaska has 142 cabins and Chugach National Forest in southcentral Alaska has 36 cabins. Most cabins have a 7-day limit for stays during the spring and summer and a 10-night limit for the fall and winter.

Most of the cabins are only accessible by plane or boat, a few by hiking trail. The average cabin size is 12 by 14 feet. All the cabins have tables, wood bunks, and a heating stove. Most of the stoves are wood, some are oil. The cabins usually sleep four to six people. You must supply your own bedding, cookware, food, cooking stove, transportation, and stove oil if using an oil-heated cabin. Firewood is usually cut and stored on site for use as are splitting mauls and axes. There are pit toilets, but no garbage dumps. Pack your garbage out. Skiffs are provided at most cabins located on lakes.

Cabin reservations are mandatory and can be made in person or by mail 180 days prior to use. You must have a permit for the specific length of occupancy. There is a 3-day limit May to August on hike-in cabins.

For cabin reservations and information, contact the U.S. Forest Service, Tongass National Forest Office of Information, Box 1628, Juneau 99802; Chugach National Forest, 2221 East Northern Lights Boulevard, Suite 230, Anchorage 99504; or stop by the district ranger offices in Cordova, Ketchikan, Seward, Sitka, Petersburg, Juneau and Wrangell.

Furs and Trapping

According to the state fur bearer biologist, the major sources of harvested Alaska furs are the Yukon and Kuskokwim valleys. The Arctic provides limited numbers of arctic fox, wolverine and wolf, but the gulf coast areas and Southeast are more productive. Southeastern Alaska is a good source of mink and otter.

Trapping is seasonal work, and most trappers work summers at fishing or other employment.

State regulated fur bearers are: beaver; coyote; red (includes cross, black, or silver color phases) and arctic (white or blue) fox; lynx; marmot; marten; mink; muskrat; raccoon; river (land) otter; squirrel (parka or ground, flying and red); weasel; wolf; and wolverine. Very little harvest or use is made of parka squirrels and marmots. Flying squirrels are not caught deliberately, and raccoons, introduced in a couple coastal locations years ago, appear to have been extirpated.

Prices for raw skins depend on the buyer, quality of fur, and market demand. According to *Alaska Trapper and Dog Mushing News,* 1981-82 average pelt prices were: beaver, $25.42; coyote, $61.87; lynx, $275.86; marten, $42.34; mink, $46.43; muskrat, $3.05; otter, $41.43; red fox, $88.86; red squirrel, $1.00; weasel (ermine), 88¢; white fox, $34.56; wolf, $227.50; and wolverine, $232.24.

Glaciers and Ice Fields

The greatest concentrations of glaciers are in the Alaska Range, Wrangell Mountains, and the coastal ranges of the Chugach, Coast, Kenai and Saint Elias mountains, where annual precipitation is high. All of Alaska's well-known glaciers fall within these areas. According to the U.S. Geological Survey, distribution of glacier ice is as follows:

Map Key/ Region	Approximate square miles
1 North	
Brooks Range	279
2 West	
Seward Peninsula	1.2
Kilbuk-Wood River mountains	89
3 Southwest	
Aleutian Islands	371
Alaska Peninsula	483
4 Interior	
Alaska Range	5,367
Talkeetna Mountains	309
Wrangell Mountains	3,205
5 Southcentral	
Kenai Mountains	1,776
Chugach Mountains	8,340
6 Southeast	
Saint Elias Mountains	4,556
Coast Mountains	4,055
Total	28,842

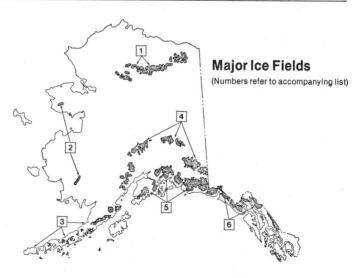

Major Ice Fields

(Numbers refer to accompanying list)

Glaciers cover approximately 28,800 square miles — or 3 percent — of Alaska, which is 128 times more area covered by glaciers than the rest of the United States. There are an estimated 100,000 glaciers in Alaska, ranging from tiny cirque glaciers to huge valley glaciers.

Glaciers are formed where, over a number of years, more snow falls than melts. Alaska's glaciers fall into roughly five general categories: alpine, valley, piedmont, ice fields and icecaps. Alpine (mountain and cirque) glaciers head high on the slopes of mountains and plateaus. Valley glaciers are an overflowing accumulation of ice from mountain or plateau basins. Piedmont glaciers form when one or more glaciers flow into a fan-shaped ice mass (called a piedmont lobe) at the foot of a mountain range. Ice fields develop when large valley glaciers interconnect, leaving only the highest peaks and ridges to rise above the ice surface. Icecaps are snow- and ice-filled basins or plateaus.

Most of Alaska's major rivers originate at glaciers. The runoff from glaciers is naturally regulated: because clean (new) snow reflects most of the sun's energy, the more snowfall, the less melt and runoff there is. The converse is also true: the less precipitation, the more runoff. This is opposite to the regime of a nonglacial-fed stream.

Alaska's better-known glaciers accessible by road are: Worthington and Black Rapids (Richardson Highway); Matanuska (Glenn Highway); Portage (Seward Highway); and Mendenhall (Glacier Highway). In addition, Childs and Sheridan glaciers may be reached by car from Cordova, and Valdez Glacier is only a few miles from the town of Valdez. The sediment-covered terminus of Muldrow Glacier in Denali National Park and Preserve is visible at a distance for several miles from the park road.

Many spectacular glaciers in Glacier Bay National Park and Preserve and in Prince William Sound are accessible by tour boat.

Glacier ice often appears blue because its great thickness absorbs all the colors of the spectrum except blue, which is reflected back to the observer.

- About three-fourths of all the fresh water in Alaska is stored as glacial ice, many times greater than the volume of water stored in all the state's lakes, ponds, rivers and reservoirs.
- Longest valley glacier in North America is Hubbard, 92 miles in length (heads in Canada).
- Longest glacier is Bering (including Bagley Icefield), over 100 miles in length.
- Southernmost active tidewater glacier in North America is LeConte.
- Greatest concentration of tidewater-calving glaciers is Prince William Sound, with 20 active tidewater glaciers.
- Largest glacier is Malaspina, 850 square miles; the Malaspina glacier complex (including tributary glaciers) is approximately 2,000 square miles in area. The Bering glacier complex, which includes Bagley Icefield, is approximately 2,250 square miles.
- La Perouse glacier is the only calving glacier in North America that discharges icebergs directly into the open Pacific Ocean.
- Iceberg production in Prince William Sound is expected to increase four-fold in the next 20 years as Columbia glacier retreats.
- There are more than 750 glacier-dammed lakes in Alaska, the largest being Chakachamna Lake west of Anchorage.

Related reading: *Alaska's Glaciers.* A close look at Alaska's glaciers. 144 pages, $9.95. See page 207.

Gold

The largest gold nugget ever found in Alaska was discovered near Nome. The nugget, weighing 107 ounces, 2 pennyweight, was found September 29, 1901, on Discovery Claim, Anvil Creek, Nome District. The nugget was 7 inches long, 4 inches wide and 2 inches thick.

Two other record-breaking nuggets were found in the Nome area the same month. On September 5, the largest Alaska nugget found up to that time was discovered on the Jarvis Brothers' claim on Anvil Creek. It weighed 45 ounces, and was 6¼ inches long, 3¼ inches wide, 1⅜ inches thick at one end and ½ inch thick at the other. On September 14, a larger nugget was found on the Discovery Claim; it weighed 97 ounces and broke the record of September 5 only to be superseded by the 107-ounce nugget found on the 29th.

According to *Alaska's Mineral Industry,* a publication of the state Division of Geological and Geophysical Surveys, 319 major (mechanized, nonrecreational) operators produced 174,900 troy ounces of gold in 1982. This was a 30 percent increase over 1981. Following are volume and value figures for recent years of Alaska gold production.

Gold Production in Alaska, 1980-82

Year	Volume (in troy ounces)	Value
1980	75,000	$32,000,000
1981	134,000	55,200,000
1982	174,900	69,960,000

The chart below shows the fluctuation in the price of gold after the gold standard was lifted in 1967. Note that these are average annual prices and do not reflect the highest or lowest prices during the year.

Average Annual Price of Gold, per Troy Ounce

Prior to 1934	$20.67	1975	$161.49
1934 to 1967	35.00	1976	125.32
1968	39.26	1977	148.31
1969	41.51	1978	193.55
1970	36.41	1979	307.50
1971	41.25	1980	569.73
1972	58.60	1981	548.90
1973	97.81	1982	461.00
1974	159.74		

Gold Strikes and Rushes

1848 First Alaska gold discovery (Russian on Kenai Peninsula)
1861 Stikine River near Telegraph Creek, British Columbia
1872 Cassiar district in Canada (Stikine headwaters country)
1872 Near Sitka
1874 Windham Bay near Juneau
1880 Gold Creek at Juneau

1886	Fortymile discovery
1887	Yakutat beach areas and Lituya Bay
1893	Mastodon Creek, starting Circle City
1895	Sunrise district on Kenai Peninsula
1896	Klondike strike, Bonanza Creek, Canada
1898	Anvil Creek, Nome; Atlin district, British Columbia
1900	Porcupine rush out of Haines
1902	Fairbanks (Felix Pedro, Pedro Dome)
1906	Innoko
1907	Ruby
1908	Iditarod
1913	Marshall
1913	Chisana
1914	Livengood

Related reading: *In Search of Gold, The Alaska Journals of Horace S. Conger, 1989-1899,* by Carolyn Jean Holeski and Marlene Conger Holeski, 314 pages, $9.95; *Gold Hunting in Alaska,* as told by Joseph Grinnell, edited by Elizabeth Grinnell, 80 pages, $7.95; *The Gold Hustlers,* by Lewis Green, 339 pages, $7.95. See pages 207-10.

Government

The capital of Alaska is in Juneau. In November 1976 Alaskan voters chose Willow as their new capital site. In a second election six years later concerning the capital move, voters chose to keep Juneau as the capital city.

Alaska is represented in the U.S.Congress by two senators and one representative.

A governor and lieutenant governor are elected by popular vote for four-year terms on the same ticket. The governor is termed strong because of extensive powers given under the constitution. He administers 14 major departments: Administration, Commerce and Economic Development, Community and Regional Affairs, Education, Environmental Conservation, Fish and Game, Health and Social Services, Labor, Law, Military Affairs, Natural Resources, Public Safety, Revenue, and Transportation and Public Facilities.

The legislature is bicameral, with 20 senators elected from 14 senate districts for four-year terms, and 40 representatives from 27 election districts for two-year terms. Under the state constitution, redistricting is accomplished every 10 years, after the reporting of the decennial federal census. The latest redistricting occurred in 1981 and was accomplished by the governor's office with assistance of an advisory apportionment board. The judiciary consists of a state supreme court, court of appeals, superior court, district courts, and magistrates. (See also *Alaska's Public Officials* and *Courts.*)

Local government is by a system of organized boroughs, much like counties in other states. Several areas of the state are not included in any borough because of sparse population. Boroughs generally provide a more limited number of services than cities. There are three classes. First- and second-class boroughs have three mandatory powers: education, land use planning and tax assessment and collection. The major

76

difference between the two classes is how they may acquire other powers. Both classes have separately elected borough assemblies and school boards. A third-class borough has two mandatory powers: operation of public schools and taxation. All boroughs may assess, levy, and collect real and personal property taxes.

Incorporated cities are small units of local government, serving one community. There are two classes. First-class cities, generally urban areas, have six-member councils and a separately elected mayor. Taxing authority is somewhat broader than second-class cities, and responsibilities are broader. A first-class city that has adopted a home rule charter is called a home rule city; adoption allows the city to revise its ordinances, such that the powers it assumes are those not prohibited by law or charter. Second-class cities, generally places with fewer than 400 people (but not less than 25), are governed by a seven-member council, one of whom serves as mayor. Taxing authority is limited. A borough and all cities located within it may unite in a single unit of government called a unified municipality.

There is also one community organized under federal law. Originally an Indian reservation, Metlakatla was organized so municipal services could effectively be provided to its residents.

In 1983 there were 155 incorporated municipalities: 3 unified home rule municipalities, 1 home rule borough, 6 second-class boroughs, 1 third-class borough, 12 home rule cities, 21 first-class cities, 111 second-class cities and 1 community, Metlakatla, organized under federal law.

Borough Addresses and Contact

Bristol Bay Borough
Contact: Borough Clerk
P.O. Box 189
Naknek 99633
Telephone: 268-4224

City and Borough of Juneau
Contact: City-Borough Manager
155 South Seward Street
Juneau 99801
Telephone: 586-3300

City and Borough of Sitka
Contact: Administrator
P.O. Box 79
Sitka 99835
Telephone: 747-3294

Fairbanks North Star Borough
Contact: Clerk
P.O. Box 1267
Fairbanks 99707
Telephone: 452-4761

Kenai Peninsula Borough
Contact: Borough Clerk
P.O. Box 850
Soldotna 99669
Telephone: 262-4441

Ketchikan Gateway Borough
Contact: Borough Manager
344 Front Street
Ketchikan 99901
Telephone: 225-6151

Kodiak Island Borough
Contact: Borough Mayor or Borough Clerk
P.O. Box 1246
Kodiak 99615
Telephone: 486-5736

Matanuska-Susitna Borough
Contact: Borough Manager
Box B
Palmer 99645
Telephone: 745-4801

Haines Borough
Contact: Borough Secretary
Box H
Haines 99827
Telephone: 766-2711

Municipality of Anchorage
Contact: Mayor's Office or
Manager's Office
Pouch 6-650
Anchorage 99502
Telephone: 264-4431

North Slope Borough
Contact: Borough Mayor
P.O. Box 69
Barrow 99723
Telephone: 852-2611

Highways

As of December 31, 1981, the state Department of Transportation and Public Facilities showed 13,698.9 miles of highways, including those in national parks and forests (2,004), and 1,416 miles of ferry routes. Of the total, 3,092.3 miles were unpaved, 2,384.7 miles were paved, 834.4 were municipal roads, 1,349.1 were borough roads, and 2,618.3 were listed as "other." Alaska's relative sparseness of roadway is accentuated by a comparison to Austria, a country only one-eighteenth the size of Alaska but with nearly twice as much public road.

Major Highways in Alaska

The following chart lists major highways in Alaska, their route numbers, the year the highway opened to vehicle traffic, and their total length *within Alaska* (most of the Alaska Highway, Haines Highway, and Klondike Highway 2 lie within Canada). Also indicated is whether the highway is open all year or closed in winter. (See also *Alaska Highway* and *Dalton Highway*.)

Major Highways in Alaska

	Route #	Year Completed	Total length (miles) paved	gravel	Open
Alaska	2	1942	298.2*		All yr.
Copper River	10	see note	12.4	35.7	All yr.
Dalton		1974		416	All yr.
Denali	8	1957		135	Apr.-Oct.
Edgerton	10	1923	19	14	All yr.
Elliott	2	1959	28	124	Apr.-Oct.
George Parks	3	1971	322.7		All yr.
Glenn	1	1942	328*		All yr.
Haines	7	1947	40.5		All yr.
Klondike	2	1978		14.6	Apr.-Oct.
Richardson	4	1923	368*		All yr.
Seward	1&9	1951	127		All yr.
Steese	6	1928	43.8	118.2	Apr.-Oct.
Sterling	1	1950	135.8		All yr.
Taylor	5	1953		161	Apr.-Oct.

*The Richardson shares a common alignment with the Alaska Highway (for 98 miles) and with the Glenn (for 14 miles).
NOTE: Construction on the Copper River Highway — which was to link up with Chitina on the Edgerton — was halted by the 1964 Good Friday earthquake which damaged the Million Dollar Bridge.

Related reading: *The MILEPOST®:* All-the-North Travel Guide®. A 500-page comprehensive travel guide with mile-by-mile logs of all access highways and travel by air, rail, water. Includes accommodations, cities, villages, parks, wildlife; hints for fishermen, bicyclists, hikers. Numerous photos and maps. *Adventure Roads North,* from the editors of *The MILEPOST®.* Tracing the history of Alaska's highways. Color photography, 224 pages. $14.95. See pages 207-10.

Hiking

A variety of hiking trails for all levels of ability may be found in the state. The experienced hiker with proper topographic maps will find some of the best Alaska hiking is cross-country above tree line. Using both maps and tide tables, it is also feasible to hike along ocean shorelines at low tide.

Hikers in Alaska must plan for rapidly changing, inclement weather. Take rain gear. If staying overnight in the back country, it's wise to carry a tent if a cabin is unavailable. Above tree line, snow can be encountered at any time of year.

Sporting goods stores in Alaska feature an excellent selection of hiking equipment. In addition, back-country guides often furnish equipment on escorted expeditions.

Information on hiking in Alaska's national parks and monuments is available from the state office of the National Park Service, 2525 Gambell Street, #107, Anchorage 99503, or from park headquarters for the area you're interested in. (See *National Parks, Preserves, and Monuments.*)

The Alaska Division of Parks (see *State Park System*) has information on hiking on the lands managed by that agency.

The U.S. Fish and Wildlife Service (see *National Wildlife Refuges*) offers some back-country information on the areas they administer.

The U.S. Forest Service (see *National Forests*) offers information on back-country travel in the Chugach (Prince William Sound, Copper River Delta and northeastern Kenai Peninsula) and Tongass (southeastern Alaska) national forests. The Forest Service maintains extensive trail networks in both these areas.

History

6,000-11,000 years ago — Human culture in southeastern, Aleutians, interior, and northwestern arctic Alaska.

6,000 years ago — Most recent migration from Siberia across the land bridge.

3,000-5,000 years ago — Human culture on the Bering Sea coast.

200-300 years ago — Tlingits and Haidas arrive.

1725 — Vitus Bering sent by Peter the Great to explore the North Pacific.

1741 — On a later expedition, Bering in one ship and Alexei Chirikof in another discover Alaska. Chirikof, according to ship logs, probably sees land on July 15 a day ahead of his leader, who was perhaps 300 miles or more to the north of him. Georg Steller goes ashore on Kayak Island, becoming the first white man known to have set foot on Alaska soil.

1743 — Russians begin concentrated hunting of sea otter, continuing until the species is almost decimated; fur seal hunting begins later.

1774-94 — Explorations of Alaska waters by Juan Perez, James Cook and George Vancouver.

1784 — First Russian settlement in Alaska, at Three Saints Bay, Kodiak Island.

1794 — Vancouver sights Mount McKinley.

1799 — Alexander Baranof establishes the Russian post known today as Old Sitka; a trade charter is granted to the Russian-American Company.

1821 — Foreign vessels prohibited from trade in Alaska waters, making the Russian-American Company the sole trading firm.

1824-42 — Russian exploration of the mainland leads to discovery of the Kuskokwim, Nushagak, Yukon and Koyukuk rivers.

1847 — Fort Yukon established by Hudson's Bay Company.

1848 — First mining in Alaska, on the Kenai Peninsula.

1853 — Russian explorers-trappers find the first oil seeps in Cook Inlet.

1857 — Coal mining begins at Coal Harbor, Kenai Peninsula, to supply steamers.

1859 — Baron Edoard de Stoeckl, minister and charge d'affaires of the Russian delegation to the United States, is given authority to negotiate the sale of Alaska.

1867 — United States buys Alaska from Russia for $7.2 million; treaty signed March 30, formal transfer takes place on October 18 at Sitka. Fur seal population begins to stabilize. U.S. Army is given jurisdiction over the Department of Alaska the following year.

1872 — Gold discovered near Sitka. Later discoveries include Windham, 1874, and Juneau, 1880; Fortymile, 1886; Circle City, 1893; Sunrise District (Kenai Peninsula), 1895; Nome, 1898; Fairbanks, 1902; Innoko, 1906; Ruby, 1907; Iditarod, 1908; Marshall, 1913; Chisana, 1913; and Livengood, 1914.

1878 — First salmon canneries at Klawock and Old Sitka.

1887 — Tsimshians, under Father William Duncan, arrive at Metlakatla from British Columbia.

1891 — First oil claims staked in Cook Inlet area.

1897-1900 — Klondike gold rush in Yukon Territory; heavy traffic through Alaska.

1902 — First oil production, at Katalla; telegraph from Eagle to Valdez completed.

1906 — Peak gold production year; Alaska granted a nonvoting delegate to Congress.

1911 — Copper production begins at Kennicott.

1912 — Territorial status for Alaska; first territorial legislature is convened the following year.

1913 — First airplane flight in Alaska, at Fairbanks, first auto trip from Fairbanks to Valdez.

1914 — President Wilson authorizes construction of the Alaska Railroad.

1916 — First bill proposing Alaska statehood introduced in Congress; peak copper production year.

1922 — First pulp mill starts production, Speel River, near Juneau.

1923 — President Warren Harding drives spike completing the Alaska Railroad.

1930 — The first "talkie" motion picture is shown in Fairbanks, featuring the Marx Brothers in *The Coconuts.*

1935 — Matanuska Valley Project begins, which establishes farming families in Alaska. First Juneau to Fairbanks flight.

1936 — All-time record salmon catch in Alaska — 126.4 million fish.

1940 — Military build-up in Alaska; Fort Richardson, Elmendorf Air Force Base established. At this point there are only about 40,000 non-Native Alaskans and 32,458 Natives. Pan American Airways inaugurates twice-weekly service between Seattle, Ketchikan and Juneau, using Sikorsky flying boats.

1942 — Dutch Harbor bombed and Attu and Kiska islands occupied by Japanese forces. Alaska Highway built; first overland connection to Lower 48.

1943 — Japanese forces driven from Alaska.

1944 — Alaska-Juneau Mine shuts down.

1953 — Oil well drilled near Eureka, on the Glenn Highway, marking the start of modern oil history; first plywood mill at Juneau; first big pulp mill at Ketchikan.

1957 — Kenai oil strike.

1958 — Statehood measure passed by Congress; statehood proclaimed officially January 3, 1959. Sitka pulp mill opens.

1964 — Good Friday earthquake, March 27, causes heavy damage throughout the gulf coast region; 131 people lost their lives.

1967 — Alaska Centennial celebration; Fairbanks flood.

1968 — Oil and gas discoveries at Prudhoe Bay on the North Slope; $900 million North Slope oil lease sale the following year; pipeline proposal follows.

1971 — Congress approves Alaska Native Land Claims Settlement Act, granting title to 40 million acres of land and providing more than $900 million in payment to Alaska Natives.

1974 — Trans-Alaska pipeline receives final approval; construction build-up begins.

1975 — Population and labor force soar with construction of pipeline; Alaska Gross Products hits $5.8 billion — double the 1973 figure.

1976 — Voters select Willow area for new capital site.

1977 — Completion of the trans-Alaska pipeline from Prudhoe Bay to Valdez; shipment of first oil by tanker from Valdez to Puget Sound.

1978 — 200-mile fishing limit goes into effect; President Jimmy Carter withdraws 56 million acres creating 17 new national monuments as of December 1, 1978.

1979 — State of Alaska files suit to halt the withdrawal of 56 million acres of Alaska land by President Carter under the Antiquities Act.

1980 — Special session of the Alaska legislature votes to repeal the state income tax and provides for refunds of 1979 taxes. Legislature establishes a Permanent Fund as a repository for one-fourth of all royalty oil revenues for future generations. Census figures show Alaska's population grew by 32.4 percent during the 1970s. The Alaska Lands Act of 1980 puts 53.7 million Alaska acres into the national wildlife refuge system, parts of 25 rivers to the national wild and scenic rivers system, 3.3 million acres to national forest lands, and 43.6 million acres to national park land.

1981 — Legislature puts on the ballot a constitutional amendment proposal to limit state spending. Secretary of the Interior James Watt initiates plans to sell oil and gas leases on 130 million acres of Alaska's nonrestricted federal land and announces a tentative schedule to open 16 offshore areas of Alaska as part of an intense national search for oil and gas on the outer continental shelf.

1982 — Oil revenues for state decrease. Vote for funding of capital move from Juneau to Willow defeated. First permanent fund dividend checks of $1,000 each are mailed to every six-month resident of Alaska.

Related reading: *Bits and Pieces of Alaskan History.* Material published over the years in *ALASKA®* magazine's "From Ketchikan to Barrow®." Vol. I, 208 pages, Vol. II, 216 pages, $14.95 each. *The Copper Spike,* by Lone E. Janson. Turn-of-the-century railroad building to the copper deposits at Kennicott. 176 pages, $9.95. *Early Visitors to Southeastern Alaska; Nine Accounts,* compiled and edited by R.N. De Armond. Firsthand accounts of exploration in Alaska during the eighteenth and nineteenth centuries, with original woodcuts by Dale De Armond. 214 pages, $5.95. *E.T. Barnette: The Strange Story of the Man Who Founded Fairbanks,* by Terrence Cole. 176 pages, $7.95. *The Lost Patrol,* by Dick North. A Mounty patrol that perished on the trail. 138 pages, $4.95. *13 Years of Travel & Exploration in Alaska, 1877-1889,* by W. H. Pierce. Northern History Library. 106 pages, $3.95. *This Old House: The Story of Clara Rust,* by Jo Anne Wold. A family in the early days of Fairbanks. 262 pages, $6.95. *A Whaler and Trader in the Arctic, 1895 to 1944,* by Arthur James Allen. 213 pages, $5.95. *Along Alaska's Great River* by Frederick Schwatka. The thrilling accounts of the author's military exploration of the Yukon River. 96 pages, $7.95. See pages 207-10.

Holidays, 1984

New Year's Day — traditional	January 1
— holiday	January 2
Lincoln's Birthday — traditional	February 12
— holiday	February 13
Washington's Birthday — holiday	February 20
— traditional	February 21
Seward's Day*	March 26
Memorial Day	May 28
Independence Day	July 4
Labor Day	September 3
Alaska Day*	October 18
Veterans Day — traditional	November 11
— holiday	November 12
Thanksgiving Day	November 22
Christmas Day	December 25

*Seward's Day commemorates the signing of the treaty by which the United States bought Alaska from Russia, signed on March 30, 1867. Alaska Day is the anniversary of the formal transfer of the territory and the raising of the U.S. flag at Sitka on October 18, 1867.

Hooligan

Smelt, also known as eulachon or candlefish (because the oily little fish can be burned like a candle). These small fish, known as "ooligan" in southeastern Alaska, are caught by dip-netting as they travel upriver to spawn.

Hospitals and Health Facilities

Alaska has numerous hospitals, nursing homes, and other health facilities. (See also *Pioneers' Homes.*) The only hospital in the state currently offering tertiary (specialized) care units is Providence Hospital in Anchorage, with its thermal unit (burn and frostbite), cancer treatment center, and neonatal intensive care nursery.

Municipal, Private, and State Hospitals

Anchorage, Alaska Psychiatric Institute (200 beds), 2900 Providence Drive, 99508.

Anchorage, Alaska Treatment Center (out-patient rehabilitation facility), 3710 East 20th Avenue, 99504.

Anchorage, Humana Hospital (99 beds), 2841 DeBarr Road, Pouch 8 AH, 99508.

Anchorage, Providence Hospital (250 beds), 3200 Providence Drive, 99504.

Cordova, Cordova Community Hospital (22 beds), Box 160, 99574.

Fairbanks, Fairbanks Memorial Hospital (155 beds), 1560 Cowles Street, 99701.

Glennallen, Faith Hospital (6 beds), c/o Central Alaskan Missions, Inc., Box 5, 99588.

Homer, South Kenai Peninsula Hospital (17 beds), Box 375, 99603.

Juneau, Bartlett Memorial Hospital (67 beds), 3260 Hospital Drive, 99801.

Juneau, Juneau Regional Rehabilitation Hospital (17 alcoholism treatment beds), 3250 Hospital Drive, 99801.
Ketchikan, Ketchikan General Hospital (92 beds), 3100 Tongass Avenue, 99901.
Kodiak, Kodiak Island Hospital (44 beds), Box 1187, 99615.
Nome, Norton Sound Regional Hospital (22 beds), Box 966, 99672.
Palmer, Valley Hospital (30 beds), Box H, 99645.
Petersburg, Petersburg General Hospital (25 beds), Box 589, 99833.
Seward, Seward General Hospital (33 beds), Box 365, 99664.
Sitka, Sitka Community Hospital (24 beds), Box 500, 99835.
Soldotna, Central Peninsula General Hospital (30 beds), Box 1268, 99669.
Valdez, Harborview Developmental Center (state operated residential center for the mentally handicapped; 96 beds), Box 487, 99686.
Valdez, Valdez Community Hospital (15 beds), Box 550, 99686.
Wrangell, Wrangell General Hospital (23 beds), Box 80, 99929.

U.S. Public Health Service Hospitals
Anchorage, Alaska Native Medical Center (170 beds), Box 7-741, 99510.
Barrow, Alaska Native Hospital (14 beds), 99723.
Bethel, Yukon-Kuskokwim Delta Hospital (50 beds), 99559.
Dillingham, Bristol Bay Area Hospital (29 beds), 99576.
Kotzebue, Alska Native Hospital (31 beds), 99752.
Mount Edgecumbe, Alaska Native Hospital (78 beds), 99835.

Military Hospitals
Adak, Branch Hospital, Box 11, FPO Seattle 98791.
Eielson AFB, Eielson Air Force Base Clinic, 99702.
Elmendorf AFB, Elmendorf Air Force Base Hospital (95 beds), 99506.
Fort Greely, Fort Greely Army Health Center (emergency support only; 2 beds), 98733.
Fort Wainwright, Bassett Army Hospital (130 beds), 99703.
Kodiak, Kodiak Coast Guard Dispensary (16 beds), Box 2, 99619.

Nursing Homes
Anchorage, Our Lady of Compassion (216 beds), 4895 Cordova Street, 99503.
Fairbanks, Careage North (101 beds), 1949 Gillam Way, Box 847, 99701.
Juneau, Saint Ann's Nursing Home (42 beds), 415 Sixth Street, 99801.
Ketchikan, Island View Manor (44 beds), 3100 Tongass Avenue, 99901.
Seward, Wesleyan Nursing Home (64 beds), Box 456, 99664.

Hostels

Alaska has 12 youth hostels, located as follows:
Anchorage Youth Hostel, P.O. Box 4-1226, Anchorage 99509. Located at 32d and Minnesota Drive.
Bear Creek Camp and Hostel, Box 334, Haines 99827. Located along Small Tract Road, one mile from town.
Delta Youth Hostel, Box 971, Delta Junction 99737. Located three miles in from Milepost 272 of Richardson Highway.
Granite Creek Ranch Youth Hostel, P.O. Box 31, Sutton 99674. Located at Mile 64.1 of Glenn Highway.
Homer Youth Hostel, P.O. Box 3366, Homer 99603. Located at 243 West Pioneer Street.
Fairbanks Youth Hostel, P.O. Box 1738, Fairbanks 99707. Located at Musher's Hall, four miles in on Farmer's Loop Road.

Juneau Youth Hostel, P.O. Box 1543, Juneau 99802. Located in Northern
Light United Church, 11th and A streets.
Ketchikan Youth Hostel, P.O. Box 8515, Ketchikan 99901. Located in
United Methodist Church, Grant and Main streets.
Kodiak Hostel Inn, Box 2912, Kodiak 99615. Location pending.
Sitka Youth Hostel, Box 2645, Sitka 99835. Located in Sitka United
Presbyterian Church, 505 Sawmill Creek Boulevard.
Tok Youth Hostel Campground, c/o General Delivery, Tok 99780. Located
one mile south of Mile 1322 Alaska Highway.
Soldotna International Youth Hostel, P.O. Box 327, Soldotna 99669.

The hostels in Anchorage, Haines, Homer, Fairbanks and Soldotna are
open year-round. All others are open only in the summer. The Soldotna
hostel requires reservations. Opening and closing dates, maximum
length of stay, and hours may vary depending on the hostel.

Hostels are available to anyone with a valid membership card issued by
one of the 48 associations affiliated with the International Youth Hostel
Federation. Membership is open to all ages, and some hostels (including
Anchorage) accept nonmembers. By international agreement, each youth
hostel member joins the association of his own country. A valid membership card, which ranges from $7 to $140, depending on age and duration
of membership, entitles a member to use hostels in 61 countries.

Hostel memberships and a guide to American youth hostels can be pur-
chased from the national offices (American Youth Hostels, 1332 I Street
N.W., Suite 800, Washington, D.C. 20005 or from local hostels. For more
information regarding Alaska youth hostels write Alaska Council, AYH,
P.O. Box 4-1461, Anchorage 99509 or Department of Natural Resources,
Division of Parks, 619 Warehouse Avenue, Suite 210, Anchorage 99501.

Hot Springs

The U.S. Geological Survey identifies 79 thermal springs in Alaska.
Almost half of these hot springs occur along the volcanic Alaska Peninsula and Aleutian Chain. The second greatest regional concentration of
springs is in southeastern Alaska. Hot springs are scattered throughout
the Interior and western Alaska, as far north as the Brooks Range and as
far west as the Seward Peninsula.

Early miners and trappers were quick to use the naturally occurring
warm waters for baths. Today approximately 25 percent of the recorded
thermal springs are used for bathing, irrigation, or domestic use.
However, only a handful can be considered developed resorts.

Resorts (with swimming pools, changing rooms and lodging) are found
at Chena Hot Springs, a 62-mile drive east of Fairbanks, and Circle Hot
Springs, 136 miles by road from Fairbanks. The less-developed Manley
Hot Springs, at the small community of the same name at the end of the
Elliott Highway, is privately owned and the primitive bathhouse is used
mainly by local residents. Developed, but not easily accessible, is Melozi
Hot Springs at Melozi Hot Springs Lodge, some 200 miles northwest of
Fairbanks by air. The community of Tenakee Springs on Chichagof Island
in southeastern Alaska maintains an old bathhouse near the waterfront.
Temperature of the hot springs here is 106° F/41° C. The state Marine
Highway System provides ferry service to Tenakee. On Baranof Island in
Southeast there are two hot springs accessible by private boat or by air;
both have bathhouses.

Hunting

There are 26 game management units in Alaska and a wide variety in both seasons and bag limits. Current copies of the *Alaska Hunting Regulations* and a map delineating game unit boundaries are available from the Alaska Department of Fish and Game (P.O. Box 3-2000, Juneau 99802) or from Fish and Game offices and sporting goods stores throughout the state.

Regulations

A hunting or trapping license is required for all residents and nonresidents with the exception of Alaska residents under 16 years of age and Alaska residents 60 years of age who have resided in the state for 30 or more consecutive years.

Resident hunting licenses (valid for calendar year) cost $12; trapping license (valid October 1 to September 30), $3; hunting and trapping license, $15; hunting and sport fishing license, $22; hunting, trapping and sport fishing license, $25.

Nonresident hunting licenses (valid for calendar year) cost $60; hunting and sport fishing license, $90; hunting and trapping license, $200.

Military personnel stationed in Alaska may purchase a small game hunting license for $12, and a small game hunting and sport fishing license for $22. Military personnel must purchase a nonresident license and pay nonresident fees for big game, unless they are hunting big game on military property.

Licenses may be obtained from any designated issuing agent or by mail from the Licensing Section, Alaska Department of Revenue, 1107 West Eighth Street, Juneau 99801. Licenses are not available at Fish and Game offices.

Big game tags and fees are required for residents hunting musk ox and brown/grizzly bear and for nonresidents hunting any big game animal. These nonrefundable, nontransferable, metal locking tags (valid for calendar year) must be purchased prior to the taking of the animal. A tag may, however, be used for any species for which the tag fee is of equal or less value. Fees quoted below are for *each* animal.

All residents (regardless of age) and nonresidents intending to hunt brown/grizzly bear must purchase tags (resident, $25; nonresident, $250). Both residents and nonresidents are also required to purchase musk ox tags (resident, $500 each bull taken on Nunivak Island or in Arctic National Wildlife Refuge, $25 each bull from Nelson Island, $25 cow; nonresident, $1,100).

Nonresident tag fees for other big game animals are as follows: deer, $135; wolf or wolverine, $150; black bear, $200; elk or goat, $250; caribou or moose, $300; bison, $350; and sheep, $400.

In addition, residents and nonresidents intending to hunt big game must pay a permit application fee of $5 for all species for which a limited drawing is conducted (except musk ox, for which the fee is $10).

Nonresidents hunting brown/grizzly bear or Dall sheep are required to have a guide or be accompanied by an Alaska resident relative over 19 years of age within the second degree of kindred (includes parents, grandparents, children, grandchildren, sisters or brothers). Nonresident aliens hunting big game and walrus must have a guide. A current list of registered Alaska guides is available from the Department of Commerce, Guide Licensing and Control Board, Pouch D, Juneau 99811 for $2 or check "The Guide Post®" in *ALASKA®* magazine.

Residents and nonresidents 16 years of age or older hunting waterfowl must have a signed federal migratory bird hunting stamp (duck stamp).

Trophy Game

Record big game in Alaska as recorded by the Boone and Crockett Club in the latest (1981) edition of *Record Big Game of North America* are as follows:

Black bear: skull 13 7/16 inches long, 8 6/16 inches wide (1966).

Brown bear (coastal region): skull 17 15/16 inches long, 12 13/16 inches wide (1952).

Grizzly bear (inland): skull 16 10/16 inches long, 9 14/16 inches wide (1970).

Polar bear: skull 18 8/16 inches long, 11 7/16 inches wide (1963). It is currently illegal for anyone but an Alaskan Eskimo, Aleut, or Indian to hunt polar bear in Alaska.

Bison: right horn 18 1/8 inches long, base circumference 15 inches; left horn 21 inches long, base circumference 15 2/8 inches; greatest spread 31 7/8 inches (1977).

Barren Ground caribou: right beam 51 2/8 inches, 22 points; left beam 51 5/8 inches, 23 points (1967).

Moose: right palm length 49 5/8 inches, width 20 6/8 inches; left palm length 49 6/8 inches, width 15 6/8 inches; right beam 18 points, left 16 points; greatest spread 77 inches (taken using an airplane in 1978).

Mountain goat: right horn 11 5/8 inches long, base circumference 5 6/8 inches; left horn 11 5/8 inches long, base circumference 5 5/8 inches (1933).

Musk ox: right horn 26 6/8 inches, left horn 26 4/8 inches, tip-to-tip spread 26 7/8 inches (1976).

Dall sheep: right horn 48 5/8 inches long, base circumference 14 5/8 inches; left horn 47 7/8 inches long, base circumference 14 6/8 inches (1961).

Related reading: *Alaska Game Trails With a Master Guide,* compiled by Charles J. Keim; foreword by Lowell Thomas, Sr. True stories about a legendary Alaska guide, Hal Waugh. 310 pages, $6.95. *Alaska Bear Tales,* by Larry Kaniut. 138 pages, $9.95. *Fair Chase With Alaskan Guides,* by Hal Waugh and Charles J. Keim. Outdoor adventure stories. 206 pages, $5.95.

Selected Alaska Hunting & Fishing Tales, Volume 4, edited by Jim Rearden. First-person adventure tales. 140 pages, $4.95. See pages 207-10.

Hypothermia

(See also *Chill Factor.*)

The body's reaction when it is exposed to cold and cannot maintain normal temperatures. In an automatic survival reaction, blood flow to the extremities is shut down in favor of preserving warmth in the vital organs. As internal temperature drops, judgment and coordination become impaired. Allowed to continue, hypothermia leads to stupor, collapse, and death. Immersion hypothermia occurs in cold water.

Ice

(See also *Glaciers.*)

Icebergs

Icebergs are formed in Alaska wherever glaciers reach salt water or a freshwater lake. Some accessible places to view icebergs include Glacier Bay, Icy Bay, Yakutat Bay, Taku Inlet, Endicott Arm, portions of northern Prince William Sound (College Fiord, Barry Arm, Columbia Bay), Mendenhall Lake, and Portage Lake.

If icebergs contain little or no sediment, approximately 75 percent to 80 percent of their bulk may be underwater. The more sediment an iceberg contains, the greater its density, and an iceberg containing large amounts of sediment will float slightly beneath the surface. Glaciologists of the U.S. Geological Survey believe that some of these "black icebergs" may actually sink to the bottom of a body of water. Since salt water near the faces of glaciers may be liquid to temperatures as low as 28°F, and icebergs melt at 32°F, some of these underwater icebergs may remain unmelted indefinitely.

Alaska's icebergs are comparatively small compared to the icebergs found near Antarctica and Greenland. One of the larger icebergs ever recorded in Alaska was formed in May 1977 in Icy Bay. Glaciologists measured it at 346 feet long, 297 feet wide, and 99 feet above the surface of the water.

Sea Ice

Sea water typically freezes at -1.8° C or 28.8° F. The first indication that sea water is freezing is the appearance of frazil, tiny needlelike crystals of pure ice, in shallow coastal areas of low current or areas of low salinity, such as near the mouths of rivers. Continued freezing turns the frazil into a soupy mass called grease ice and eventually into an ice crust approximately four inches thick. More freezing, wind and wave action thicken the ice and break it into ice floes ranging from a few feet to several miles across. In the Arctic Ocean, ice floes can be 10 feet thick. Most are criss-crossed with 6- to 8-foot-high walls of ice caused by the force of winds.

Sea salt that is trapped in the ice during freezing is leached out over time, making the older ice least saline. Meltwater forming in ponds on multi-year-old ice during summer months is a fresh water source for native marine life.

Refreezing of meltwater ponds and the formation of new ice in the permanent ice pack (generally north of 72° north latitude) begins in mid-September. While the ice pack expands southward, new ice freezes to the coast (shorefast ice) and spreads seaward. Where the drifting ice pack grinds against the relatively stable shorefast ice tremendous walls or ridges of ice are formed, some observed to be 100 feet thick and grounded in 60 feet of water. They are impenetrable by all but the most powerful icebreakers. By late March the ice cover has reached its maximum extent, approximately from Port Heiden on the Alaska Peninsula in the south to the northern Pribilof Islands and northwestward to Siberia. In Cook Inlet, sea ice, usually no more than two feet thick, can extend as far south as Anchor Point and Kamishak Bay on the east and west sides of the inlet respectively. The ice season usually lasts from mid-November to mid-March.

In 1954 the navy began observing and forecasting sea ice conditions in support of the construction of defense sites along the arctic coast. In 1969 the National Weather Service began a low-profile sea ice reconnaissance program, which expanded greatly during the summer of 1975, when during a year of severe ice, millions of dollars of material had to be shipped to Prudhoe Bay. Expanded commercial fisheries in the Bering Sea also heightened the problem of sea ice to crabbing and bottom fish trawling operations. In 1976, headquarters for a seven-day-a-week ice watch was established at Fairbanks and then moved to Anchorage in 1981.

The National Weather Service operates a radio facsimile broadcast service making current ice analysis charts, special oceanographic charts, and standard weather charts available to the public via standard radios equipped with "black box" receivers. Commercial fishing operators, particularly in the Bering Sea, use the radio-transmitted charts to steer clear of problem weather and troublesome ice formations. More information is available from the National Weather Service in Kodiak or Anchorage.

Related reading: *Icebound in the Siberian Arctic,* by Robert J. Gleason. Rescue of a ship by early aviators. 164 pages, $4.95. See page 209.

Ice Fog

A fog of tiny, spherical ice crystals formed when air just above the ground becomes so cold it can no longer retain water vapor. Most common in arctic and subarctic regions in winter when clear skies create an air inversion. Surface heat radiates into space, forming a warm-air cap that contains cold air at low elevations. Most noticeable when man-made pollutants are also trapped at low levels by the air inversion.

Iceworm

Although generally regarded as a hoax, iceworms actually exist. These small, thin, segmented black worms, usually less than one inch long, thrive at temperatures just above freezing. Observers as far back as the 1880s report that at dawn, dusk or on overcast days, the tiny worms, all belonging to the genus *Mesenchytraeus,* may literally carpet the surface of glaciers. When sunlight strikes them, they burrow back down into the ice.

The town of Cordova commemorates its own version of the iceworm each February in the Iceworm Festival, when a 150-foot-long, multilegged "iceworm" marches in a parade down Main Street.

Iditarod Trail Sled Dog Race

The first race, conceived and organized by Joe Redington, Sr., of Knik, began in Anchorage on March 3, 1973, and ended April 3, 1973, in Nome. Of the 34 who started the race, 22 finished. The Iditarod has been run every year since its inception in 1973. In 1976 it was declared Alaska's official sled dog race by Gov. Jay Hammond. That year also, Congress designated the Iditarod as a National Historic Trail.

Following the old dog team mail route blazed in 1910 from Knik to Nome, the trail crosses two mountain ranges, follows the Yukon River for about 150 miles, runs through several bush villages, and crosses the pack ice of Norton Sound.

Strictly a winter trail because the ground is mostly spongy muskeg swamps, the route attracted national attention in 1925 when sled dog mushers, including the famous Leonhard Seppala, relayed 300,000 units of life-saving diphtheria serum to epidemic-threatened Nome. However, as the airplane and snowmobile replaced the sled dog team, the trail fell into disuse. Thanks to Redington, the trail has been assured a place in Alaska history.

Each year the Iditarod takes a slightly different course, following an alternate southern route in odd years (see map). While the route is traditionally described as 1,049 miles long (a figure that was selected because Alaska is the 49th state), actual distance is close to 1,200 miles.

In 1983, 68 mushers started the world's longest and richest sled dog race. Of those, 54 finished the Anchorage to Nome ordeal. The last die-hard to finish, Scott Cameron of Palmer, arrived in Nome a week after Wasilla's Dick Mackey secured first place for the second time. The Iditarod purse ($100,000 in 1982 and again in 1983) is divided among the first 20 finishers. And the race can be close: in 1982, second-place finisher Susan Butcher was only 3 minutes and 43 seconds behind winner Rick Swenson.

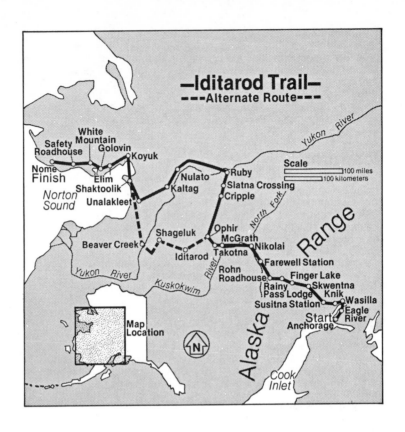

All-Time Winners and Times

Year	Musher	Days	Hrs.	Min.	Sec.	Prize
1983	Dick Mackey, Wasilla	12	14	10	44	$24,000
1982	Rick Swenson, Eureka	16	4	40	10	24,000
1981	Rick Swenson, Eureka	12	8	45	2	24,000
1980	Joe May, Trapper Creek	14	7	11	51	12,000
1979	Rick Swenson, Eureka	15	10	37	47	12,000
1978	Dick Mackey, Wasilla	14	18	52	24	12,000
1977	Rick Swenson, Eureka	16	16	27	13	9,600
1976	Jerry Riley, Nenana	18	22	58	17	7,000
1975	Emmitt Peters, Ruby	14	14	43	45	15,000
1974	Carl Huntington, Galena	20	15	2	7	12,000
1973	Dick Willmarth, Red Devil	20	—	49	41	12,000

1983 Results

Place	Musher	Days	Hrs.	Min.	Sec.	Prize
1	Dick Mackey	12	14	10	44	$24,000
2	Eep Anderson	12	15	50	36	16,000
3	Larry Smith	12	20	19	56	12,000
4	Herbie Nayokpuk	12	22	4	28	8,000
5	Rick Swenson	13	2	49	46	6,000
6	Lavon Barve	13	3	0	49	5,000
7	Duane Halverson	13	4	42	0	4,000
8	Sonny Lindner	13	5	28	20	3,600
9	Susan Butcher	13	10	25	32	3,200
10	Roger Legaard	13	11	33	45	2,800
11	Joe Runyan	13	12	39	34	2,000
12	Guy Blankenship	13	12	59	0	1,900
13	Dave Monson	13	14	8	54	1,800
14	Sue Firmin	13	17	28	52	1,700
15	Dee Dee Jonrowe	13	18	10	25	1,600
16	Howard Albert	13	22	11	39	1,500
17	Bruce Denton	14	0	37	7	1,400
18	Dave Olson	14	3	35	29	1,300
19	Emmitt Peters	14	3	36	20	1,200
20	John Barron	14	5	44	30	1,000

Igloo

In Alaska, this dwelling is traditionally made of driftwood, whalebone and sod. It was the Canadian Eskimos, not those of Alaska, who built the well-known houses of snow and ice. Alaska Natives, however, did sometimes build temporary shelters and storehouses of snow.

Industry

Oil and gas mining is by far the largest income producer in Alaska. As measured by gross state product — the value of all goods and services produced in a state in a given year — oil and gas mining accounted for $10,852 million in current dollars in 1981, the most current figures available. The entire mining industry produced $10,913.6 million. The next most productive sectors of the economy are government, which generated $1,872 million, and services, at $967 million. Gross state product figures are prepared by the Institute of Social and Economic Research, University of Alaska.

Fiscal budgets provide another perspective on the importance of oil and gas to the state's economy. Approximately 85 percent of the state's 1984 fiscal year budget (July 1983 to July 1984) came from the oil and gas industry. This figure is estimated to be 87 percent for 1985.

With the major exception of oil and gas, industries yielding the highest gross state product are also among the top employers. According to statistics provided by the Department of Labor, local, state, and federal governments (excluding uniformed military) employ by far the greatest number in the state. The three levels of government employed an average of more than 61,000 people in 1982. Following government in rank by average number of people employed annually came retail and wholesale trade; services and miscellaneous; transportation, communications, and utilities; construction; manufacturing; finance, insurance, and real estate; and mining.

Information Sources

Agriculture: State Division of Agriculture, Pouch A, Wasilla 99687; Cooperative Extension Service, University of Alaska, Fairbanks 99701.

Alaska Natives: Alaska Federation of Natives, 2550 Denali Street, Suite 1606, Anchorage 99503.

Boating, Canoeing, and Kayaking: U.S. Fish and Wildlife Service, 1011 East Tudor, Anchorage 99503; State Division of Parks, 619 Warehouse Avenue, Suite 210, Anchorage 99501.

Business: Alaska Department of Commerce and Economic Development, Pouch D, Juneau 99801; State Chamber of Commerce, 310 Second Street, Juneau 99801.

Camping and Hiking: State Division of Parks, 619 Warehouse Avenue, Suite 210, Anchorage 99501; Bureau of Land Management, 701 C Street, Box 13, Anchorage 99513; State Division of Tourism, Pouch E-101, Juneau 99811; Supervisor, Chugach National Forest, 2221 East Northern Lights Boulevard, Suite 238, Anchorage 99508; National Park Service, 2525 Gambell Street, Anchorage 99501; Supervisor, Tongass National Forest, P.O. Box 1628, Juneau 99802.

Census Data: Alaska Department of Labor, Administrative Services Division, P.O. Box 1149, Juneau 99811.

Climate: State Climatologist, University of Alaska Arctic Environmental and Data Center, 707 A Street, Anchorage 99501.

Education: Alaska Department of Education, Pouch F, Juneau 99811; U.S. Bureau of Indian Affairs, Box 3-8000, Juneau 99802.

Gold panning: State Division of Geological and Geophysical Surveys, Mines Information Office, 3327 Fairbanks Street, Anchorage 99503; Bureau of Land Management, 701 C Street, Box 13, Anchorage 99513.

Health: State Department of Health and Social Services, Pouch H-01, Juneau 99811.

Housing: State Housing Authority, Box 100080, Anchorage 99510.

Hunting and Fishing Regulations: State Department of Fish and Game, P.O. Box 3-2000, Juneau 99802.

Job Opportunities: State Employment Service, Box 3-7000, Juneau 99802.

Labor: State Department of Labor, Box 1149, Juneau 99811.

Land: State Division of Lands, Pouch 7-005, Anchorage 99510; Bureau of Land Management, 701 C Street, Box 13, Anchorage 99513.

Legislature: Legislative Information Office, 1024 West Sixth Avenue, Anchorage 99501; Legislative Information Office, Eskimo Building, 333 Front Street, P.O. Box 667, Kotzebue 99752.

Military: Department of the Air Force, Headquarters, Alaskan Air Command, Elmendorf Air Force Base 99506; Department of the Army, Headquarters, 172d Infantry Brigade (Alaska), Fort Richardson 99505; State Department of Military Affairs, Office of the Adjutant General,

3601 C Street, Anchorage 99503; Department of Transportation, U.S. Coast Guard, 17th Coast Guard District, P.O. Box 3-5000, Juneau 99802.

Mines and Petroleum: State Division of Geological and Geophysical Surveys, 3001 Porcupine Drive, Anchorage 99501; Mines Information Office, 3327 Fairbanks Street, Anchorage 99503; Alaska Miners Association, 509 West Third Avenue, Suite 17, Anchorage 99501; Alaska Oil and Gas Association, 505 West Northern Lights Boulevard, Anchorage 99503.

River Running: National Park Service, 2525 Gambell Street, Anchorage 99503; Alaska Wilderness Guides Association, 360 K Street, Suite 246, Anchorage 99501.

Travel and Visitor Information: State Division of Tourism, Pouch E-101, Juneau 99811; Marine Highway Systems, Pouch R, Juneau 99811.

Islands

Southeastern Alaska contains about 1,000 of the state's 1,800 named islands, rocks and reefs; several thousand remain unnamed. There are more than 200 islands in the Aleutian Island chain in southwestern Alaska. Of the state's 10 largest islands, six are in southeastern Alaska. Of the remainder, Unimak is in the Aleutians, Nunivak and Saint Lawrence are in the Bering Sea off the west coast of Alaska, and Kodiak is in the Gulf of Alaska. The state's 10 largest islands, according to U.S. Geological Survey and Bureau of Land Management figures, are:

	Square Miles			Square Miles
Kodiak	3,588		Baranof	1,636
Prince of Wales	2,731*		Nunivak	1,600**
Chichagof	2,062		Unimak	1,600
Saint Lawrence	1,780**		Revillagigedo	1,134
Admiralty	1,709		Kupreanof	1,084

*The figure 2,770 square miles reported in earlier editions of The ALASKA ALMANAC® included associated islands.
**Estimate

Related reading: *Admiralty: Island in Contention,* southeastern Alaska's wilderness island and its future. 78 pages, $5.00. *Islands of the Seals, The Pribilofs.* 128 pages, color photography, $9.95. *The Aleutians.* 224 pages, color photography, $14.95. See pages 207-10.

Ivory

Eskimos traditionally carved ivory to make such implements as harpoon heads, dolls and *ulu* handles. For the past 80 years, however, most carvings have been made to be sold. The bulk of the ivory used today comes from walrus tusks and teeth. Fossil ivory is also used; it may be black, dark brown or beige, depending on the moisture conditions and soil in which it is found. Etching originally was done with hand tools and the scratches were filled in with soot. Today modern power tools supplement the hand tools and carvers color the etching with India ink. The most active carvers live on Saint Lawrence Island, the Seward Peninsula and Little Diomede Island.

Walrus may be taken by only Alaska Natives (Aleuts, Eskimos, and Indians) who dwell on the coast of the North Pacific Ocean or the Arctic Ocean for subsistence purposes or for the creation and sale of authentic Native articles of handicrafts or clothing.

Raw walrus ivory or other parts can be sold by only an Alaska Native to an Alaska Native within Alaska or to a registered agent for resale or transfer to an Alaska Native within the state. Only authentic Native processed ivory articles of handicrafts or clothing may be sold or transferred to a non-Native, or sold in interstate commerce.

Beach ivory, which is found on the beach within one-fourth mile of the ocean, may, however, be kept by anyone. This ivory must be registered by all non-Natives with the U.S. Fish and Wildlife Service or the National Marine Fisheries Service within 30 days of discovery. Beach-found ivory must remain in the possession of the finder even if carved or scrimshawed.

Carved or scrimshawed walrus ivory (authentic Native handicraft) or other marine mammal parts made into clothing or other authentic Native handicrafts may be exported from the United States to a foreign country, but the exporter must first obtain an export permit from the USFWS. Even visitors from the Lower 48 simply traveling through, or stopping in, Canada on their way home are required to have a USFWS export and/or transit permit. Cost is $25. Mailing the carved ivory home will avoid the need for an export/transit permit. Importation of walrus or other marine mammals is illegal except for scientific research purposes or for public display once a permit is granted.

For further information contact: Special Agent-in-Charge, U.S. Fish and Wildlife Service, 1011 East Tudor Road, Anchorage 99503, phone (907) 263-3311; or Senior Resident, U.S. Fish and Wildlife Service, 1412 Airport Way, Fairbanks 99701, phone (907) 456-4839.

Jade

Most Alaskan jade is found near the Dall, Shungnak, and Kobuk rivers and Jade Mountain, all north of the Arctic Circle. The stones occur in various shades of green, brown, black, yellow, white, and even red. The most valuable are those that are marbled black, white, and green. Gem-quality jade, about one-fourth of the total mined, is used in jewelry making. Fractured jade is used for clock faces, table tops, book ends, and other items. Jade is the Alaska state gem.

Kuspuk

Eskimo woman's parka, often made with a loosely cut back so that an infant may be carried piggyback-style. Parkas are made from rabbit or fox skins; traditionally, the fur lining faces inward. The ruffs are generally wolverine or wolf fur. An outer shell, called a *qaspeq*, is worn over a fur parka to keep it clean and prevent wearing. This outer shell is usually made of brightly-colored corduroy, cotton print, or velveteenlike material, and may be trimmed with rickrack.

Labor and Employer Organizations

The Alaska Department of Labor directory *Labor Unions and Employer Groups* lists the following organizations:

Anchorage

Alaska Public Employees Association
Alaska State District Council of Laborers
American Federation of Government Employees Council 121
Anchorage Independent Longshore Union Local No. 1
Anchorage Musicians Association Local No. 650
Anchorage Typographical Union Local No. 823
Asbestos Workers Local No. 97
Associated General Contractors of America
Bartenders' International Union Local No. 883
Bricklayers and Allied Craftsmen Local No.1
Brotherhood of Railroad Trainmen Lodge No. 999
Construction and General Laborers Local No. 341
Hotel, Motel, Restaurant and Construction Camp Employees Local No. 878
International Alliance of Theatrical Stage Employees and Motion Picture Machine Operators Local No. 770
International Association of Bridge, Structural and Ornamental Ironworkers Local No. 751
International Association of Firefighters Local No. 1264
International Association of Machinists and Aerospace Workers Local No. 601

International Brotherhood of Boilermakers, Iron Ship Builders, Blacksmiths, Forgers and Helpers Local No. 498
International Brotherhood of Teamsters, Chauffeurs, Warehousemen and Helpers Local No. 959
International Brotherhood of Painters and Allied Trades Local No. 1140
Laundry and Dry Cleaning International Union Local No. 333
National Electrical Contractors Association
Operative Plasterers' and Cement Masons' International Association Local No. 867
Piledrivers, Bridge, Dock Builders and Drivers Local No. 2520

Public Employees Local No. 71
Retail Clerks Union Local No. 1496
Roofers Union Local No. 190
Sheet Metal Workers' International Association Local No. 23
United Association of Plumbers and Steamfitters Local No. 367
United Brotherhood of Carpenters and Joiners Local No. 1281
Western Alaska Building and Construction Trades Council
Cordova
Copper River and Prince William Sound Cannery Workers' Union
Cordova District Fisheries Union
International Longshoremen's and Warehousemen's Union Local No. 66
Dillingham
Western Alaska Cooperative Marketing Association
Dutch Harbor
International Longshoremen's and Warehousemen's Union
Fairbanks
Alaska Public Employees Association
Construction and General Laborers Local No. 942
Fairbanks Central Labor Council
Fairbanks Joint Crafts Council
Hotel, Motel, Restaurant, Construction Camp Employees and Bartenders
    Local No. 879
International Association of Firefighters Local No. 1324
International Brotherhood of Electrical Workers Local No. 1547
International Brotherhood of Teamsters, Chauffeurs, Warehousemen and
    Helpers Local No. 959
International Printing and Graphic Communications Union Local No. 704
International Union of Operating Engineers Local No. 302
Musicians' Protective Union Local No. 481
NEA-Alaska (Fairbanks Education Association)
Operative Plasterers' and Cement Masons' International Association
    Local No. 867
Public Employees Local No. 71
Retail Clerks International Association Local No. 1689
Sheet Metal Workers' International Association Local No. 72
Technical Engineers Local No. 959
United Association of Journeymen and Apprentices of the Plumbing and
    Pipefitting Industry Local No. 375
United Brotherhood of Carpenters and Joiners Local No. 1243
Haines
International Longshoremen's and Warehousemen's Union Local No. 65
Juneau
Alaska Public Employees Association
Associated General Contractors of America
Bartenders' International Union Local No. 869
Hotel and Restaurant Employees' Union Local No. 871
Inland Boatmen's Union of the Pacific
International Brotherhood of Electrical Workers Local No. 1547
International Brotherhood of Teamsters, Chauffeurs, Warehousemen and
    Helpers Local No. 959
International *Longshoremen's* and Warehousemen's Union Local No. 16
International Longshoremen's and *Warehousemen's* Union Local No. 41
International Union of Operating Engineers Local No. 302
Juneau Central Labor Council

Juneau and Vicinity Building and Construction Trades Council
Laborers International Union Local No. 942
Musicians' Protective Union
NEA-Alaska
National Federation of Federal Employees Local No. 251
Public Employees Local No. 71
United Association of Journeymen and Apprentices of the Plumbing and
    Pipefitting Industry Local No. 262
United Brotherhood of Carpenters and Joiners Local No. 2247
Ketchikan
Alaska Loggers Association
Association of Western Pulp and Paper Workers Local No. 783
Bartenders and Culinary Workers Union Local No. 867
International Brotherhood of Electrical Workers Local No. 1547
International Brotherhood of Teamsters, Chauffeurs, Warehousemen and
    Helpers Local No. 959
International *Longshoremen's* and Warehousemen's Union Local No. 62
International Longshoremen's and *Warehousemen's* Union Local No. 61
International Woodworkers of America Local No. 3-193
Ketchikan Central Labor Council
United Brotherhood of Carpenters and Joiners Local No. 1501
Kodiak
United Brotherhood of Carpenters and Joiners Local No. 2161
Inland Boatmens' Union of the Pacific
Palmer
United Mineworkers Local No. 7901
Wood, Wire, and Metal Lathers International Union Local No. 529
Pelican
International Longshoremen's and Warehousemen's Union Local No. 83
Petersburg
International Longshoremen's and *Warehousemen's* Union Local No. 85
Petersburg Fishermen's Union
United Industrial Workers
Seldovia
United Cannery Workers of Lower Cook Inlet
Seward
International Longshoremen's and Warehousemen's Union Local No. 60
Sitka
Hotel, Motel and Culinary Workers' and Bartenders' Union Local No. 873
International Longshoremen's and Warehousemen's Union Local No. 84
International Union, United Paperworkers Local No. 962
Retail Clerks International Association Local No. 1394
United Brotherhood of Carpenters and Joiners Local No. 466
Skagway
United Transportation Union Local No. 1787
Wrangell
International Longshoremen's and Warehousemen's Union Local No. 87
United Paperworkers' International Union Local No. 1341

Lakes

    There are 94 lakes with surface areas of more than 10 square miles among Alaska's more than 3 million lakes. According to a 1963 report of the U.S. Geological Survey, the 10 largest (larger than 20 acres) natural freshwater lakes are:

Lake	Square Miles	Lake	Square Miles
Iliamna	1,000	Clark	110
Becharof	458	Dall	100
Teshekpuk	315	Upper Ugashik	75
Naknek	242	Lower Ugashik	72
Tustumena	117	Kukaklek	72

Land

At first glance it seems odd that such a huge country as Alaska has not been more heavily settled. Thousands of acres of forest and tundra, miles and miles of rivers and streams, hidden valleys, bays, coves and mountains, are spread across an area so vast that it staggers the imagination. Yet, over two-thirds of the population of Alaska remains clustered around two major centers of commerce and survival. Compared to the settlement of the western Lower 48, Alaska is not settled at all.

Visitors flying over the state are impressed by immense areas showing no sign of humanity. Current assessments indicate that approximately 160,000 acres of Alaska have been cleared, built on or otherwise directly altered by man, either by settlement or resource development, including mining, pipeline construction, and agriculture. In comparison to the 375 million acres of land which comprise the total of the state, the settled or altered area currently amounts to less than 1/20th of a percent.

There are significant reasons for this lack of development in Alaska. Frozen for long periods in the dark of the Arctic, much of the land cannot support quantities of people or industry and where the winters are "warm," the mountains, glaciers, rivers and oceans prevent easy access for commerce and trade.

The status of land, especially in Alaska, is constantly changing. In most places, the free market affects patterns of land ownership, but in Alaska, all land ownership patterns until recently were the result of a century-long process of a single landowner, the United States government.

The Statehood Act signaled the beginning of a dramatic shift in land ownership patterns. It authorized the state to select a total of 104 million of the 375 million acres of land and inland waters in Alaska. Under the Submerged Lands Act, the state also has title to submerged lands under navigable inland waters. In passing the Statehood Act, Congress cited economic independence and the need to open Alaska to economic development as the primary purposes for large Alaska land grants.

The issue of the Native claims in Alaska was cleared with the passage of the Alaska Native Claims Settlement Act (ANCSA) on December 18, 1971. This act of Congress provided for creation of Alaska Native village and regional corporations, and gave the Alaska Eskimos, Aleuts and Indians nearly $1 billion and the right to select 44 million acres from a land "pool" of some 116 million acres.

Immediately after the passage of the settlement act, the state filed for the selection of an additional 77 million acres of land before the creation of some Native withdrawals and withdrawals for study as National Interest Lands. The Department of the Interior refused to recognize these selections. In September 1972 the litigation initiated by the state was resolved by a settlement affirming state selection of 41 million acres.

Section 17 of the settlement act, in addition to establishing a Joint Federal-State Land Use Planning Commission, directed the secretary of the interior to withdraw from public use up to 80 million acres of land in Alaska for study as possible national parks, wildlife refuges, forests, and wild and scenic rivers. These were the National Interest Lands Congress

was to decide upon as set forth in Section 17(d)(2) of the settlement act, by December 18, 1978. The U.S. House of Representatives passed a bill (HR39) which would have designated 124 million acres of national parks, forests and wildlife refuges, and designated millions of acres of these and existing parks, forests and refuges as wilderness. Although a bill was reported out of committee, it failed to pass the Senate before Congress adjourned.

In November 1978 the secretary of the interior published a draft environmental impact supplement which listed the options that the executive branch of the federal government could take to protect federal lands in Alaska until the Ninety-sixth Congress could consider the creation of new parks, wildlife refuges, wild and scenic rivers and forests. In keeping with this objective, the secretary of the interior withdrew from most public uses about 114 million acres of land in Alaska, under provisions of the 1976 Federal Land Policy and Management Act. On December 1, 1978, the president, under the authority of the 1906 Antiquities Act, designated 56 million acres of these lands as National Monuments.

In February 1980 the House of Representatives passed a modified HR39. In August 1980 the Senate passed a compromise version of the Alaska lands bill which created 106 million acres of new conservation units and affected a total of 131 million acres of land in Alaska. In November 1980 the House accepted the Senate version of the Alaska National Interest Lands Conservation Act, which Pres. Jimmy Carter signed into law on December 2, 1980. This is also known as the d-2 lands bill or the compromise HR39. (Please see also following sections: *National Parks, Preserves, and Monuments; National Wilderness Areas; National Wildlife Refuges; National Forests;* and *National Wild and Scenic Rivers.*)

Alaska's land will continue to be a controversial and complex subject for some time. Implementation of the d-2 issue, and distribution of land to the Native village and regional corporations, the state of Alaska, and private citizens in the state will require time. Numerous land issues created by large land exchanges, conflicting land use and management policies, and overlapping resources will require constant cooperation between landowners if the issues are going to be solved successfully.

Acquiring Land for Private Use

The easiest and fastest way to acquire land for private use is by purchase from the private sector: through real estate agencies or directly from individuals. Because of speculation, land claim conflicts and delays involving Native, state and federal groups, however, private land is considered by many people to be in short supply and often is very expensive.

Private land in Alaska, excluding land held by Native corporations, is estimated to be more than one million acres, but less than 1 percent of the state. Much of this land passed into private hands through the federal Homestead Acts and other public land laws as well as the land disposal programs of the state, boroughs or communities. Most private land is located along Alaska's small road network. Compared to other categories of land, it is highly accessible and constitutes some of the prime settlement land.

Following are programs that are, or soon will be, in effect for the sale of state land. A one-year residency is required for all but the auction program.

Auction: The state has been selling land by public auction since statehood. The state may sell full surface rights, lease of surface or subsurface rights, or restricted title at an auction. There is a minimum bid of fair market value, and the high bidder is the purchaser. Participants must be 18.

Homesite: The homesite program was passed in 1977. Under its provisions Alaskans are eligible for up to five acres. The land is free, but the individual must pay the cost of the survey and platting. Persons enrolled in this program must live on the homesite for 35 months within seven years of entry and construct a permanent, single-family dwelling on the site within five years (this is called "proving up" on the land).

Remote Parcels: The remote parcel program replaced the old open-to-entry program. It permits entry upon designated areas to stake a parcel of up to 5, 20 or 40 acres depending on the area and to lease the area for five years with an option for a five-year renewal. Rental under the lease is $10 per acre per year. The lease is not transferable. During the lease period the lessee must survey the land. He may then apply to purchase the land at the fair market value at the time of his initial lease application. The state will finance the sale over a period of 20 years.

Remote parcels no longer will be offered by the state as of July 1, 1984, as the program will be replaced by the 1983 homesteading bill. Alaskans leasing remote parcels, but who have not yet purchased them, may continue under the remote parcel program or opt to obtain title by meeting homesteading requirements.

Lottery: One year of residency is required to participate in the lottery program. Successful applicants are determined by a drawing and pay the appraised market value of the land. They repay the state over a period of up to 20 years, with interest set at the current federal land loan bank rate. Lotteries require a 5 percent down payment.

The state offered 100,000 acres of land to private ownership in each fiscal year from July 1, 1979, to July 1, 1982. Disposal levels from that time forward have been based on an annual assessment of the demand for state land. Sales are scheduled for fall and spring.

On April 1, 1983, the Department of Natural Resources discontinued a program that provided Alaska residents who were registered voters a 5-

percent-per-year-of-residency discount (up to $25,000) on the sale of land purchased from the state. Fifteen-year veteran residents had been eligible for up to $37,500 on this one-time program.

Homestead: In July 1983 Gov. Bill Sheffield signed into law a bill creating a new homesteading program. Department of Natural Resource officials hope the first homesteads will be offered as early as the spring or summer of 1984. Effective July 1, 1984, the homestead program will replace that for remote parcels.

Under the new law, residents of at least one year, who are 18 years or older, will have a chance to receive up to 40 acres of nonagricultural land or up to 160 acres of agricultural land without paying for the acreage itself. The homesteader, however, must survey, occupy and improve the land in certain ways and within specific time frames to receive title.

The homestead act also allows homesteaders to purchase parcels at fair market value without occupying or improving the land. This option requires only that nonagricultural land be staked, brushed and surveyed, and that parcels designated for agricultural use also meet clearing requirements.

After homesteading areas have been designated, homesteaders must stake the corners and flag the boundaries of the land, pay a fee of five dollars per acre, and personally file a description of the land with the state. Title then may be acquired either by purchasing the land (after brushing, surveying and clearing); brushing the boundaries within 90 days after issuance of the entry permit; completing an approved survey of the land within two years, unless a one-year extension is granted; erecting a habitable permanent dwelling on the homestead within three years; living on the parcel for not less than 25 months within five years; and clearing and either putting into production or preparing for cultivation 25 percent of the land within five years if it is classified for agricultural use.

Up-to-date information and applications for state programs are available from the Alaska Division of Land and Water Management:

Northcentral District
4420 Airport Way
Fairbanks 99701

Southcentral District Office
3601 C Street
Anchorage, 99510

Southeastern District Office
Marine View Apts., #407
230 South Franklin
Juneau 99801

Languages

Besides English, Alaska's languages include Haida, Tlingit, Tsimshian, Aleut, several dialects of Eskimo, and several dialects of Athabascan.

Mammals

Large Land Mammals

Black bear — Highest densities found in Southeast, Prince William Sound, and southcentral coastal mountains and lowlands. Also occur in interior and western Alaska. Absent from Southeast islands north of Frederick Sound (primarily Admiralty, Baranof, and Chichagof) and

Kodiak archipelago. Not commonly found west of about Naknek Lake on the Alaska Peninsula, in the Aleutian Islands, or on the open tundra sloping into the Bering Sea and Arctic Ocean.

Brown/grizzly bear — Found in most of Alaska. Absent from Southeast islands south of Frederick Sound and from the Aleutians (except for Unimak Island).

Polar bear — There are two groups in Alaska's arctic rim: an eastern group found largely in the Beaufort Sea, and a western group found in the Chukchi Sea between Alaska and Siberia. The latter group are the largest polar bears in the world. Old males can exceed 1,500 pounds.

American bison — In 1928, 23 bison were transplanted from Montana to Delta Junction to restore Alaska's bison population which had died out some 500 years before. Today, several hundred bison graze near Delta Junction; other herds are at Farewell, Chitina, and Nabesna.

Barren Ground caribou — At least 13 distinct herds: Adak, Alaska Peninsula, Arctic, Beaver, Chisana, Delta, Kenai, McKinley, Mentasta, Mulchatna, Nelchina, Porcupine, and Fortymile. Porcupine and Fortymile herds range into Canada.

Sitka blacktail deer — Coastal rain forests of southeastern Alaska; expanded by transplants to Yakutat area, Prince William Sound, and Kodiak and Afognak islands.

Roosevelt elk — Transplanted in 1928 from Olympic Peninsula, Washington, to Raspberry and Afognak islands.

Moose — Found from the Unuk River in Southeast to the arctic slope. Most abundant in second-growth birch forests, on timber line plateaus, and along major rivers of Southcentral and Interior. Not found on islands in Prince William Sound or Bering Sea, most major islands in Southeast nor on Kodiak or Aleutians group.

Mountain goat — Found in mountains throughout Southeast and north and west along coastal mountains to Cook Inlet and Kenai Peninsula; successfully transplanted to Kodiak and Baranof islands.

Musk ox — First transplanted to Nunivak Island and from there to arctic slope around Kavik, Seward Peninsula, Cape Thompson, and Nelson Island.

Dall sheep — Found in all major mountain ranges in Alaska except the Aleutian Range south of Iliamna Lake.

Wolf — Found throughout Alaska except Bering Sea islands, some Southeast and Prince William Sound islands, and the Aleutian Islands. Classified as big game and as fur bearer. Inhabits a variety of climates and terrains.

Wolverine — Found throughout Alaska and on some Southeast islands; abundant in the Interior and on the Alaska Peninsula. Shy, solitary creatures; not abundant in comparison with other fur bearers. Member of the weasel family. Classified as big game and as fur bearer.

Fur Bearers

Beaver — Found in most of mainland Alaska from Brooks Range to middle of Alaska Peninsula. Abundant in some major mainland river drainages in Southeast and on Yakutat forelands. Successfully transplanted to Kodiak area. Beaver dams are sometimes destroyed to allow salmon upstream; however, the beavers can rebuild their dams quickly and usually do so on the same site.

Coyote — Relative newcomer to Alaska, showing up shortly after the turn of the century, according to old-timers and records. Not abundant on a statewide basis, but common in Tanana, Copper, Matanuska, and Susitna river drainages and on Kenai Peninsula. As far west as Alaska Peninsula and the north side of Bristol Bay.

Fox — Arctic (white and blue phases): Almost entirely along the arctic coast as far south as the northwestern shore of Bristol Bay. Introduced to Pribilof and Aleutian islands where blue color phase, most popular with fox farmers, predominates. White color phase occurs naturally on Saint Lawrence and Nunivak islands. **Red:** Found throughout Alaska except for most areas of Southeast and Prince William Sound.

Hoary marmot — Present throughout most of the mountain regions of Alaska and along the Endicott Mountains east into Canada. Does not inhabit lower elevations.

Lynx — Found throughout Alaska, except on Yukon-Kuskokwim Delta, southern Alaska Peninsula, and along coastal tidelands. Relatively scarce along northern gulf coast and southeastern Alaska.

Marten — Ranges throughout timbered Alaska, except north of the Brooks Range, on treeless sections of the Alaska Peninsula, and on the Yukon-Kuskokwim Delta. Successfully introduced to Prince of Wales, Baranof, Chichagof and Afognak islands in this century. Absent from Prince William Sound and Kodiak Island.

Muskrat — Found throughout all of mainland Alaska south of the Brooks Range except for the Alaska Peninsula west of the Ugashik lakes. Introduced to Kodiak Island, Afognak and Raspberry islands. Absent from most other Alaska islands.

Raccoon — Not native to Alaska and considered an undesirable addition because of impact on native fur bearers. Found on west coast of Kodiak Island, on Japonski and Baranof islands, and other islands off Prince of Wales Island in Southeast.

River Otter — Occurs throughout the state except on Aleutian Islands, Bering Sea islands, and on the arctic coastal plain east of Point Lay. Most abundant in southeastern Alaska, Prince William Sound coastal areas, and on the Yukon-Kuskokwim Delta.

Squirrel — Northern Flying: Occurs in interior, southcentral and southeastern Alaska where forests are sufficiently dense to provide suitable habitat. Not found in areas lacking coniferous forests. **Red:** Found in spruce forests, especially along rivers, from Southeast north to the Brooks Range. Absent from Seward Peninsula, Yukon-Kuskokwim Delta, and Alaska Peninsula south of Naknek River.

Weasel — Least weasel and short-tailed weasel are found throughout Alaska, except for Bering Sea and Aleutian islands. Short-tailed weasels are brown with white underparts in summer, becoming snow-white in winter (designated ermine).

Other Small Mammals

Bat — There are five common bat species in Alaska.

Northern hare (or tundra hare) — Inhabits western and northern coastal Alaska. Weighs 12 pounds or more and measures 2½ feet long.

Snowshoe hare (or varying hare) — Occurs throughout Alaska except for lower portion of Alaska Peninsula, Arctic coast, and most islands; scarce in southeastern Alaska. Cyclic population highs and lows of hares occur roughly every 10 years. Reddish brown color in summer, white in winter. Named for their big hind feet, covered with coarse hair in winter, which make for easy travel over snow.

Brown lemming — Found throughout northern Alaska and the Alaska Peninsula. Not present in Southeast, Southcentral or Kodiak archipelago. Population undergoes cyclic highs and lows.

Collared lemming — Found from Brooks Range north and from lower Kuskokwim River drainage north.

Northern bog lemming (sometimes called lemming mice) — Tiny mammals, rarely observed, occur in meadows and bogs across most of Alaska.

Deer mouse — Inhabit timber and brush in southeastern Alaska.

House mouse — Found in Alaska seaports and large communities in Southcentral.

Meadow jumping mouse — Found in southern third of Alaska from Alaska Range to Gulf of Alaska.

Collared pika — Found in central and southern Alaska; most common in Alaska Range.

Porcupine — Found in most wooded regions of mainland Alaska.

Norway rat — Came to Alaska on whaling ships to Pribilof Islands in mid-1800s; great numbers of these rats thrived in the Aleutians (the Rat Islands group is named for the Norway rats). Found in virtually all Alaska seaports and in Anchorage and Fairbanks and other population centers with open garbage dumps.

Bushy-tailed woodrat — Found along mainland coast of southeastern Alaska. Commonly named pack rats, they carry off objects such as coins, buttons, or bits of broken glass, often leaving a stick or similar object in their place.

Shrews — Seven species range in Alaska.

Meadow vole (or meadow mouse) — Seven species attributed to Alaska range throughout the state.

Red-backed vole — Found throughout Alaska from Southeast to Norton Sound.

Woodchuck — Found in eastern Interior between Yukon and Tanana rivers, from east of Fairbanks to Alaska-Canada border. Large, burrowing squirrels, also called ground hogs.

Marine Mammals

Marine mammals found in Alaska waters are as follows: **dolphin,** Grampus, Pacific white-sided, and Risso's; **Pacific walrus; porpoise,** dall and harbor; **sea otter; seal,** harbor, larga, northern elephant, northern fur, Pacific bearded *(oogruk),* ribbon, ringed, and spotted; **Steller sea lion;** and

whale, Baird's beaked (giant bottlenose), beluga, narwhal, blue, bowhead, Cuvier's beaked (goose-beaked), fin or finback, gray, humpback, killer, minke or little piked, northern right, pilot, sei, sperm, and Stejneger's (or Bering Sea) beaked.

The Marine Mammal Protection Act, passed by Congress on December 21, 1972, provided for a complete moratorium on the taking and importation of all marine mammals. The purpose of the act was to give protection to population stocks of marine mammals that "are, or may be, in danger of extinction or depletion as a result of man's activities." Congress further found that marine mammals have "proven themselves to be resources of great international significance, aesthetic and recreational as well as economic, and it is the sense of the Congress that they should be protected and encouraged to develop to the greatest extent feasible commensurate with sound policies of resource management and that the

primary objective of their management should be to maintain the health and stability of the marine ecosystem. Whenever consistent with this primary objective, it should be the goal to obtain an optimum sustainable population keeping in mind the carrying capacity of the habitat."

At the present time, the U.S. Fish and Wildlife Service (Department of the Interior) is responsible for the management of polar bear, sea otter, and walrus in Alaska. The National Marine Fisheries Service (Department of Commerce) is responsible for the management of all other marine mammals. The state of Alaska assumed management of walrus in April 1976, and relinquished it back to the USFWS in July 1979. However, an amendment to the Marine Mammal Protection Act in 1981 makes it easier for states to assume management of marine mammals and Alaska is currently going through the necessary steps to assume management of marine mammals in Alaska.

Excluded from the moratorium on the taking and importation of all marine mammals are Alaska Natives (Indian, Aleut, or Eskimo) who reside in Alaska and dwell on the coast of the North Pacific Ocean or Arctic Ocean. Under federal management, Alaska Natives may take marine mammals for "subsistence purposes" or for "creating and selling authentic Native articles of handicrafts and clothing" provided in each case it is "not accomplished in a wasteful manner." Provisions also allow that only authentic Native articles of handicraft and clothing may be sold to non-Natives other than edible portions sold in Native villages and towns in Alaska.

In anticipation of the transfer of marine mammal management to the state, the Alaska Department of Fish and Game hunting regulations give tag fees for polar bear and walrus. However, it is currently illegal for anyone but an Alaska Native to take marine mammals.

(See also *Whales.*)

Related reading: *Alaska Mammals,* Jim Rearden, chief editor. *The* book on Alaska's wildlife. 184 pages, $12.95. *Alaska Whales and Whaling.* Includes coverage of all whales occurring in Alaskan waters. 144 pages, $12.95. See page 207.

Metric Conversions

Metrics, as in the rest of the United States, are slow in coming to Alaska. These conversion formulas will help to prepare for the metric system and to understand measurements in neighboring Yukon Territory. Approximate conversions from customary to metric and vice versa...

	When you know:	You can find:	If you multiply by:
Length	inches	millimeters	25.4
	feet	centimeters	30.5
	yards	meters	0.9
	miles	kilometers	1.6
	millimeters	inches	0.04
	centimeters	inches	0.4
	meters	yards	1.1
	kilometers	miles	0.6
Area	square inches	square centimeters	6.5
	square feet	square meters	0.09
	square yards	square meters	0.8
	square miles	square kilometers	2.6
	acres	square hectometers (hectares)	0.4
	square centimeters	square inches	0.16
	square meters	square yards	1.2
	square kilometers	square miles	0.4
	square hectometers (hectares)	acres	2.5
Weight	ounces	grams	28.4
	pounds	kilograms	0.45
	short tons	megagrams (metric tons)	0.9
	grams	ounces	0.04
	kilograms	pounds	2.2
	megagrams (metric tons)	short tons	1.1

Liquid Volume	ounces	milliliters	29.6
	pints	liters	0.47
	quarts	liters	0.95
	gallons	liters	3.8
	milliliters	ounces	0.03
	liters	pints	2.1
	liters	quarts	1.06
	liters	gallons	0.26

Temperature

		% (after subtracting 32)
degrees Fahrenheit	degrees Celsius	
degrees Celsius	degrees Fahrenheit	% (then add 32)

Celsius -40 -30 -20 -10 0 10 20 30 40
Fahrenheit -40 -30 -20 -10 0 10 20 30 40 50 60 70 80 90 100

Mileage Chart

	Alaska Boundary	Anchorage	Chicago, IL	Circle	Dawson Creek, BC	Delta Junction	Eagle	Edmonton, AB	Fairbanks	Glennallen	Great Falls, MT	Haines	Haines Jct., YT	Homer	Livengood	Los Angeles, CA	New York, NY	Palmer	Paxson	Portage	Seattle, WA	Seward	Tok	Valdez	Whitehorse, YT
Alaska Boundary		421	3506	463	1221	201	242	1591	298	232	2106	364	205	648	380	3208	4347	373	274	469	2063	550	93	347	304
Anchorage	421		3927	523	1642	340	503	2012	358	189	2527	785	626	227	440	3629	4768	40	259	48	2484	129	328	304	725
Chicago, IL	3506	3927		3969	2285	3707	3748	1915	3804	3738	1400	3460	3301	4154	3886	2095	840	3879	3780	3975	2103	4056	3599	3853	3202
Circle	463	523	3969		1684	262	545	2054	165	413	2569	827	668	750	223	3671	4810	483	343	571	2526	652	370	528	767
Dawson Creek, BC	1221	1642	2285	1684		1422	1463	370	1519	1453	885	1175	1016	1869	1601	1987	3126	1594	1495	1690	842	1771	1314	1568	917
Delta Junction	201	340	3707	262	1422		283	1792	97	151	2307	565	406	567	179	3409	4548	292	81	388	2264	469	108	266	505
Eagle	242	503	3748	545	1463	283		1833	380	314	2348	606	447	730	462	3450	4589	455	356	551	2305	632	175	429	546
Edmonton, AB	1591	2012	1915	2054	370	1792	1833		1889	1823	515	1545	1386	2239	1971	2088	2756	1964	1865	2060	943	2141	1684	1938	1287
Fairbanks	298	358	3804	165	1519	97	380	1889		248	2404	662	503	585	82	3506	4645	389	178	406	2361	487	205	363	602
Glennallen	232	189	3738	413	1453	151	314	1823	248		2338	596	437	416	330	3440	4579	141	70	237	2295	318	139	115	536
Great Falls, MT	2106	2527	1400	2569	885	2307	2348	515	2404	2338		2060	1901	2754	2486	1848	2241	2479	2380	2575	703	2656	2199	2453	1802
Haines	364	785	3460	827	1175	565	606	1545	662	596	2060		159	1012	744	3162	4301	737	638	833	2017	914	457	711	258
Haines Jct., YT	205	626	3301	668	1016	406	447	1386	503	437	1901	159		853	585	3003	4142	578	479	674	1858	755	298	552	99
Homer	648	227	4154	750	1869	567	730	2239	585	416	2754	1012	853		667	3856	4995	267	486	179	2711	172	555	531	952
Livengood	380	440	3886	223	1601	179	462	1971	82	330	2486	744	585	667		3588	4727	400	260	488	2443	569	287	445	684
Los Angeles, CA	3208	3629	2095	3671	1987	3409	3450	2088	3506	3440	1848	3162	3003	3856	3588		2915	3581	3482	3677	1145	3758	3301	3555	2904
New York, NY	4347	4768	840	4810	3126	4548	4589	2756	4645	4579	2241	4301	4142	4995	4727	2915		4720	4621	4816	2944	4897	4440	4694	4043
Palmer	373	40	3879	483	1594	292	455	1964	389	141	2479	737	578	267	400	3581	4720		211	88	2436	169	280	256	677
Paxson	274	259	3780	343	1495	81	356	1865	178	70	2380	638	479	486	260	3482	4621	211		307	2337	388	181	185	578
Portage	469	48	3975	571	1690	388	551	2060	406	237	2575	833	674	179	488	3677	4816	88	307		2532	81	376	352	773
Seattle, WA	2063	2484	2103	2526	842	2264	2305	943	2361	2295	703	2017	1858	2711	2443	1145	2944	2436	2337	2532		2613	2156	2410	1759
Seward	550	129	4056	652	1771	469	632	2141	487	318	2656	914	755	172	569	3758	4897	169	388	81	2613		457	433	854
Tok	93	328	3599	370	1314	108	175	1684	205	139	2199	457	298	555	287	3301	4440	280	181	376	2156	457		254	397
Valdez	347	304	3853	528	1568	266	429	1938	363	115	2453	711	552	531	445	3555	4694	256	185	352	2410	433	254		651
Whitehorse, YT	304	725	3202	767	917	505	546	1287	602	536	1802	258	99	952	684	2904	4043	677	578	773	1759	854	397	651	

Military

Until the rapid escalation of war in Europe in 1940-41, Congress saw little need for a strong military presence in Alaska. Spurred by World War II and a growing realization that Alaska could shorten the route to Asia for friend and foe, the government built and now maintains units of the air force, army, navy, and Coast Guard at dozens of installations across the state and on floating units in Alaskan waters. At the state level are Air National Guard and Army National Guard units. (See *National Guard.*)

The Army Corps of Engineers has three offices in Alaska: the Alaska District Office at Elmendorf Air Force Base, the Denali Area Office at Fort Richardson, and the Fairbanks Resident Office at Fort Wainwright. A small number of project offices are scattered across the state at Corps construction sites. Clear, Alaska, is the site of one of three Ballistic Missile Early Warning System stations (the others are in Greenland and England). Operating since 1961, the BMEW station's three 400-foot-wide, 165-foot-high radar screens scan the skies from the North Pole to China. Designed to give the U.S. at least a 15-minute warning before the missiles hit, the BMEWS replaced the earlier Distant Early Warning (DEW) Line, which was designed to detect bombers crossing into North American air space but was ineffective in detecting ballistic missiles.

The 172d Infantry Brigade is the army force in Alaska. Headquartered at Fort Richardson near Anchorage, the brigade also maintains fighting forces at Fort Wainwright, near Fairbanks, and Fort Greely, near Delta Junction. The brigade, which is under the command of a brigadier general, is responsible for the ground defense of Alaska. Two infantry battalions, a support battalion, and an artillery battalion at Fort Richardson and an infantry battalion and artillery battalion at Fort Wainwright serve this purpose. They are supported by an aviation battalion that has helicopter forces at both posts, and by the U.S. Army Communications Command-Alaska, which oversees all army communications in the state. The Northern Warfare Training Center, which trains soldiers, guardsmen and representatives from other services in arctic combat and survival, and the Cold Regions Test Center, where equipment is tested for cold weather use, are the principal activities at Fort Greely.

Small-scale, brigade-wide training exercises are held several times a year, as are joint exercises with the air force. (Training at company and battalion levels occurs more regularly.) Every other year the brigade participates in a major winter exercise sponsored by the U.S. Readiness Command. The most recent was in January and February 1983 when several thousand soldiers, airmen, marines, sailors and national guardsmen were deployed to Alaska for Joint Readiness Exercise Brim Frost 83. Brim Frost took place in the center of the state, northwest of Delta Junction during a month-long period that included a five-day mock war.

The brigade also provides support to the civilian community. In 1982, army aircraft rescued 15 persons from wilderness emergencies and another 116 were evacuated in M.A.S.T (Military Assistance to Safety of Traffic) helicopter missions. As of June 30, 1983, only two recorded rescues had taken place for the year, but 37 persons had been evacuated by M.A.S.T. crews stationed at Fort Wainwright.

The air force is represented in Alaska by the Alaska Air Command, which has headquarters at Elmendorf Air Force Base and stations throughout the state. Its mission is to train and employ combat-ready, tactical air forces to preserve the national sovereignty of United States lands, water, and air space.

Total Military Expenditures in Alaska by Agency Fiscal Year 1982
(in millions of dollars)

Service	Pay	Construction	Operations & Maintenance	Other Procurement	Total
Air Force	$318.1	$19.0	$219.9	$101.9	$ 658.9
Army	196.0	15.1	79.5	65.4	356.0
Coast Guard	41.7	11.6	33.0	9.8	96.1
Corps of Engineers	14.8	16.4	1.1	.9	33.2
National Guard	24.9	3.0	21.2	—	49.1
Navy	21.7	39.7	11.8	10.5	83.7
Total	617.2	104.8	366.5	188.5	1,277.0

Military Expenditures in Alaska For Fiscal Years 1978 to 1982
(in millions of dollars)

	1978	1979	1980	1981	1982
Military Payroll	$326.3	$326.1	$ 319.8	$ 390.3	$ 440.6
Civilian Payroll	122.5	123.6	129.6	146.0	156.1
Operations & Maintenance	190.8	215.6	303.1	308.3	366.5
Construction	32.8	66.7	78.6	94.1	104.8
Subtotal Appropriated Funds	672.4	732.0	831.1	938.7	1,068.0
Exchange & Nonappropriated Payrolls	17.2	17.1	23.6	21.4	20.5
Other Procurement	135.0	149.0	168.2	194.4	188.5
Subtotal Other	152.2	166.1	191.3	215.8	209.0
Total	824.6	898.1	1,022.9	1,154.5	1,277.0

The total population of the uniformed services in Alaska on September 30, 1982, was approximately 74,285. Population figures include active duty personnel, Department of Defense Civil Service employees, Nonappropriated Fund and Exchange personnel, and dependents. Of the total, 23,215 were active duty uniformed personnel and 4,810 were Civil Service employees of the Department of Defense. The total makes up approximately 17 percent of Alaska's population.

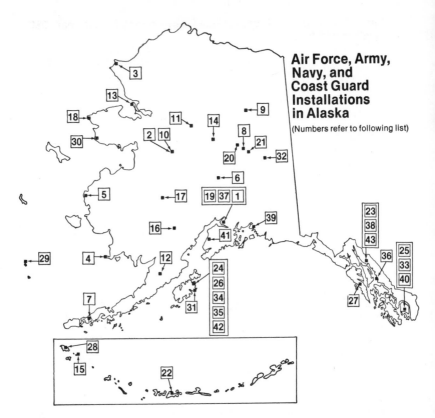

Air Force, Army, Navy, and Coast Guard Installations in Alaska

(Numbers refer to following list)

Map Key	Installation	Military Personnel
Air Force		
1	Elmendorf AFB	5,957
2	Campion AFS	17
3	Cape Lisburne AFS	12
4	Cape Newenham AFS	10
5	Cape Romanzof AFS	12
6	Clear AFS	126
7	Cold Bay AFS	15
8	Eielson AFB	3,221
9	Fort Yukon AFS	17
10	Galena Airport	302
11	Indian Mountain AFS	15
12	King Salmon	314
13	Kotzebue AFS	17
14	Murphy Dome AFS	42

Map Key	Installation	Military Personnel
15	Shemya AFB	533
16	Sparrevohn AFS	23
17	Tatalina AFS	20
18	Tin City AFS	13
Army		
19	Fort Richardson	5,341
20	Fort Greely	781
21	Fort Wainwright	2,659
Navy		
22	Adak	1,677
Coast Guard		
23	17th District Office Juneau	202
24	Kodiak Support Center	304
25	Base/Group Ketchikan	103

Map Key	Installation	Military Personnel	Map Key	Installation	Military Personnel
26	Air Station Kodiak	319	39	Marine Safety Office Valdez	16
27	Air Station Sitka	122	40	Detachment Ketchikan	6
28	LORAN Station Attu	24	41	Detachment Kenai	4
29	LORAN Station Saint Paul	17	42	Detachment Kodiak	2
30	LORAN STATION Port Clarence	28	43	Station Juneau	14
31	LORAN STATION Narrow Cape	11	**U.S. Coast Guard Cutters**		
32	LORAN STATION Tok	12	—	*Firebush*	55
33	LORAN STATION Shoal Cove	15	—	*Ironwood*	55
34	Communication Station Kodiak	39	—	*Laurel*	55
			—	*Sedge*	55
35	LORAN Monitoring Station Kodiak	16	—	*Storis*	77
			—	*Sweetbrier*	56
36	Five Finger Light Station	4	—	*Woodrush*	55
37	Marine Safety Office Anchorage	25	—	*Cape Carter*	15
			—	*Cape Romain*	14
38	Marine Safety Office Juneau	12	—	*Elderberry*	6
			—	*Yocona*	72

The U.S. Coast Guard's LORAN (Long Range Navigation) stations are a system of ground stations that transmit pulsed radio signals. The signals may be used by air, land, and sea navigators as an aid in determining their position.

Minerals

In 1970, there were 300 people employed in mining in Alaska, according to the state Division of Geological and Geophysical Surveys. The early years of the decade were relatively quiet in the industry, with exploration primarily limited to geological reconnaissance. Late in 1974, restrictions on gold in the United States were lifted, and the price of gold soared, spurring a revival of gold mining in the state.

By 1981, several large deposits containing minerals such as copper, chromite, molybdenum, nickel, and uranium were the subject of serious exploration. Estimated exploration costs were in excess of $100 million for 1981, and more than 3,000 people were employed in the industry. However, total expenditures for mineral exploration in Alaska dropped significantly during 1982 to $45.6 million, or approximately 59 percent of that reported for 1981.

In 1974, after three years exploration, U.S. Borax determined it had located one of the largest molybdenum deposits in the world at what is now known as Quartz Hill, approximately 45 miles east of Ketchikan. Molybdenum is essential to making specialty steel. Based on more than 250,000 feet of diamond core drilling through 1982, U.S. Borax estimates a mineral deposit in excess of 1.5 billion tons of minable ore. Core drilling in 1982 amounted to 20,000 feet. The number of employees on the project averaged 40 during the year but reached 100 at certain periods. U.S. Borax estimates total project expenditures through 1982 at approximately $62 million. The current timetable calls for commencement of production in 1987-88.

The Usibelli mine near Healy continues as the state's single commercial coal mine. Exploration and planning continues for huge coal deposits west of Anchorage in the Beluga coal field. Testing also continues in the Bering River coal field about 70 miles east of Cordova.

Huge reserves of copper, lead, zinc, and barite in the Brooks Range are held by several giant corporations, but activity has generally been limited to exploration and definition of the resource.

The major mining effort in the state (excluding oil, gas, and coal) is sand, gravel, and stone. A production value of nearly $115 million was recorded in 1981, although peak levels in excess of $200 million were recorded during the oil pipeline construction period in 1975 and 1976. Production value in 1982 was more than $106 million.

Gold is second at $70 million, and all others — silver, tungsten, platinum, tin — total about $1.7 million.

(See also *Coal, Oil and Gas* and *Gold*.)

Miscellaneous Facts

State capital: Juneau.

Land area: 591,004 square miles or 378,242,560 acres — largest state in the union; one-fifth the size of the Lower 48.

Area per person: There are 1.5 square miles for each person in Alaska. New York has .003 square miles per person.

Diameter: East to west, 2,400 miles; north to south, 1,420 miles.

Coastline: 6,640 miles, point to point; as measured on the most detailed maps available, including islands, Alaska has 33,904 miles of shoreline. Estimated tidal shoreline, including islands, inlets and shoreline to head of tidewater is 47,300 miles.

Adjacent salt water: North Pacific Ocean, Bering Sea, Chukchi Sea, Arctic Ocean.

Alaska/Canada border: 1,538 miles long; Length of boundary between the Arctic Ocean and Mount Saint Elias, 647 miles; Southeast border with British Columbia and Yukon Territory, 710 miles; water boundary, 181 miles.

Geographic center: 63°50′ north, 152° west, about 60 miles northwest of Mount McKinley.

Northernmost point: Point Barrow, 71°23′ north.

Southernmost point: Tip of Amatignak Island, Aleutian Chain, 51°13′05″ north.

Easternmost and westernmost points: It all depends on how you look at it. The 180th meridian — halfway around the world from the prime meridian at Greenwich, England, and the dividing line between east and west longitudes — passes through Alaska. According to one view, therefore, Alaska has both the easternmost and westernmost spots in the country! The westernmost is Amatignak Island, 179°10′ west; and the easternmost is Pochnoi Point, 179°46′ east. On the other hand, if you are facing north, east is to your right and west to your left. Therefore, the westernmost point is Cape Wrangell, Attu Island, 172°27′ east; and the easternmost is in southeastern Alaska near Camp Point, 129°59′ west.

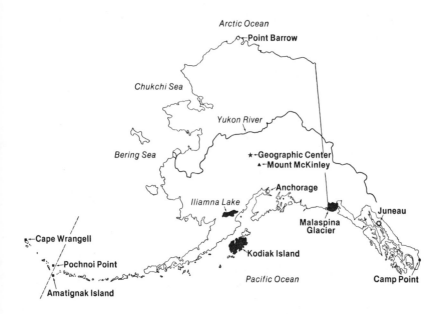

Farthest north supermarket: In Barrow; constructed on stilts to prevent snow build-up, at a cost of $4 million.

Tallest mountain: Mount McKinley, 20,320 feet.

Largest natural freshwater lake: Iliamna, 1,000 square miles.

Longest river: Yukon, 1,400 miles in Alaska; 1,875 total.

Largest glacier: Malaspina, 850 square miles.

Largest city in population: Anchorage, population 200,503.

Largest city in area: Juneau with 3,108 square miles (also largest city in square miles in North America).

Typical Alaskan: According to 1980 census figures, 26 years old and male. (About 53 percent of Alaskans are male, the highest percentage of any state.) Median age: 26.1 years, second only to Utah as the state with the youngest population.

Oldest building: Erskine House in Kodiak, built by the Russians, probably between 1793 and 1796.

World's largest and busiest seaplane base: Lake Hood, accommodating more than 800 takeoffs and landings on a peak summer day.

World's largest concentration of bald eagles: Along Chilkat River, just north of Haines. More than 3,500 bald eagles gather here in fall and winter months for late salmon runs.

Median income: $31,037, highest in the nation in fiscal year 1982.

Per capita personal income: $13,763, highest in the nation.

Miss Alaska

The legislature has declared that the young woman selected as Miss Alaska each year will be the state's official hostess. Holders of the title are selected in Anchorage each spring in a competition sponsored by the

nonprofit Miss Alaska Scholarship Pageant organization. Title holders since 1959:

1983	Jennifer Smith, Soldotna
1982	Kristan Sapp, Wasilla
1981	Laura Trollan, Juneau
1980	Sandra Lashbrook, Chugiak-Eagle River
1979	Lila Oberg, Matanuska Valley
1978	Patty-Jo Gentry, Fairbanks
1977	Lisa Granath, Kenai
1976	Kathy Tebow, Anchorage
1975	Cindy Suryan, Kodiak
1974	Darby Moore, Kenai
1973	Virginia Adams, Anchorage
1972	Deborah Wood, Elmendorf Air Force Base
1971	Linda Joy Smith, Elmendorf Air Force Base
1970	Virginia Walker, Kotzebue
1969	Gwen Gregg, Elmendorf Air Force Base
1968	Jane Haycraft, Fairbanks
1967	Penny Ann Thomasson, Anchorage
1966	Nancy Lorell Wellman, Fairbanks
1965	Mary Ruth Nidiffer, Alaska Methodist University
1964	Karol Rae Hommon, Anchorage
1963	Colleen Sharon Kendall, Matanuska Valley
1962	Mary Dee Fox, Anchorage
1961	Jean Ann Holm, Fairbanks
1960	June Bowdish, Anchorage
1959	Alansa Rounds Carr, Ketchikan

Mosquitoes

At least 25 species of mosquitoes are found in Alaska (the number may be as high as 40), the females of all species feeding on people, other mammals or birds. Males and females eat plant sugar, but only the females suck blood, which they use for egg production. The itch that follows the bite comes from an anticoagulant injected by the mosquito. No Alaska mosquitoes carry diseases. The insects are present from April through September in many areas of the state. From Cook Inlet south, they concentrate on coastal flats and forested valleys. In the Aleutian Islands, mosquitoes are absent or present only in small numbers. The most serious mosquito infestations occur in moist areas of slow-moving or standing water such as found in the fields, bogs and forests of interior Alaska, from Bristol Bay eastward. Mosquitoes are most active at dusk and dawn; low temperatures and high winds decrease their activity. Mosquitoes may be controlled by draining their breeding areas or spraying with approved insecticides. When traveling in areas of heavy mosquito infestations, it is wise to wear protective clothing, carefully screen living and camping areas and use a good insect repellent.

Mount McKinley

Mount McKinley in the Alaska Range is the highest mountain on the North American continent. The South Peak is 20,320 feet high; the North Peak has an elevation of 19,470 feet. The mountain was named in 1896 for William McKinley of Ohio, who at the time was the Republican candidate for president. An earlier name had been Denali, a Tanaina Indian word meaning "the big one" or "the great one." The state of Alaska officially renamed the mountain Denali in 1975 and the state Geographic Names Board claims the proper name for the mountain is Denali. However, the federal Board of Geographic Names has not taken any action, and congressional legislation has been introduced to retain the name McKinley in perpetuity.

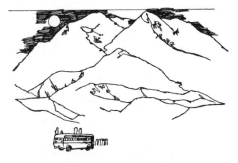

Mount McKinley is within Denali National Park and Preserve (formerly Mount McKinley National Park). The park entrance is about 237 miles north of Anchorage and 121 miles south of Fairbanks via the George Parks Highway. (A 90-mile gravel road runs west from the highway through the park; vehicle traffic on the park road is restricted.) The park is also accessible via The Alaska Railroad and by aircraft. The mountain and its park are the top tourist attractions in Alaska. The finest times to see McKinley up close are on summer mornings. August is best, according to statistics based on six summers of observation by park ranger Rick McIntyre. The mountain is rarely visible the entire day. The best view is from Eielson Visitor Center, located about 66 miles from the park entrance and 33 miles northeast of the summit. The center, open from early June through the second week in September, is accessible via free shuttle bus provided by the park.

Mountain climbers reported 1983 to be a particularly good year for attempting Mount McKinley. By season's end, 709 climbers had attempted the peak, of which 456, or roughly 67 percent, were successful. This compares to 1982 figures of 310 persons out of 696 reaching the top, for a success rate of 44 percent. Exceptionally good weather is the reason for the high results of 1983.

Related reading: *A Tourist Guide to Mount McKinley,* revised in 1980, by Bradford Washburn. 82 pages, $5.95. See page 210.

Mountains

Of the 20 highest mountains in the United States, 17 are in Alaska, which has 19 peaks over 14,000 feet. The U.S. Geological Survey lists them as follows:

Map Key	Elevation
1 McKinley, South Peak*	20,320
1 McKinley, North Peak*	19,470
2 Saint Elias**	18,008
3 Foraker	17,400
4 Blackburn	16,390
5 Bona	16,421
6 Sanford	16,237
1 South Buttress	15,885
7 Vancouver**	15,700
8 Churchill	15,638

Map Key	Elevation
9 Fairweather**	15,300
10 Hubbard**	15,015
11 Bear	14,831
1 East Buttress	14,730
12 Hunter	14,573
13 Alverstone**	14,565
1 Browne Tower	14,530
14 Wrangell	14,163
15 Augusta**	14,070

*Note: The two peaks of Mount McKinley are known collectively as the Churchill Peaks.
**On Alaska-Canada border.

Other Well-Known Alaska Mountains

	Elevation
Augustine Volcano	4,025
Deborah	12,339
Devils Paw	8,584
Devils Thumb	9,077
Doonerak	7,610
Drum	12,010

	Elevation
Edgecumbe	3,201
Hayes	13,832
Kates Needle	10,002
Marcus Baker	13,176
Shishaldin	9,372

Mountain Ranges

	Elevation
Ahklun Mountains	1,000-3,000
Alaska Range	to 20,320
Aleutian Range	to 7,585
Askinuk Mountains	to 2,342
Baird Mountains	to 4,300
Bendeleben Mountains	to 3,730
Brabazon Range	to 5,515
Brooks Range	4,000-9,000
Chigmit Mountains	to 5,000
Chugach Mountains	to 13,176
Coast Mountains	to 18,000
Darby Mountains	to 3,083

	Elevation
Davidson Mountains	to 5,540
De Long Mountains	to 4,888
Endicott Mountains	to 7,000
Fairweather Range	to 15,300
Igichuk Hills	to 2,000
Kaiyuh Mountains	1,000-2,844
Kenai Mountains	to 6,000
Kiglapak Mountains	to 1,070
Kigluaik Mountains	to 4,714
Kuskokwim Mountains	to 3,973
Lookout Range	to 2,400
Mentasta Mountains	4,000-7,000

	Elevation		Elevation
Moore Mountains	to 3,000	Talkeetna Mountains	6,000-8,800
Nutzotin Mountains	5,000-8,000	Waring Mountains	to 1,800
Ray Mountains	2,500-5,500	Waxell Ridge	4,000-10,000
Romanzof Mountains	to 8,700	White Mountains	to 5,000
Saint Elias Mountains	to 18,000	Wrangell Mountains	to 16,421
Schwatka Mountains	to 8,800	York Mountains	to 2,349
Shublik Mountains	to 4,500	Zane Hills	to 4,053
Sischu Mountains	to 2,422		

Related reading: *Wrangell-Saint Elias: International Mountain Wilderness.* A colorful and in-depth look at this vast area that encompasses both Canadian and U.S. territory. 144 pages, $9.95. See page 210.

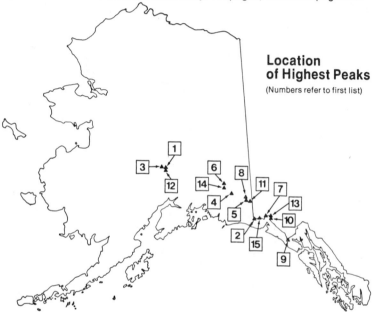

Location of Highest Peaks

(Numbers refer to first list)

Mukluks

Lightweight boots designed to provide warmth in extreme cold. Eskimo mukluks are traditionally made with *oogruk* (bearded seal) skin bottoms and caribou tops and trimmed with fur. (Mukluk is also another name for *oogruk*.) Athabascan mukluks are traditionally made of moose hide and trimmed with fur and beadwork.

Muktuk

This Eskimo delicacy consists of the outer skin layers of whales. The two species of whales most often used for muktuk are the bowhead whale and the beluga, or white whale. The outer skin layers consist of a corky protective layer, the true skin and the blubber. In the case of beluga muktuk, the outer layer is white, the next layer is black and the blubber is pink. It may be eaten fresh, frozen, cooked or pickled.

Museums, Cultural Centers, and Repositories

Cultural Resources in Alaska: A Guide to People and Organizations, published by Heritage Conservation and Recreation Service, Alaska Regional Office, U.S. Department of the Interior, May 1981, and *Worlds of Alaska,* published by Alaska State Division of Tourism, Pouch E, Juneau 99811, list the following museums, cultural centers, and repositories:

Alaska Historical Library, Pouch G, Juneau 99811
Alaska Indian Arts, Inc., Box 271, Port Chilkoot, Haines 99827
Alaskaland, 410 Cushman, Fairbanks 99701
Alaska Resources Library, 701 C Street, Anchorage 99513
Alaska State Archives, Pouch C-0207, Juneau 99811
Alaska State Museum, Pouch FM, Juneau 99811
Anchorage Historical and Fine Arts Museum, 121 West Seventh Avenue, Anchorage 99503
Assumption of the Virgin Mary Church, phone (907) 283-4122 in Kenai
Baranof Museum, 101 Marine Way, Kodiak 99615
Bear Tribal House, Wrangell 99929
Bristol Bay Museum, Naknek 99633
Carrie M. McLain Memorial Museum, Box 53, Nome 99762
Clausen Memorial Museum, Second and F streets, Petersburg 99833
Collections of the Cook Inlet Historical Society, 121 West Seventh Avenue, Anchorage 99503
Cordova Museum, Box 391, Cordova 99574
Cripple Creek Resort, Ester 99725
Damon Memorial Museum, Soldotna 99669
Dillingham Heritage Museum, Box 202, Dillingham 99576
Dinjii Zhuu Enjit Museum, Box 42, Fort Yukon 99740
Duncan Cottage Museum, Box 282, Metlakatla 99926
Eagle Historic District—Mule Barn Museum, Eagle 99738
Erskine House, Box 61 Marine Way, Kodiak 99615
Father Hubbard Memorial Museum, Taku Harbor, Alaska 99850
Fort Kenay Museum and Visitor Information Center, Box 1348, Kenai 99611
Fort Richardson Fish and Wildlife Center, Building 600, Fort Richardson 99505
Hoonah Indian Association Cultural Center, Box 144, Hoonah 99829
House of Wickersham, Juneau. For information, write Alaska Tour and Marketing Services, Suite 312, Park Place Building, Seattle, Washington 98101
Juneau Mining Museum, 490 South Franklin Street, Juneau 99801
Kenai Museum, Box 1348, Kenai 99611
Ketchikan Indian Museum, P.O. Box 5454, Ketchikan 99901
Klawock Totem Park, Box 113, Klawock 99925
Last Chance Mining Museum, 155 South Seward Street, Juneau 99801
Living Museum of the Arctic, Kotzebue 99752
Matanuska Valley Museum, Greater Palmer Chamber of Commerce, Palmer 99645

NARL Museum, Naval Arctic Research Laboratory, Barrow 99723
National Bank of Alaska Heritage Library, 303 West Northern Lights Boulevard, Anchorage 99501
Pioneer Park Memorial Museum, 1126 Sixth Avenue, Fairbanks 99701
Pratt Museum of Homer, Box 682, Homer 99603
Rasmusson Library, University of Alaska, Fairbanks, Fairbanks 99701
Resurrection Bay Historical Society Museum, Box 871, Seward 99664

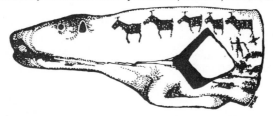

Saint Herman's Theological Seminary, Box 728, Kodiak 99615
Sheldon Jackson Museum, Box 479, Sitka 99835
Sheldon Museum and Cultural Center, Box 25, Haines 99827
Soapy Smith Museum, Box 492, Skagway 99840
Southeast Alaska Indian Cultural Center, P.O. Box 944, Sitka 99835
Talkeetna Historical Society Museum, Box 76, Talkeetna 99676
Tongass Historical Society Museum, 629 Dock Street, Ketchikan 99901
Totem Bight, Ketchikan. For information, write Alaska Division of Parks, Pouch M, Juneau 99811
Totem Heritage Center, 601 Deermount, Ketchikan 99901
Trail of '98 Museum, Box 415, Skagway 99840
Transportation Museum of Alaska, Star Route Box S-875, Palmer 99645
Unalaska Museum, Box 6, Unalaska 99685
U.S. Historical Aircraft-Maritime Museum, P.O. Box 6813, Anchorage 99502
University of Alaska Museum, Fairbanks 99701
Valdez Heritage Archives Alive, P.O. Box 6, Valdez 99686
Valdez Heritage Center, Box 307, Valdez 99686
Wasilla Museum, Box 874, Wasilla 99687
Whittier Historical Museum, Box 728, Whittier 99502
Wildlife Museum, Elmendorf Air Force Base, Anchorage 99506
Wrangell Museum, Box 13, Wrangell 99929
Yugtarvik Regional Museum, P.O. Box 388, Bethel 99559

Mushrooms

More than 500 different species of mushrooms abide in Alaska, and, while most are not common enough to be seen and collected readily by the amateur mycophile (mushroom hunter), many edible and choice species shoot up in any available patch of earth. Alaska's "giant arc of mushrooms" extends from Southeast's panhandle through Southcentral, the Alaska Peninsula and the Aleutian Chain and is prime mushroom habitat. Interior, western and northern Alaska also support mushrooms in abundance.

Mushroom seasons vary considerably according to temperature, humidity and available nutrients, but most occur from June through September. In a particularly cold or dry season, the crop will be scant.

A few Alaska mushroom species are considered "sickeners," and while no deadly poisonous mushrooms have been reported in the state, they may occur, especially in Southeast, which has a climate similar to Washington and northern Oregon where severely poisonous species do occur. Play it safe and be sure you know your species before foraging.

Related reading: *The Alaskan Mushroom Hunter's Guide* by Ben Guild; illustrated by Jack VanHoesen. All major families of Alaska mushrooms. 286 pages, $13.95. See page 207.

Muskeg

Deep bogs where little vegetation can grow except for sphagnum moss, black spruce, dwarf birch and a few other shrubby plants. Such swampy areas cover much of Alaska.

Musk Ox

Stocky, shaggy, long-haired mammals of extreme northern latitudes, musk ox remain in the open through Alaska's long winters. Their name is misleading, for the creatures do not give musk and are more closely related to sheep and goats than to cattle. Adult males may weigh 500 to 900 pounds; females between 250 to 500 pounds. Both sexes have horns which droop down from their forehead and curve back up at the tips.

The soft underhair of musk ox is called *qiviut* and grows next to the skin, protected by long guard hairs. It is shed naturally every spring. Oomingmak, Musk Ox Producers' Co-operative, maintains a musk ox farm at Unalakleet, where workers gather the *qiviut* for cottage industry use. The hair is spun into yarn in Rhode Island and sent back to Alaska, where the co-operative arranges for knitters in villages in western Alaska, where jobs are scarce, to knit the yarn into clothing at their own pace.

Each village keeps its own distinct signature pattern for scarves knitted from *qiviut*. Villagers also produce stoles, tunics, hats, and a smoke ring, which is a circular scarf that fits a person's head like a hood.

When threatened by wolves or other predators, musk ox form circles or lines with their young in the middle. These defensive measures did not protect them from man and his gun, however. Musk ox were eliminated from Alaska in about 1865, when hunters shot and killed a herd of 13. The species was reintroduced to the territory in the 1930s when 34 musk ox were purchased from Greenland and brought to the University of Alaska at Fairbanks. In 1935-36, the 31 remaining musk ox at the university were shipped to Nunivak Island in the Bering Sea, where the herd eventually thrived. Animals from the Nunivak herd have been transplanted to areas along Alaska's western and northern coasts; at least five herds — approximately 1,000 musk ox — now exist in the state.

National Forests

Alaska's two national forests, the Tongass in Southeast, and the Chugach in Southcentral, are the nation's largest and second-largest national forests respectively. The Alaska National Interest Lands Conservation Act of 1980 — also referred to as the Alaska d-2 lands bill or lands act — increased the acreage and changed the status of certain lands in Alaska's national forests. (See also *Land; National Wilderness Areas;* and map on pages 134-35.)

The Alaska d-2 lands bill created approximately 5.5 million acres of wilderness (consisting of 14 units) within the 17-million-acre Tongass National Forest. It also added three new areas to the forest: the Juneau Icefield, Kates Needle, and parts of the Brabazon Range, totaling more than one million acres.

The lands bill also provided extensive additions to the Chugach National Forest. These additions, totaling about two million acres, include the Nellie Juan area east of Seward, College Fiord extension, Copper/Rude rivers addition, and a small extension at Controller Bay southeast of Cordova.

The following charts show the effect of the Alaska lands act on the Tongass and Chugach national forests.

	Tongass	Chugach
Total acreage before act	15,555,388	4,392,646
Total acreage after act	16,954,713	5,940,040*
Wilderness acreage created	5,453,366	none created
Wilderness Study	none created	2,019,999 acres
Wild and Scenic River Study	Situk River**	none created

*The lands act provides for additional transfers of national forest land to Native corporations, the state, and the Fish and Wildlife Service of an estimated 296,000 acres on Afognak Island and an estimated 242,000 acres to the Chugach Native Corporation.
** The lands act provides for a maximum of 640 acres on each side of the river, for each mile of river length.

Wilderness Units in Tongass National Forest	Acres
Admiralty Island National Monument*	937,396
Coronation Island Wilderness	19,232
Endicott River Wilderness	98,729
Maurelle Islands Wilderness	4,937
Misty Fiords National Monument*	2,142,243
Petersburg Creek-Duncan Salt Chuck Wilderness	46,777
Russell Fiord Wilderness	348,701
South Baranof Wilderness	319,568
South Prince of Wales Wilderness	90,996
Stikine-LeConte Wilderness	448,841
Tebenkof Bay Wilderness	66,839
Tracy Arm-Fords Terror Wilderness	653,179
Warren Island Wilderness	11,181
West Chichagof-Yakobi Wilderness	264,747
Total Acreage	5,453,366

*Designated monuments under d-2 bill; first areas so designated in the National Forest system.

National Guard

The Department of Military Affairs administers the Alaska Army National Guard and the Air National Guard. The guard is charged with performing military reconnaissance, surveillance and patrol operations in Alaska; providing special assistance to civil authorities during natural disasters or civil disturbances; and augmenting regular army and air force in times of national emergency.

The Alaska Air National Guard has a headquarters unit, a tactical airlift group, and several support elements. All units are based at Kulis Air National Guard Base on the west side of Anchorage International Airport.

Authorized staffing is 710 military personnel, with about 25 percent of those full-time technicians. The eight C-130 Hercules cargo aircraft assigned to the guard logged more than 4,200 hours of flight time in support of state and air force missions in 1982.

The major unit of the Alaska Army National Guard, with a muster of 2,300, is the 207th Infantry Group, consisting of five Scout Battalions and detachments in 86 communities across the state. In addition, it has an airborne element, an air traffic control detachment, and an aviation detachment. The Scout Battalions are authorized one Twin Otter aircraft and two helicopters in their aviation sections. In all, the Alaska Army National Guard operates 46 aircraft.

The scout teams are a unique element in the Alaska Army National Guard, performing a full-time active mission of intelligence gathering. Many scouts are subsistence hunters and whalers and, as such, they constantly comb the coastal zones, off-shore waters, and inland areas. Reports of Soviet naval and air activities are common since Alaska and the USSR are separated by less than 50 miles across the Bering Strait.

National Guard Stations

Map Key		Map Key	
1	Akiachak	22	Gambell
2	Akiak	23	Golovin
3	Alakanuk	24	Goodnews Bay
4	Ambler	25	Haines
5	Anchorage	26	Hoonah
6	Angoon	27	Hooper Bay
7	Arctic Village	28	Huslia
8	Barrow	29	Juneau
9	Bethel	30	Kake
10	Brevig Mission	31	Kaltag
11	Buckland	32	Kasigluk
12	Chefornak	33	Kenai
13	Chevak	34	Ketchikan
14	Deering	35	Kiana
15	Delta Junction	36	Kipnuk
16	Eek	37	Kivalina
17	Elim	38	Kodiak
18	Emmonak	39	Kongiganak
19	Fairbanks	40	Kotlik
20	Fort Yukon	41	Kotzebue
21	Galena	42	Koyuk

National Guard Stations in Alaska

(Numbers refer to preceding list)

National Historic Places

Historic Places can be districts, sites, buildings, structures, or objects significant in American history, architecture, archaeology, and culture. The register is an official list of properties, recognized by the federal government, as worthy of preservation. Listing on the register begins with owner's consent and entails a nomination process with reviews by the state historic preservation officer, the Alaska Historic Sites Advisory Committee, and the keeper of the national register. Limitations will *not* be placed on a listed property: the federal government will not attach restrictive covenants to the property or seek to acquire it.

Listing on the register means that a property is accorded national recognition for its significance in American history or prehistory. Other benefits include tax credits on income-producing properties and automatic qualification for federal matching funds for preservation, maintenance and restoration work. Listed properties are also guaranteed a full review process for potential adverse effects by federally funded, licensed, or otherwise assisted projects. Such a review usually takes place while the project is in the planning stage: alternatives are sought to avoid, if at all possible, damaging or destroying the particular property in question.

Southcentral

AHRS Site KOD-207, Long Island	Kodiak area
Alaska Nellie's Homestead	Lawing vicinity
Alex, Mike, Cabin	Eklutna
American Cemetery	Kodiak
Anchorage City Hall	Anchorage
Anderson (Oscar) House	Anchorage
Ascension of Our Lord Chapel	Karluk
Assumption of the Virgin Mary, Church of	Kenai
Ballaine House	Seward
Beluga Point Archaeological Site	North Shore, Turnagain Arm
Bering Expedition Landing	Kayak Island
Campus Center Archaeological Site	Anchorage
Cape Saint Elias Lighthouse	Cordova
Chilkat Oil Refinery Site	Katalla
Chitina Tin Shop	Chitina
Chugach Island Archaeological Site	Kachemak Bay
Coal Village	Kachemak Bay
Cooper Landing Post Office	Cooper Landing
Copper River and Northwestern Railway	Chitina vicinity
Cordova Post Office	Cordova
Crow Creek Mine	Girdwood
Cunningham-Hall PT-6 NC692W (aircraft)	Palmer
Dakah Den'nin's Village Site	Chitina
Diversion Tunnel, Lowell Creek	Seward
Eklutna Power Plant	Eklutna

Erskine House	Kodiak
Federal Building (Old)	Anchorage
Fort Abercrombie	Kodiak
Fourth Avenue Theatre	Anchorage
Gakona Roadhouse	Gakona
Government Cable House	Seward
Hirshey Mine	Hope vicinity
Holy Resurrection, Church of the	Kodiak
Holy Transfiguration of Our Lord Chapel	Ninilchik
Hope Historic District	Hope vicinity
Independence Mines	Hatcher Pass
Kaguyak Village Site	Kodiak Island
Kennecott Mines	McCarthy vicinity
Knik Site	Knik vicinity
KOD-011 Archaeological Site	Kodiak
KOD-171 Archaeological Site	Kodiak
KOD-233 Archaeological Site	Kodiak
Kodiak Oil Site	Kodiak vicinity
Lauritsen Cabin	Seward Highway
McCarthy General Store	McCarthy
McCarthy Power Plant	McCarthy
Moose River Site, Naptowne	Kenai area
Nabesna Gold Mine	Nabesna area
Nativity of Holy Theotokos	Afognak Island
Nativity of Our Lord Chapel	Ouzinkie
Old St. Nicholas Russian Orthodox Church	Eklutna
Palmer Depot	Palmer
Palugvik Site	Hawkins Island
Pioneer School House	Anchorage
Protection of the Theotokos Chapel	Akhiok
Rebarchek (Raymond), Colony Farm	Palmer area
Reception Building	Cordova
Red Dragon Historic District	Cordova
St. Michael the Archangel Church	Cordova
St. Nicholas Chapel	Seldovia
St. Peter's Episcopal Church	Seward
SS. Sergius and Herman of Valaam Church	English Bay
SS. Sergius and Herman of Valaam Chapel	Kodiak Island
Selenie Lagoon Archaeological Site	Port Graham vicinity
Sourdough Lodge	Gulkana vicinity
Susitna River Bridge, Alaska Railroad	Talkeetna vicinity
Swetman House	Seward

Tangle Lakes Archaeological District	Paxson vicinity
Teeland's General Store	Wasilla
Three Saints Site	Kodiak Island
Tunnel #1, Alaska Central Railroad	Seward vicinity
United Protestant Church	Palmer
Van Gilder Hotel	Seward
Victor Holm Cabin	Cohoe
Wasilla Community Hall	Wasilla
Wasilla Depot	Wasilla
Wasilla Elementary School	Wasilla
Yukon Island, Main Site	Yukon Island

Southeast

Alaska Native Brotherhood Hall	Sitka
Alaska Steam Laundry	Juneau
Alaska Totems	Ketchikan
Alaskan Hotel	Juneau
American Flag Raising Site	Sitka
Bergmann Hotel	Juneau
Bering Expedition Landing	Kayak Island
Burkhart-Dibrell House	Ketchikan
Cable House and Station	Sitka
Cape Spencer Lighthouse	Cape Spencer
Chief Shakes House	Wrangell
Chilkoot Trail, Mile 0 to Canadian Border	Chilkoot Pass Area
Crab Bay Petroglyph	Crab Bay
Davis, J.M., House	Juneau
Dyea Site	Dyea
Eldred Rock Lighthouse	Lynn Canal
Emmons House	Sitka
Father William Duncan Cottage	Metlakatla
Fort Durham, Taku Harbor	Juneau vicinity
Fort William H. Seward	Haines
Government Indian School	Haines
Government School	Sitka
Governor's Mansion	Juneau
Hidden Falls Site	Sitka vicinity
Holy Trinity Church	Juneau
Klondike Gold Rush National Historic Park	Skagway area
Mills, May, House	Sitka
Mills, W.P., House	Sitka
New Russia Archaeological Site	Yakutat
Pleasant Camp	Haines Highway

Redoubt St. Archangel Michael Site, Old Sitka	Sitka vicinity
Russian Bishop's House	Sitka
Russian Mission Orphanage	Sitka
St. John the Baptist Church	Angoon
St. Michael's Cathedral	Sitka
St. Nicholas Church (Russian Orthodox)	Juneau
St. Peter's Church	Sitka
Saxman Totem Park	Ketchikan
See House	Sitka
Sheldon Jackson Museum	Sitka
Sitka National Cemetery	Sitka
Sitka National Historical Park	Sitka
Sitka Pioneers' Home	Sitka
Skagway and White Pass District	Taiya Inlet, Lynn Canal
Sons of Norway Hall	Petersburg
Totem Bight	Ketchikan
U.S. Army Corps of Engineers, Storehouse #3	Portland Canal
U.S. Army Corps of Engineers, Storehouse #4	Hyder
Walker-Broderick House	Ketchikan
Wickersham, House of	Juneau
Wrangell Public School	Wrangell

Western

Amaknak Bridge Site	Unalaska vicinity
Ananiulak Island Archaeological District	Aleutian Islands
Archaeological Site 49 Af3	Katmai National Park and Preserve
Archaeological Site 49 Mk10	Katmai National Park and Preserve
Atka B-24 Liberator	Aleutian Islands
Brooks River Archaeological District	Katmai National Park and Preserve
Cape Krusenstern Archaeological District	Kotzebue vicinity
Cape Nome Mining District Discovery Sites	Nome
Cape Nome Roadhouse	Nome vicinity
Carrighar (Sally) House	Nome
Chaluka Site	Umnak Island
Christ Church Mission	Anvik
Chugachik Island Archaeological Site	Aleutian Islands
Discovery Saloon	Nome
Donaldson, Lieutenant, C.V.	Nome
Elevation of Holy Cross Church	South Naknek
Fort St. Michael Site	Nome vicinity
Fur Seal Rookeries	Pribilof Islands
Gambell Sites	St. Lawrence Island
Holy Ascension, Church of	Unalaska

Holy Resurrection Church	Belkofski
Iyapana, John, House	Little Diomede Island
Iyatayet Archaeological Site	Norton Sound
Kijik Historic District	Lake Clark vicinity
Kolmakov Redoubt Site, Kuskokwim River	Aniak vicinity
Kukak Village Site 49 Mk6	Katmai National Park and Preserve
McClain (Carrie) House	Nome
Norge Landing Site	Teller
Old Savonski Site	Naknek vicinity
Onion Portage Archaeological Site	Kiana vicinity
Pilgrim Hot Springs	Seward Peninsula
Port Moller Hot Springs Village Site	Alaska Peninsula
Presentation of Our Lord Chapel	Nikolai
Redoubt St. Michael Site	Nome vicinity
St. George the Great Martyr Orthodox Church	St. George Island
St. Jacob's Church	Napaskiak
St. John the Baptist Chapel	Naknek
St. John the Theologian Church	Perryville
St. Nicholas Chapel	Ekuk
St. Nicholas Chapel	Igiugig
St. Nicholas Chapel	Nondalton
St. Nicholas Chapel	Pedro Bay
St. Nicholas Chapel	Pilot Point
St. Nicholas Chapel	Sand Point
St. Nicholas Chapel	Nikolski
SS. Constantine and Helen Chapel	Lime Village
St. Seraphim Chapel	Lower Kalskag
St. Sergius Chapel	Chuathbaluk
SS. Peter and Paul Church	St. Paul Island
Savonski River Archaeological District	Naknek vicinity
Sir Alexander Nevsky Chapel	Akutan
Sitka Spruce Plantation	Amaknak Island
Solomon Roadhouse	Solomon
Takli Island Archaeological District	Katmai National Park and Preserve
TEMNAC P-38G Lightning plane	Aleutian Islands
Transfiguration of Our Lord Chapel	Nushagak
Wales Site	Wales vicinity

Interior

Archaeological Site	Fort Greely
Archaeological Site KAR-037	Karluk
Central Roadhouse	Central
Chatanika Gold Camp	Chatanika

Chena Pump House	Fairbanks
Chugwater Archaeological Site	Fairbanks
Clay Street Cemetery	Fairbanks
Creamer's Dairy	Fairbanks
Cripple Creek Site	Steese Highway
Davis, Mary Lee, House	Fairbanks
Dry Creek Site	Healy vicinity
Davidson Ditch	Steese Highway
Eagle Historic District	Eagle
Fairview Inn	Talkeetna
Federal Building, U.S. Post Office, Courthouse	Fairbanks
Harding Car	Alaskaland, Fairbanks
Immaculate Conception Church	Fairbanks
Joslin, Falcon, House	Fairbanks
The Kink	Fortymile River
Masonic Temple	Fairbanks
Mission Church	Arctic Village
Mission House (Old)	Fort Yukon
Nenana Depot	Nenana
Oddfellows Hall (First Avenue Bathhouse)	Fairbanks
Porcupine Historic District	Northeastern Alaska
Rainey's Cabin	Fairbanks
Rika's Landing	Delta
Ruby Roadhouse	Ruby
Steele Creek Roadhouse	Fortymile
Sternwheeler *Nenana*	Fairbanks
Sullivan Roadhouse	Fort Greely
Tanana Mission	Tanana
Teklanika Archaeological District	Denali National Park and Preserve
Thomas (George C.) Library	Fairbanks
U.S. Bureau of Mines Safety Car #5	Suntrana
Wickersham House	Fairbanks

Far North

Aluakpak Site	Wainwright vicinity
Anaktuuk Site	Wainwright vicinity
Atanik	Wainwright vicinity
Avalitkuk Site	Wainwright vicinity
Birnirk Site	Barrow
Gallagher Flint Station Archaeological Site	Sagwon
Ipiutak Archaeological Site	Point Hope
Ivishaat Site	Wainwright vicinity
Kanitch	Wainwright vicinity

Leffingwell Camp	Flaxman Island
Napanik Site	Wainwright vicinity
Negilik	Barrow
Point Barrow Refuse/Cape Smythe Whaling and Trading Station	Barrow vicinity
Rogers-Post Site	Barrow vicinity
Uyagaagruk	Wainwright vicinity

National Parks, Preserves, and Monuments

The National Park Service administers approximately 54.4 million acres of land in Alaska, consisting of 15 units classified as national parks, national preserves, and national monuments. The Alaska National Interest Lands Conservation Act of 1980 — also referred to as the Alaska d-2 lands bill or lands act (see *Land*) — created 10 new National Park Service units in Alaska and changed the size and status of the 3 existing park service units: Mount McKinley National Park, now Denali National Park and Preserve; Glacier Bay National Monument, now a national park and preserve; and Katmai National Monument, now a national park and preserve. See map on pages 134-35.

National parks are traditionally managed to preserve scenic, wildlife, and recreational values; mining, logging, hunting, and other resource exploitation are usually not permitted within park boundaries and motorized access is restricted to automobile traffic on authorized roads. However, regulations for National Park Service units in Alaska recognize that these units contain lands traditionally occupied and used by Alaska Natives and rural residents for subsistence activities. Therefore, management of some parks, preserves, and monuments in Alaska provide for subsistence hunting, fishing, and gathering activities, and the use of such motorized vehicles as snow machines, motorboats, and airplanes, where such activities are customary. In addition, the national preserves permit sport hunting.

Following is a list of National Park Service national parks, preserves, and monuments. (The U.S. Forest Service manages another two national monuments: Admiralty Island National Monument, 900,000 acres; and Misty Fiords National Monument, 2.3 million acres. Both are in Southeast and part of the National Wilderness Preservation System. See also *National Wilderness Areas*.)

National Park Service Units	Acreage, major features, recreation
Aniakchak National Monument and Preserve Superintendent, Katmai National Park and Preserve Box 7, King Salmon 99613	615,000 acres Aniakchak caldera

Bering Land Bridge National Preserve National Park Service P.O. Box 220, Nome 99762	2,770,000 acres Lava fields, archaeological sites, migratory waterfowl
Cape Krusenstern National Monument National Park Service P.O. Box 287, Kotzebue 99752	660,000 acres Archaeological sites
Denali National Park and Preserve National Park Service Denali Park 99755	5,696,000 acres Mount McKinley, abundant wildlife
Gates of the Arctic National Park and Preserve National Park Service 201 First Avenue, P.O. Box 74680 Fairbanks 99707	8,440,000 acres Brooks Range, wild and scenic rivers, wildlife
Glacier Bay National Park and Preserve National Park Service P.O. Box 1089, Juneau 99806	3,280,000 acres Glaciers, marine wildlife
Katmai National Park and Preserve National Park Service P.O. Box 7, King Salmon 99613	4,090,000 acres Valley of Ten Thousand Smokes, brown bears
Kenai Fjords National Park National Park Service P.O. Box 1727, Seward 99664	669,500 acres Fjords, Harding Icefield
Kobuk Valley National Park National Park Service P.O. Box 287, Kotzebue 99752	1,710,000 acres Archaeological sites, Great Kobuk Sand Dunes, river rafting
Klondike Gold Rush National Historical Park National Park Service P.O. Box 517, Skagway 99840	13,000 acres Chilkoot Trail
Lake Clark National Park and Preserve National Park Service 701 C Street, Box 61, Anchorage 99513	4,045,000 acres Back-country recreation, fishing, scenery
Noatak National Preserve National Park Service P.O. Box 287, Kotzebue 99752	6,560,000 acres River floating, abundant wildlife
Sitka National Historical Park National Park Service P.O. Box 738, Sitka 99835	107 acres
Wrangell-Saint Elias National Park and Preserve National Park Service P.O. Box 29, Glennallen 99588	13,188,000 acres Rugged, peaks, glaciers, expansive wilderness
Yukon-Charley Rivers National Preserve National Park Service P.O. Box 64, Eagle 99738	2,528,000 acres Back-country recreation, river floating

NATIONAL WILDLIFE REFUGE SYSTEM

1 Alaska Maritime NWR*
 a Chuckchi Sea Unit
 b Bering Sea Unit
 c Aleutian Island Unit
 d Alaska Peninsula Unit
 e Gulf of Alaska Unit
2 Alaska Peninsula
3 Arctic
4 Becharof
5 Innoko
6 Izembek
7 Kanuti
8 Kenai
9 Kodiak
10 Koyukuk
11 Nowitna
12 Selawik
13 Tetlin
14 Togiak
15 Yukon Delta
16 Yukon Flats

NATIONAL PARK SYSTEM

17 Aniakchak Nat'l Monument and Preserve
18 Bering Land Bridge Nat'l Preserve
19 Cape Krusenstern Nat'l Monument
20 Denali Nat'l Park and Preserve
21 Gates of the Arctic Nat'l Park and Preserve
22 Glacier Bay Nat'l Park and Preserve
23 Katmai Nat'l Park and Preserve
24 Kenai Fjords Nat'l Park
25 Kobuk Valley Nat'l Park
26 Lake Clark Nat'l Park and Preserve
27 Noatak Nat'l Preserve
28 Wrangell Saint Elias Nat'l Park and Preserve
29 Yukon-Charley Rivers Nat'l Preserve
30 Klondike Gold Rush Nat'l Historical Park
31 Sitka Nat'l Historical Park

BUREAU OF LAND MANAGEMENT SYSTEM

32 Steese Nat'l Conservation Areas
33 White Mountains Nat'l Recreation Area

NATIONAL WILD AND SCENIC RIVERS SYSTEM

Rivers (25)

NATIONAL FOREST SYSTEM

34 Chugach Nat'l Forest
35 Tongass Nat'l Forest
36 Admiralty Island Nat'l Monument†
37 Misty Fiords Nat'l Monument†

Wilderness

*The Alaska Maritime National Wildlife Refuge consists of all the public lands in the coastal waters and adjacent seas of Alaska consisting of islands, islets, rocks, reefs, capes and spires.
†Admiralty Island and Misty Fiords national monument wildernesses are part of the Tongass National Forest, which includes 12 other wilderness areas as well.

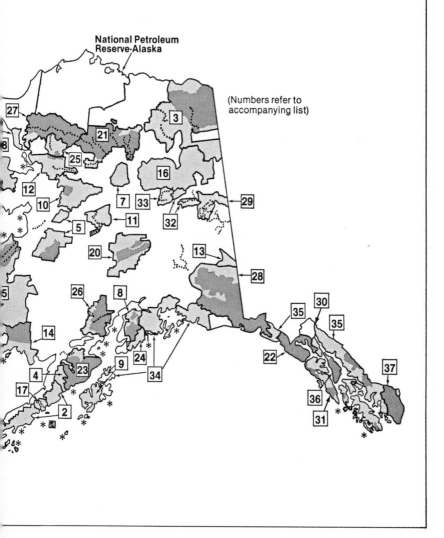

Alaska National Interest Lands

National Petroleum
Reserve-Alaska

(Numbers refer to
accompanying list)

Information on the parks, preserves, and monuments is available at the National Park Service offices and exhibit area at 2525 Gambell Street, Anchorage 99503. A permanent display of photographs from areas throughout the state may be seen there. Films about Alaska are shown daily.

Related reading: *Admiralty: Island in Contention.* Crisp text and color photos. 78 pages, $5.00. *Alaska National Interest Lands,* 240 pages, $14.95. *Glacier Bay,* by William D. Boehm. Color photos. Flora, fauna, history, hiking, cruise information. 134 pages, $11.95. *A Tourist Guide to Mount McKinley* (revised edition), by Bradford Washburn. 80 pages, $5.95. *Wrangell-Saint Elias: International Mountain Wilderness.* Glorious photos, full information on this incredible part of the world. 144 pages, $9.95. See pages 207-10.

National Petroleum Reserve

In 1923, Pres. Warren G. Harding signed an executive order creating Naval Petroleum Reserve Number 4 (NPR-4), the last of four petroleum reserves to be placed under control of the U.S. Navy. The Secretary of the Navy was charged to "explore, protect, conserve, develop, use, and operate the Naval Petroleum Reserves," including NPR-4, on Alaska's North Slope (see map on pages 134-35).

The U.S. Geological Survey had begun surface exploration in the area in 1901; following creation of the 23-million-acre reserve, exploration programs were conducted by the navy. From 1944 to 1953, extensive geological and geophysical surveys were conducted and 36 test wells were drilled. Nine oil and gas fields were discovered; the largest oil field, near Umiat, contains an estimated 70 million barrels of recoverable oil. Active exploration was suspended in 1953.

In 1974 the Arab oil embargo, coupled with the knowledge of large petroleum reserves at nearby Prudhoe Bay, brought about renewed interest in NPR-4, and Congress directed the navy to resume its exploration program.

In 1977, all lands within NPR-4 were redesignated as the National Petroleum Reserve-Alaska (NPR-A) and jurisdiction was transferred to the secretary of the interior. In 1981, Congress authorized the secretary of the interior to prescribe an expeditious program of competitive leasing of oil and gas tracts in the reserve, clearing the way for private development of the area's resources.

By mid-1983 three competitive bid lease sales, involving a total of 7.2 million acres of NPR-A, had been held. Dates of the sales and the number of acres involved are: January 1982, 1.5 million acres; May 1982, 3.5 million acres; and July 1983, 2.2 million acres. Additional lease sales are anticipated under a five-year development plan. All receipts from the sales are deposited with the U.S. Treasury, from which 50 percent is paid to the state of Alaska.

The Interior Department, through USGS, has continued exploration of NPR-A. Past naval explorations and those currently being conducted by USGS have resulted in the discovery of oil at Umiat and Cape Simpson and several gas fields, including Walakpa, Gubic, and Point Barrow. Data gathered thus far indicates NPR-A may contain recoverable reserves of 1.85 billion barrels of crude oil and 3.74 trillion cubic feet of natural gas.

National Wild and Scenic Rivers

The Alaska National Interest Lands Conservation Act of December 2, 1980, gave wild and scenic river classification to 13 streams within the National Park System, 6 in the National Wildlife Refuge System, and 2 in Bureau of Land Management Conservation and Recreation areas. The remaining 5 rivers are located outside designated preservation units. Twelve more rivers were designated for further study and possible wild and scenic classification. See map, pages 134-35.

The criteria for wild and scenic river classification are not just for its float trip possibilities. Scenic features, wilderness characteristics and other recreational opportunities that would be impaired by alteration, development or impoundment are also considered.

Rivers are classified into three categories under the Wild and Scenic Rivers Act. The wild classification is most restrictive of development or incompatible uses — it stresses the wilderness aspect of the rivers. The scenic classification permits some intrusions upon the natural landscape, and recreational classification is the least restrictive category. A specified amount of land back from the river's banks is also put in protected status to ensure access, use and the preservation of aesthetic values for the public.

For those desiring to float these rivers, special consideration must be given to put-in and take-out points as most of the new wild and scenic rivers are not accessible by road. This means that voyagers and their crafts have to be flown in and picked up by charter bush planes. Because Federal Aviation Administration regulations prohibit the lashing of canoes and kayaks on pontoons of floatplanes when carrying passengers, inflatable rafts and folding canvas or rubber kayaks are often more convenient and less expensive to transport.

Further information on rivers and river running can be obtained from offices of the National Park Service, 2525 Gambell Street, #107, Anchorage 99503; the U.S. Fish and Wildlife Service, 1011 East Tudor Road, Anchorage 99503; and the Bureau of Land Management, P.O. Box 13, Anchorage 99513.

Rivers within National Park Areas

Alagnak	Katmai National Preserve
Alatna	Gates of the Arctic National Park
Aniakchak	Aniakchak National Monument Aniakchak National Preserve
Charley	Yukon-Charley Rivers National Preserve
Chilikadrotna	Lake Clark National Park and Preserve
John	Gates of the Arctic National Park and Preserve
Kobuk	Gates of the Arctic National Park and Preserve
Mulchatna	Lake Clark National Park and Preserve

Noatak	Gates of the Arctic National Park and Noatak National Preserve
North Fork Koyukuk	Gates of the Arctic National Park and Preserve
Salmon	Kobuk Valley National Park
Tinayguk	Gates of the Arctic National Park and Preserve
Tlikakila	Lake Clark National Park

Rivers within National Wildlife Refuges

Andreafsky	Yukon Delta National Wildlife Refuge
Ivishak	Arctic National Wildlife Refuge
Nowitna	Nowitna National Wildlife Refuge
Selawik	Selawik National Wildlife Refuge
Sheenjek	Arctic National Wildlife Refuge
Wind	Arctic National Wildlife Refuge

Rivers within Bureau of Land Management Units

Beaver Creek — The segment of the main stem from confluence of Bear and Champion creeks within White Mountains National Recreation Area and Yukon Flats National Wildlife Refuge.

Birch Creek — The segment of the main stem from the south side of Steese Highway downstream to approximately Twelvemile House on Steese Highway, within Steese National Conservation Area.

Rivers outside of designated preservation units

Alagnak — Those segments or portions of the main stem and Nonvianuk tributary lying outside and westward of Katmai National Park and Preserve.

Delta River — The segment from and including all of the Tangle Lakes to a point one-half mile north of Black Rapids.

Fortymile River — The main stem within the state of Alaska, plus tributaries.

Gulkana River — The main stem from the outlet of Paxson Lake to the confluence with Sourdough Creek; various segments of the west fork and middle fork.

Unalakleet River — Approximately 65 miles of the main stem.

Rivers designated for study for inclusion in Wild and Scenic Rivers System

Colville River	Porcupine River
Etivluk-Nigu Rivers	Sheenjek River (lower segment)
Kanektok River	Situk River
Kisaralik River	Squirrel River
Koyuk River	Utukok River
Melozitna River	Yukon River (Ramparts section)

National Wilderness Areas

Passage of the Alaska National Interest Lands Conservation Act, on December 2, 1980, added millions of acres to the National Wilderness Preservation System. Administration of these wilderness areas is the responsibility of the agency under whose jurisdiction the land is situated. Agencies which administer wilderness areas in Alaska include the National Park Service, U.S. Fish and Wildlife Service, and the U.S. Forest Service. Although the Bureau of Land Management has authority to manage wilderness in the public domain, no BLM wilderness areas exist in Alaska. See map on pages 134-35.

Wilderness allocations to different agencies in Alaska are:

Agency	Approximate Acreage
U.S. Forest Service	5,453,366
National Park Service	33,120,000
U.S. Fish and Wildlife Service	18,560,000

Wilderness, according to the Wilderness Act of 1964, is land sufficient in size to enable the operation of natural systems without undue influence from activities in surrounding areas, and should be places in which man himself is a visitor who does not remain. Alaska wilderness regulations follow the stipulations of the Wilderness Act as amended by the Alaska lands act. Specifically designed to allow for Alaska conditions, the rules are considerably more lenient about transportation access, man-made structures, and use of mechanized vehicles. The primary objective of a wilderness area continues to be the maintenance of the wilderness character of the land. In Alaska wilderness areas, the following uses and activities are permitted:

- Fishing, hunting and trapping will continue on lands within the national forests, national wildlife refuges, and national park preserves. National park wilderness does not allow these activities.
- Subsistence uses, including hunting, fishing, trapping, berry gathering, and use of timber for cabins and firewood will be permitted in wilderness areas by all agencies.
- Public recreation cabins in wilderness areas in national forests, national wildlife refuges, and national park preserves will continue to be maintained and may be replaced. A limited number of new public cabins may be added if needed.
- Existing special use permits and leases on all national forest wilderness lands for cabins, homesites or similar structures will continue. Use of temporary campsites, shelters, and other temporary facilities and equipment related to hunting and fishing on national forest lands will continue.
- Fish habitat enhancement programs, including construction of buildings, fish weirs, fishways, spawning channels, and other accepted means of maintaining, enhancing, and rehabilitating fish stocks will be allowed in national forest wilderness areas. Reasonable access including use of motorized equipment will be permitted.
- Special use permits for guides and outfitters operating within wilderness areas in the national forests will be allowed to continue.
- Private, state, and Native lands surrounded by wilderness areas will be guaranteed access through the wilderness area.
- Use of airplanes, motorboats, and snow machines where *traditional* as a means of access into wilderness areas will be allowed to continue.

National Wildlife Refuges

There are approximately 76 million acres of National Wildlife Refuge lands in Alaska administered by the U.S. Fish and Wildlife Service. (National wildlife refuge acreage in Alaska increased nearly fourfold with the signing of the Alaska d-2 lands bill — Alaska National Interest Lands Conservation Act — in December 1980.) Wildlife refuges are designed to protect the habitats of representative populations of land and marine mammals, other marine animals, and birds. Thus the 16 refuges vary widely in size, depending upon the life cycles and habitat requirements of a particular species. See map on pages 134-35.

Among the public recreational uses permitted within national wildlife refuges are sightseeing, nature observation and photography, sport hunting and fishing, boating, camping, hiking, and picnicking. Trapping can be carried out under applicable state and federal laws. Commercial fishing, including use of motorized vehicles, is allowed.

Subsistence living activities within national wildlife refuges are all protected under the d-2 lands bill. Use of snowmobiles, motorboats and other means of surface transportation traditionally relied upon by local rural residents for subsistence is generally permitted. Aircraft access to wildlife refuges is allowed, and off-road vehicles may be used on special routes and in areas designated by the refuge manager.

National Wildlife Refuge administrative address	Acreage and major features
Alaska Maritime National Wildlife Refuge Operations Manager South 1011 East Tudor Road Anchorage 99503	3,548,956 acres Sea birds, sea lions, sea otters, harbor seals
Alaska Peninsula National Wildlife Refuge Operations Manager South 1011 East Tudor Road Anchorage 99503	3,500,000 acres Brown bears, caribou, moose, sea otters, bald eagles, peregrine falcons
Arctic National Wildlife Refuge Refuge Manager Room 226, Federal Building & Courthouse, 101 12th Avenue Fairbanks 99701	18,054,624 acres Caribou, polar bears, grizzly bears, wolves, Dall sheep, peregrine falcons
Becharof National Wildlife Refuge Refuge Manager P.O. Box 211, King Salmon 99613	1,200,000 acres Brown bears, bald eagles caribou, moose, salmon
Innoko National Wildlife Refuge Operations Manager North 1011 East Tudor Road Anchorage 99503	3,850,000 acres Migratory birds, beavers
Izembek National Wildlife Refuge Refuge Manager Pouch 2, Cold Bay 99571	320,893 acres Black brant, brown bears
Kanuti National Wildlife Refuge Operations Manager North 1011 East Tudor Road Anchorage 99503	1,430,000 acres Migratory water birds, fur bearers, moose

National Wildlife Refuge administrative address	Acreage and major features
Kenai National Wildlife Refuge Refuge Manager Box 2139, Soldotna 99669	1,970,000 acres Moose, salmon, mountain goats, Dall sheep, bears
Kodiak National Wildlife Refuge Refuge Manager Box 825, Kodiak 99615	1,865,000 acres Brown bears, blacktail deer, bald eagles, salmon
Koyukuk National Wildlife Refuge Operations Manager North 1011 East Tudor Road Anchorage 99503	3,550,000 acres Wolves, caribou, bear, moose
Nowitna National Wildlife Refuge Operations Manager North 1011 East Tudor Road Anchorage 99503	1,560,000 acres Migratory waterfowl, caribou, moose, bears, fur bearers
Selawik National Wildlife Refuge Operations Manager North 1011 East Tudor Road Anchorage 99503	2,150,000 acres Migratory water birds
Tetlin National Wildlife Refuge Operations Manager North 1011 East Tudor Road Anchorage 99503	700,000 acres Migratory waterfowl, Dall sheep
Togiak National Wildlife Refuge Operations Manager South 1011 East Tudor Road Anchorage 99503	4,105,000 acres Nearly every major wildlife species of Alaska is represented
Yukon Delta National Wildlife Refuge Refuge Manager Box 346, Bethel 99559	19,624,458 acres Migratory birds, musk ox are found on Nunivak Island
Yukon Flats National Wildlife Refuge Refuge Manager Room 226, Federal Building & Courthouse, 101 12th Avenue Fairbanks 99701	8,630,000 acres Waterfowl

Native People

Alaska's 64,000 Native people make up about 13 percent of the state's total population. Of those, roughly 34,000 are Eskimos, 22,000 are Indians, and 8,000 are Aleuts. Although many live in widely scattered villages along the coastline and great rivers of Alaska, in 1980, 9,000 Native persons lived in Anchorage, and Fairbanks had a Native population of nearly 3,000.

At the time of European discovery in 1741, the Eskimo, Indian, and Aleut people lived within well-defined regions, with little mixing of ethnic groups. But they shared a number of characteristics: all were hunting and gathering people who did not practice agriculture.

In southeastern Alaska, the salmon, deer, and other plentiful foods permitted the Tlingit, Tsimshian, and Haida Indians to settle in permanent villages and develop a culture rich in art. The Athabascan Indians of the Interior took advantage of seasonal abundance of fish, waterfowl, and other game. Coastal Eskimos and Aleuts subsisted primarily on the rich resources of the rivers and the sea.

Traditional Native Distribution

The Tsimshians migrated in 1887 from their former home in British Columbia to Annette Island, under Anglican minister Father William Duncan. About 1,000 now live in Metlakatla. As are most southeastern people, they are primarily fishermen.

Between 700 and 800 Haidas live in Alaska, about 200 of whom live in Hydaburg on the south end of Prince of Wales Island. They emigrated from Canada in the 1700s. Haidas excelled in the art of totem carving and are noted for precise and delicate working of wood, bone, and shell.

About 10,000 Tlingits live thoughout southeastern Alaska; another 1,000 live in other parts of the state, primarily in the Anchorage area. Tlingits, who arrived from Canada before the first European contact, commercially dominated the interior Canadian Indians, trading eulachon oil, copper pieces, and Chilkat blankets for various furs. Like the Haidas, they are part of the totem culture; totems are used to provide a historic record of major events in the life of a family or clan.

Athabascan Indians, who occupied the vast area of interior Alaska, were nomadic people whose principal source of food was land animals. Hard times and famines were frequent for all Athabascans except the Tanaina and Ahtna groups who lived along the Gulf of Alaska and could rely on salmon as their basic food.

142

The Aleuts have traditionally lived on the Alaska Peninsula and along the Aleutian Chain. When the Russians reached the Aleutians in the 1740s, practically every island was inhabited. Today, there are only a few permanent Aleut settlements, including two on the Pribilof Islands, where the Natives work handling seal herds for the government.

The Aleuts lived in permanent villages, taking advantage of sea life and land mammals for food. Their original dwellings were large, communal structures, housing as many as 40 families, although after Russian occupation they lived in much smaller houses, called *barabaras.* Today many Aleuts are commercial fishermen.

The Eskimos have traditionally lived in villages along the harsh Bering Sea and Arctic Ocean coastlines, and along a thin strip of the Gulf of Alaska coast, including Kodiak Island. They took salmon, waterfowl, berries, ptarmigan, and a few caribou, but it was the sea and its whales, walruses, and seals which provided the foundation for their existence. Houses were igloos — dwellings built partially underground and covered with sod. They did not build snow igloos.

Rapid advances in communications, transportation, and other services to remote villages have altered Native life in Alaska. Economic changes, from a subsistence to a cash economy, were brought about by the passage in 1971 of the Alaska Native Claims Settlement Act. The act gave Alaska Natives $962.5 million and 40 million acres of land as compensation for the loss of lands historically occupied by their people.

Native Regional Corporations

Twelve regional business corporations were formed under the 1971 Alaska Native Claims Settlement Act to manage money and land received

Arctic Slope Regional Corporation

NANA Regional Corporation

Bering Straits Native Corporation

Doyon Limited

Alaska Native Regional Corporations

Calista Corporation

Cook Inlet Region Incorporated

Ahtna Incorporated

Bristol Bay Native Corporation

Chugach Natives Incorporated

Sealaska Corporation

The Aleut Corporation

Koniag Incorporated

from the government. A thirteenth corporation was organized for those Natives residing outside Alaska. Following is a list of corporations and the area or region each administers:

Ahtna Incorporated (Copper River Basin), Drawer G, Copper Center 99573 or 1577 C Street, Suite 256, Anchorage 99501.

Aleut Corporation (Aleutian Islands), 2550 Denali, Suite 900, Anchorage 99503.

Arctic Slope Regional Corporation (Arctic Alaska), P.O. Box 129, Barrow 99723, or 313 E Street, Anchorage 99501.

Bering Straits Native Corporation (Seward Peninsula), P.O. 1008, Nome 99762 or P.O. Box 3396, Anchorage 99510.

Bristol Bay Native Corporation (Bristol Bay area), P.O. Box 198, Dillingham 99576 or 445 East Fifth, Anchorage 99501.

Calista Corporation (Yukon-Kuskokwim Delta), P.O. Box 648, Bethel 99559 or 516 Denali Street, Anchorage 99501.

Chugach Natives, Incorporated (Prince William Sound), 903 West Northern Lights Boulevard, Suite 201, Anchorage 99503.

Cook Inlet Region, Incorporated (Cook Inlet region), 2525 C Street, P.O. Drawer 4-N, Anchorage 99509.

Doyon Limited (Interior Alaska), 201 First Avenue, Fairbanks 99701.

Koniag, Incorporated (Kodiak area), P.O. Box 746, Kodiak 99615.

NANA Regional Corporation, Incorporated (Kobuk region), P.O. Box 49, Kotzebue 99752 or 4706 Harding Drive, Anchorage 99503.

Sealaska Corporation (southeastern Alaska), One Sealaska Plaza, Suite 400, Juneau 99801.

The 13th Regional Corporation (outside Alaska), 1800 Westlake Avenue North, Suite 313, Seattle, Washington 98109.

Regional Nonprofit Corporations

Aleutian-Pribilof Islands Association, Incorporated (Aleut Corporation), 1689 C Street, Anchorage 99501.

Association of Village Council Presidents (Calista Corporation), P.O. Box 219, Bethel 99559.

Bristol Bay Native Association (Bristol Bay Native Corporation), P.O. Box 237, Dillingham 99756.

Central Council of Tlingit-Haida Indian Tribes (Sealaska Corporation), One Sealaska Plaza, Suite 200, Juneau 99801.

Cook Inlet Native Association (Cook Inlet Region, Incorporated), 670 West Fireweed Lane, Anchorage 99503.

Copper River Native Association (Ahtna Incorporated), Drawer H, Copper Center 99573.

Inupiat Community of the Arctic Slope (Arctic Slope Regional Corporation), P.O. Box 437, Barrow 99723.

Kawerak, Incorporated (Bering Straits Native Corporation), P.O. Box 948, Nome 99762.

Kodiak Area Native Association (Koniag, Incorporated), P.O. Box 172, Kodiak 99615.

Maniilaq (formerly Mauneluk) Association (NANA Regional Corporation), P.O. Box 256, Kotzebue 99752.

North Pacific Rim Native Association (Chugach Natives, Incorporated), 903 West Northern Lights Boulevard, Suite 203, Anchorage 99503.

Tanana Chiefs Conference (Doyon, Limited), 201 First Avenue, Fairbanks 99701.

Other Native Organizations

Alaska Eskimo Whaling Commission, P.O. Box 570, Barrow 99723.

Alaska Federation of Natives, 411 West Fourth Avenue, Suite 1-A, Anchorage 99501.

Alaska Native Brotherhood, Box 112, Juneau 99801.

Alaska Native Commission on Alcoholism and Drug Abuse, P.O. Box 4-2463, Anchorage 99509.

Alaska Native Foundation, 411 West Fourth Avenue, Suite 314, Anchorage 99501.

Alaska Native Health Board, 1135 West Eighth, Suite 2, Anchorage 99501.

Central Council of Tlingit and Haida Indian Tribes of Alaska, One Sealaska Plaza, Suite 200, Juneau 99801.

Fairbanks Native Association, Incorporated, 310 First Avenue, Fairbanks 99701.

Interior Village Association, 127½ Minnie Street, Fairbanks 99701.

Inuit Circumpolar Conference, Barrow 99723.

Norton Sound Health Corporation, P.O. Box 966, Nome 99762.

Southeast Alaska Regional Health Corporation, P.O. Box 2800, Juneau 99803.

Yukon-Kuskokwim Health Corporation, P.O. Box 528, Bethel 99559.

Yupiktat Bista (a branch of the Association of Village Council Presidents), Bethel 99559.

Native Village Corporations

In addition to the 12 regional corporations managing money and land received as part of the Alaska Native Claims Settlement Act, eligible Native villages were required to form corporations and to choose lands made available by the settlement act by December 1974. The 203 Native villages which formed village corporations eligible for land and money benefits are listed below under their regional corporation.

Ahtna Incorporated: Cantwell, Chistochina, Chitina, Copper Center, Gakona, Gulkana, Mentasta Lake, Tazlina.

Aleut Corporation: Akutan, Atka, Belkofski, False Pass, King Cove, Nelson Lagoon, Nikolski, Saint George, Saint Paul, Sand Point, Unalaska, Unga.

Arctic Slope Regional Corporation: Anaktuvuk Pass, Atkasook, Barrow, Kaktovik, Nuiqsut, Point Hope, Point Lay, Wainwright.

Bering Straits Native Corporation: Brevig Mission, Council, Golovin, Inalik/Diomede, King Island, Koyuk, Marys Igloo, Nome, Saint Michael, Shaktoolik, Shishmaref, Stebbins, Teller, Unalakleet, Wales, White Mountain.

Bristol Bay Native Corporation: Aleknagik, Chignik, Chignik Lagoon, Chignik Lake, Clarks Point, Dillingham, Egegik, Ekuk, Ekwok, Igiugig, Iliamna, Ivanof Bay, Kokhanok, Koliganek, Levelock, Manokotak, Naknek, Newhalen, New Stuyahok, Nondalton, Pedro Bay, Perryville, Pilot Point, Portage Creek, Port Heiden, South Naknek, Togiak, Twin Hills, Ugashik.

Calista Corporation: Akiachak, Akiak, Alakanuk, Andreafsky, Aniak, Atmautluak, Bethel, Bill Moores, Chefornak, Chevak, Chuathbaluk, Chuloonawick, Crooked Creek, Eek, Emmonak, Georgetown, Goodnews Bay, Hamilton, Hooper Bay, Kasigluk, Kipnuk, Kongiganak, Kotlik, Kwethluk, Kwigillingok, Lime Village, Lower Kalskag, Marshall, Mekoryuk, Mountain Village, Napaimiute, Napakiak, Napaskiak, Newtok, Nightmute, Nunapitchuk, Ohogamiut, Oscarville, Paimiut, Pilot Station, Pitkas Point, Platinum, Quinhagak, Red Devil, Russian Mission, Saint Marys, Scammon Bay, Sheldons Point, Sleetmute, Stony River, Toksook Bay, Tuluksak, Tuntutuliak, Tununak, Umkumiut, Upper Kalskag.

Chugach Natives, Incorporated: Chenega, English Bay, Eyak, Port Graham, Tatitlek.

Cook Inlet Region, Incorporated: Chickaloon, Knik, Eklutna, Ninilchik, Seldovia, Tyonek.

Doyon Limited: Alatna, Allakaket, Anvik, Beaver, Bettles Field, Birch Creek, Chalkyitsik, Circle, Dot Lake, Eagle, Fort Yukon, Galena, Grayling, Healy Lake, Holy Cross, Hughes, Huslia, Kaltag, Koyukuk, Manley Hot Springs, McGrath, Minto, Nenana, Nikolai, Northway, Nulato, Rampart, Ruby, Shageluk, Stevens Village, Takotna, Tanacross, Tanana, Telida.

Koniag, Incorporated: Afognak, Akhiok, Kaguyak, Karluk, Larsen Bay, Old Harbor, Ouzinkie, Port Lions, Woody Island.

NANA Regional Corporation, Incorporated: Ambler, Buckland, Deering, Kiana, Kivalina, Kobuk, Kotzebue, Noatak, Noorvik, Selawik, Shungnak.

Sealaska Corporation: Angoon, Craig, Hoonah, Hydaburg, Kake, Kasaan, Klawock, Saxman, Yakutat.

Related reading: *Alaska's Native People,* edited by Lael Morgan. A comprehensive account of Alaska's Eskimo, Indian and Aleut peoples. 304 pages. $24.95. *Roots of Ticasuk: An Eskimo Woman's Family Story.* 120 pages, $4.95. See pages 208-10.

Nenana Ice Classic

A gigantic pool that offers more than $100,000 in cash prizes to the lucky winners who can guess the time, to the nearest minute, of the ice breakup on the Tanana River at the town of Nenana. Official breakup time each spring is established when the surging ice dislodges a tripod and breaks an attached line, which stops a clock set to Alaska standard time.

Tickets for the classic are sold for $2 each, entitling the holder to one guess. Ice Classic officials estimate $7 million has been paid to lucky guessers through the years.

The primary intention of the Ice Classic was never as a fund raiser for the town, but as a lottery, which was officially sanctioned by the first state legislature in one of its first actions back in 1959. But over the years the contest has benefited the town. Fifty-five percent of the gross proceeds goes to the winners. Nenana residents are paid salaries for ticket counting and compilation, and about 15 percent is earmarked for upkeep of the Nenana Civic Center and as donations to local groups such as the Dog Mushers, the Visitors Center, and other activities or organizations.

The U.S. Internal Revenue Service also gets a large chunk including 20 percent of the gross, withholding taxes on the $25,000 payroll, and a huge bite out of each winner's share.

Breakup times from 1918 through 1983, arranged in order of date and year, were:

April	20, 1940—	3:27 P.M.	May	6, 1954—	6:01 P.M.
	26, 1926—	4:03 P.M.		6, 1950—	4:14 P.M.
	28, 1969—	12:28 P.M.		6, 1938—	8:14 P.M.
	28, 1943—	7:22 P.M.		6, 1928—	4:25 P.M.
	29, 1983—	6:37 P.M.		7, 1965—	7:01 P.M.
	29, 1958—	2:56 P.M.		7, 1925—	6:32 P.M.
	29, 1953—	3:54 P.M.		8, 1971—	9:31 P.M.
	29, 1939—	1:26 P.M.		8, 1968—	9:26 P.M.
	30, 1981—	6:44 P.M.		8, 1966—	12:11 P.M.
	30, 1980—	1:16 P.M.		8, 1959—	11:26 A.M.
	30, 1979—	6:16 P.M.		8, 1933—	7:30 P.M.
	30, 1978—	3:18 P.M.		8, 1930—	7:03 P.M.
	30, 1951—	5:54 P.M.		9, 1955—	2:31 P.M.
	30, 1942—	1:28 P.M.		9, 1923—	2:00 P.M.
	30, 1936—	12:58 P.M.		10, 1982—	5:36 P.M.
	30, 1934—	2:07 P.M.		10, 1975—	1:49 P.M.
May	1, 1956—	11:24 A.M.		10, 1972—	11:56 A.M.
	1, 1932—	10:15 A.M.		10, 1931—	9:23 A.M.
	2, 1976—	10:51 A.M.		11, 1924—	3:10 P.M.
	2, 1960—	7:12 P.M.		11, 1921—	6:42 A.M.
	3, 1947—	5:53 P.M.		11, 1920—	10:45 A.M.
	3, 1941—	1:50 A.M.		11, 1918—	9:33 A.M.
	3, 1919—	2:33 P.M.		12, 1962—	11:23 P.M.
	4, 1973—	11:59 A.M.		12, 1952—	5:04 P.M.
	4, 1970—	10:37 P.M.		12, 1937—	8:04 P.M.
	4, 1967—	11:55 A.M.		12, 1927—	5:42 A.M.
	4, 1944—	2:08 P.M.		12, 1922—	1:20 P.M.
	5, 1963—	6:25 P.M.		13, 1948—	11:13 A.M.
	5, 1961—	11:31 A.M.		14, 1949—	12:39 P.M.
	5, 1957—	9:30 A.M.		15, 1935—	1:32 P.M.
	5, 1946—	4:40 P.M.		16, 1945—	9:41 A.M.
	5, 1929—	3:41 P.M.		20, 1964—	11:41 A.M.
	6, 1977—	12:46 P.M.			
	6, 1974—	3:44 P.M.			

In 1983, 21 persons had all or part claim to one of nine winning tickets, each ticket worth $14,777. Holders of the nine tickets were: Damon and Chris Rubio (Anchorage); Tom Waters (Fairbanks); William C. Neil (Anchorage); Bill Van Hees (Anchorage); Mr. and Mrs. J.R. Huffsmith (Anchorage); Eduardo Viralta (Anchorage); the Upesleja family (Girts, Linda, Maija and Brian — all from Fairbanks); James Eakin (Anchorage); and the Fairbanks pool of Lloyd Pike, Marjorie Pike, Joan Davis, Gene Davis, Jerry Pike, Linda Pike, Marlene Barkdahl and Scott Barkdahl. Total winnings were $133,000.

Newspapers and Periodicals

(Rates are subject to change.)

Air Alaska, Pouch 4-9007, Anchorage 99509. Monthly. Rates: free to all licensed Alaskan pilots.

Alaska Fisherman's Journal, 1115 NW 46th Street, Seattle, Washington 98107. Monthly. Rates: 12 issues (plus 4 of *Seafood Leader*); second class, $15; first class, $30, foreign, $58.

ALASKA GEOGRAPHIC®, Box 4-EEE, Anchorage 99509. Quarterly. Annual rates, including membership in The Alaska Geographic Society: $30; outside the U.S., $34.

The ALASKA JOURNAL®, Box 4-EEE, Anchorage 99509. Quarterly. Annual rates: $16; outside the U.S., $20.

Alaska Journal of Commerce and Pacific Rim Reporter, Pouch 4-9007, Anchorage 99509. Weekly. Rates: 1 year, $49; 2 years, $90.

ALASKA® magazine, Box 4-EEE, Anchorage 99509. Monthly. Annual rates: $18 ($17 for each additional subscription ordered at the same time); outside the U.S., $22.

Aleutian Eagle, P.O. Box 486, Dutch Harbor 99692. Twice monthly. Annual rates: Alaska, $30; Outside, $35.

The All-Alaska Weekly, P.O. Box 970, Fairbanks 99707. Weekly. Second-class rates: 6 months, $11; 1 year, $20.

Anchorage Daily News, Pouch 6616, Anchorage 99502. Daily including Sunday. Monthly rates: Anchorage home delivery, $4.75; second-class mail, $12.95.

The Anchorage Times, P.O. Box 40, Anchorage 99510. Daily including Sunday. Monthly rates: Anchorage home delivery, $4.75; second-class mail, $13.00.

Bering Sea Fisherman, 805 West Third Avenue, Anchorage 99501. Every two months. Annual rate: $10.

Bristol BayTimes, Box 10024, Dillingham 99576. Twice monthly. Annual rates: Alaska, $15; Outside, $20.

Cheechako News, P.O. Drawer 0, Kenai 99611. Weekly. Annual second-class rates: Alaska, $20; Outside, $25.

Chugiak-Eagle River Star, P.O. Box 1007, Eagle River 99577. Weekly. Rates: 6 months, $6.50; 1 year, $12.75.

Copper Valley Views, P.O. Box 233, Copper Center 99573. Twice monthly. Annual rate: $18.

Cordova Times, P.O. Box 200, Cordova 99574. Weekly. Annual rates: second class, $30; first class, $60.

Daily Sitka Sentinel, P.O. Box 799, Sitka 99835. Daily except Saturday and Sunday. Annual rate: Sitka, $50. Write for mailed subscription rates.

The Delta Paper, P.O. Box 988, Delta Junction 99737. Weekly. Rate: $1.10 per issue. Write for out-of-town rates.

Fairbanks Daily News-Miner, Box 710, Fairbanks 99707. Daily except Sunday. Annual second-class rate: Alaska, $131.75. Write for rates outside Alaska.

The Frontiersman, P.O. Box D, Palmer 99645. Weekly. Annual second-class rates: Matanuska-Susitna Borough, $12.50; elsewhere, $20.

Great Lander Shopping News, 3110 Spenard Road, Anchorage 99503. Weekly. Free in distribution area. Annual mail rate: third class, $20.

Homer News, P.O. Box 254, Homer 99603. Weekly. Annual rates: Kenai Peninsula Borough, $24; elsewhere, second class, $30; first class, $54.

Juneau Empire, 235 Second Street, Juneau 99801. Daily except Saturday and Sunday. Rates: Juneau, 1 month, $5.25; 1 year, $63; elsewhere, 3 months, $24.

Kadiak Times, P.O. Box 1698, Kodiak 99615. Twice weekly. Annual rates: second class, $26; first class, $39.

Ketchikan Daily News, P.O. Box 7900, Ketchikan 99901. Daily except Sunday. Annual rates: Ketchikan, $61; elsewhere, second class, $85.

Kodiak Daily Mirror, P.O. Box 1307, Kodiak 99615. Daily except Saturday and Sunday. Annual second-class rates: Alaska, $58; Outside, $84.

Kusko Courier, McGrath 99627. Write for subscription rates.

Lynn Canal News, P.O. Box 637, Haines 99827. Weekly. Annual second-class rates: Haines, $25; elsewhere, $28. First class, $40.

Metro, P.O. Box 104281, Anchorage 99510. Free distribution within Anchorage.

The MILEPOST®, Box 4-EEE, Anchorage 99509. Annual edition, available in March. $11.95 ($13.95 in Canada) plus $1.00 for fourth-class postage and handling; $3.00 for first-class mail.

Mukluk News, P.O. Box 96, Tok 99780. Twice monthly. Annual rates: first class, $24; third class, $10.

Nome Nugget, P.O. Box 610, Nome 99762. Weekly. Annual second-class rates: Alaska, $24; Outside, $28. Fifty percent discount for senior citizens.

Peninsula Clarion, P.O. Box 4330, Kenai 99611. Daily except Saturday and Sunday. Annual second-class rates: Alaska, $35; Outside, $48.

Petersburg Pilot, P.O. Box 930, Petersburg 99833. Weekly. Annual second-class rates: Petersburg, $22; elsewhere, $25. First class, $40.

The Prudhoe Bay Journal, Prudhoe Bay. Distributed free.

Senior Voice, P.O. box 10-2240, Anchorage 99510. Monthly. Annual rate for nonmembers of Older Persons Action Group, $10.

Seward Phoenix Log, P.O. Box 97, Seward 99664. Weekly. Annual second-class rates: Kenai Peninsula Borough, $20; elsewhere, $24. First class, $38.

The Skagway News, P.O. Box 1898, Skagway 99840. Twice monthly. Annual rates: Skagway, $15; elsewhere, $25.

Southeastern Log, P.O. Box 7900, Ketchikan 99901. Monthly. Annual rates: free to southeastern Alaska residents; other Alaska residents and out-of-state subscriptions, $12.

Tundra Drums, P.O. Box 868, Bethel 99559. Weekly. Annual second-class rates: Alaska, $20; elsewhere, $30. First class, $55.

Tundra Times, P.O. Box 104480, Anchorage 99510-4480. Weekly. Second-class rates: 6 months, $12; 1 year, $20.

Valdez Vanguard, P.O. Box 157, Valdez 99686. Weekly. Annual second-class rates: Valdez, $30; elsewhere, $60.

The Valley Sun, Pouch M, Wasilla 99687. Weekly. Write for subscription rates.

Wrangell Sentinel, Box 798, Wrangell 99929. Weekly. Annual rates: second class, $22; first class, $30.

No-see-ums

Aptly named because alone he is difficult to see but in his usual swarms this tiny, gray-black, silver-winged gnat is a most persistent pest and annoys all creatures. While not a disease carrier, his bites are irritating. Protective clothing, netting and a good repellent are recommended while in the bushes or near still-water ponds. Tents and recreational vehicles should be well screened.

Nuchalawoya

Nuchalawoya means "where the great waters meet" and was originally a meeting of Athabascan chiefs held near the time of the summer solstice. Today, nuchalawoya names a festival held in June at Tanana, located at the confluence of the Tanana and Yukon rivers.

Oil and Gas

Alaska's first exploratory oil well was drilled in 1898 on the Iniskin Peninsula, Cook Inlet, by Alaska Petroleum Company. According to the Alaska Oil and Gas Association, oil was encountered in this first hole at about 700 feet, but a water zone beneath the oil strata cut off the oil flow. Total depth of the well was approximately 1,000 feet.

The first commercial oil discovery was made in 1902 near Katalla, near the mouth of the Bering River east of Cordova. This field produced until 1933.

As early as 1921, oil companies surveyed land north of the Brooks Range for possible drilling sites. In 1923 the federal government created Naval Petroleum Reserve Number 4 (now known as National Petroleum Reserve-Alaska, see *National Petroleum Reserve*), a 23-million-acre area of Alaska's North Slope. Wartime needs speeded up exploration. In 1944 the navy began drilling operations on the petroleum reserve and continued until 1953, but made no significant oil discoveries.

Atlantic Richfield discovered oil in 1957 on the Kenai Peninsula, at a depth of approximately 2 miles, about 20 miles northeast of Kenai at what became known as the Swanson River Oilfield. Later, Union Oil Company found a large gas field at Kalifonsky Beach (the Kenai Gas Field), and Amoco found the first gas offshore at a location known as Middle Ground Shoals in Cook Inlet in 1962.

Currently, there are 14 production platforms in Cook Inlet, one of which produces only gas. Built to contend with extreme tides, siltation, and ice floes, the Cook Inlet platforms are in one of three successful areas of offshore oil production in the United States. Hundreds of miles of pipeline with diameters of up to 20 inches link the offshore platforms with onshore facilities at Kenai and Drift River. The deepest producing oil well in the state is in the Swanson River Oilfield on the Kenai Peninsula; total depth is 17,689 feet. A fertilizer plant, largest of its kind on the West Coast, is located at Kenai. It uses natural gas as a feed stock to manufacture ammonia and urea. Two refineries are located at Kenai; a third is at North Pole near Fairbanks. Gasoline, diesel fuel, heavy fuel oil, JP-4, Jet A-50, and asphalt are produced for use within and outside of Alaska. Crude oil topping plants located at Prudhoe Bay and at pump stations 6, 8 and 10 provide diesel oil for industrial use.

The Prudhoe Bay oil field, largest in North America, was discovered in 1968 by Atlantic-Richfield Company. Recoverable reserves were estimated to be 9.6 billion barrels of oil and 26 trillion cubic feet of natural gas. The field contains about one-quarter of the known petroleum reserves in the United States and each day produces 14 percent of U.S. production and 10 percent of U.S. consumption. The average daily production of 1.5 million barrels is transported via the trans-Alaska pipeline from Prudhoe Bay to Valdez (see *Trans-Alaska Pipeline*). In the summer of 1983 it was estimated that one-third of the Prudhoe Bay oil reserve had been pumped. A $2 billion waterflood project is under way to maximize oil recovery by forcing additional oil out of the reservoir rock and into producing wells. Sohio Alaska Petroleum Company operates the west half of the field and ARCO the east half. They operate for 11 participant companies.

The Kuparuk River Field, 40 miles west of Prudhoe Bay, is being developed by ARCO. The eventual cost of full development is expected to be approximately $7 billion, with ARCO's share being $3.9 billion. The field went into production in mid-December 1981; approximately 120,000 barrels a day are being delivered to the trans-Alaska pipeline. Production from Kuparuk is expected to reach 200,000 to 250,000 barrels a day in the late 1980s.

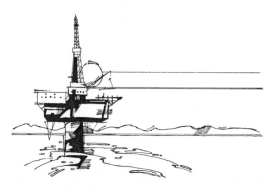

The Alaska Natural Gas Transportation System — the proposed Alaska gas pipeline — was authorized by the federal government in 1977. Estimated cost was $10 billion with a completion date in 1983. A two-year delay in the northern part of the project was announced in May 1982 by Northwest Alaskan, the consortium building the project. Recent cost estimates for the gas pipeline have risen to more than $40 billion. The completion date is now uncertain, due to problems in financing the project.

The natural gas pipeline route would follow the trans-Alaska oil pipeline corridor to near Fairbanks, then the Alaska Highway through Alaska and Yukon Territory to British Columbia; branch lines extend into Alberta. The total length of the gas pipeline (including proposed sections) will be 4,800 miles. Natural gas from Alberta gas reserves began flowing to West Coast states in October 1981.

Alaska Oil and Natural Gas (Liquid) Production
(in millions of barrels)

Year	Oil*	Natural Gas**	Year	Oil*	Natural Gas**
1972	73.6	0.562	1978	447.8	0.815
1973	73.1	0.806	1979	511.3	0.634
1974	72.2	0.793	1980	591.6	0.481
1975	72.0	0.765	1981	587.3	0.537
1976	67.0	0.770	1982	618.9	0.498
1977	171.3	0.863			

*Oil production for the years 1902-71 totaled 396,537,603 barrels; for the years 1902-82, total production amounted to 3,682,769,004 barrels.
**Natural gas (liquid) production for the years 1902-71 totaled 1,312,113 barrels; for the years 1902-82, total production was 8,837,550 barrels.
Source: *1982 Statistical Report,* Alaska Oil and Gas Conservation Commission.

Oil and gas leasing on state land in Alaska is managed by the Department of Natural Resources, Division of Minerals and Energy Management. The secretary of the interior is responsible for establishing oil and gas leasing on federal lands in Alaska including the outer-continental shelf.

Parka

Pronounced *par-kee,* this over-the-head garment worn by Eskimos was made in several versions. The work parka most often came from caribou fawn skin, while the fancy parka, reserved for special occasions, used the skin of the male ground squirrel (the male offering grayer fur than the female). Another version, the rain parka, was made from *oogruk* (bearded seal) intestine. A person's wealth was judged by the quality of his or her best parka.

Related reading: *Secrets of Eskimo Skin Sewing* by Edna Wilder. The complete book on the art of Eskimo skin sewing, with how-to-do-it instructions and things-to-make ideas. 125 pages, $6.95. See page 210.

Permafrost

Permafrost, perennially frozen ground, is defined as ground which remains frozen for two or more years. In its continuous form, permafrost underlies the entire arctic region to depths of 2,000 feet. In broad terms, continuous permafrost occurs north of the Brooks Range and in the alpine region of mountains (including those of the Lower 48).
Discontinous permafrost occurs south of the Brooks Range and north

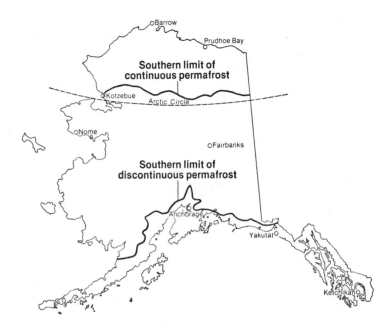

of the Alaska Range. Much of the Interior and some of Southcentral are underlain by discontinous permafrost.

Permafrost affects many man-made structures and natural bodies. It influences construction in the Arctic because building on it may cause the ground to thaw, and if the ground is ice-rich, structures will sink. Arctic and subarctic rivers typically carry 55 to 65 percent of precipitation falling onto their watersheds, roughly 30 to 40 percent more than rivers of more temperate climates. Consequently, northern streams are prone to flooding and have high silt loads. Permafrost is responsible for the thousands of lakes dotting the arctic tundra because ground water is held on the surface.

A tunnel excavated in permafrost near Fox during the early 1960s is maintained cooperatively by the University of Alaska, Fairbanks, and the U.S. Army Cold Regions Research and Engineering Laboratory. It is one of the few such tunnels in the world that offers unique research opportunities on a 40,000-year-old accumulation of sediments and ice.

The tunnel is open to the general public from June 1 through August 31 each year by appointment only through the CRREL office.

Permanent Fund

In 1976, state voters approved a constitutional amendment to establish the Alaska Permanent Fund. This provides that a percentage of all mineral lease rentals, royalties, royalty sales proceeds, federal mineral revenue sharing payments and bonuses shall be placed in a Permanent Fund. Essentially a trust fund for all Alaskans, money from the fund may be used in income-producing investments but may not be used for state operating expenses. (Interest income from the Permanent Fund can go into the state's General Fund.)

In 1980, the legislature established a Permanent Fund dividend payment program, providing for distribution of the fund's earnings (interest income and capital gains on any liquidation of assets) among the people of Alaska. Eligible residents were to receive a $50 dividend for each year of residency since 1959. The U.S. Supreme Court declared the 1980 program unconstitutional on the grounds that it discriminated against short-term residents, and in 1982 a new state program was signed into law. Under the new plan, an initial $1,000 dividend was paid to applicants who had lived in the state for at least six months prior to applying. Amounts of subsequent dividend payments are computed each fiscal year by dividing one-half of the fund's earnings by the number of applicants. In 1983, each eligible resident received a dividend check of $386.15.

Pioneers' Homes

"The state of Alaska recognizes the invaluable contributions of its older citizens and seeks to offer a place for them in which they can live in comfort and security, while remaining active members of the Alaska community. The companionship of other pioneer Alaskans whose earlier years have been spent in the exciting days of the territory is one of the advantages of living in the Pioneers' Homes." These words were taken from a state brochure describing Pioneers' Homes. The five state-supported homes offer a comfortable, secure residence for several hundred older Alaskans. The homes provide space for 363 ambulatory guests and 282 nursing spaces for bedridden and wheelchair patients.

The only requirements for admission to a Pioneers' Home are that a person be 65 years old or older and have lived continuously in Alaska for 15 years immediately prior to seeking admittance. (Some exceptions are made for Alaskans who have lived in the state more than 30 years.) No minimum or maximum income guidelines apply. Race, sex, national origin, and religion are not considered when determining eligibility. Some people are under the mistaken impression that to qualify for the Pioneers' Homes, one must be a member of the Pioneers of Alaska. This is not the case. Pioneers of Alaska is a private, fraternal organization and is not connected with the state-operated Pioneers' Homes.

The first Pioneers' Home was established in Sitka in 1913 for "indigent prospectors and others who have spent their years in Alaska." With the coming of statehood in 1959, the homes were officially opened to women and Alaska Natives.

For additional information about Pioneers' Homes, contact the Director of Pioneers Benefits, Pouch C, Department of Administration, Juneau 99811; phone (907) 465-4400.

Following are the locations of the five existing homes:

Anchorage Pioneers' Home, 923 West 11th Avenue, Anchorage 99501; phone (907) 276-3414.
Fairbanks Pioneers' Home, 2221 Egan, Fairbanks 99701; phone (907) 456-4372.
Ketchikan Pioneers' Home, 141 Bryant, Ketchikan 99901; phone (907) 225-4111.
Palmer Pioneers' Home, P.O. Box 1068, Palmer 99645; phone (907) 745-4241.
Sitka Pioneers' Home, P.O. Box 198, Sitka 99835; phone (907) 747-3213.

Place Names

Alaska has a rich international heritage of place names. Throughout the state names of British (Barrow), Spanish (Valdez), Russian (Kotzebue), French (La Perouse), American (Fairbanks), and Native Alaska (Sitka) origin dot the map. Some Alaska place names are quite common. There are about 70 streams called Bear Creek in Alaska (not to mention Bear Bay, Bear Bluff, Bear Canyon, Bear Cove, and Bear Draw) and about 50 called Moose Creek. Many place names have an unusual history. In 1910 geologist Lawrence Martin named Sherman Glacier in the Chugach Mountains after Gen. William Tecumseh Sherman, with the explanation, "He [Sherman] said 'war is hell'; so I put him on ice, near the Sheridan Glacier."

For a comprehensive listing, description, and history of Alaska's usual and unusual place names, from Aaron Creek to Zwinge Valley, see Donald Orth's *Dictionary of Alaska Place Names,* U.S. Geological Survey Professional Paper 567. (See also *Populations and Zip Codes* for pronunciations of many of Alaska's unusual place names.)

Poisonous Plants

There are poisonous plants in Alaska but not many considering the total quantity of plant species growing in the state. Baneberry *(Actaea rubra),* water hemlock *(Cicuta douglasii* and *C. mackenzieana),* and fly agaric mushroom *(Amanita muscaria)* are the most dangerous. Be sure you have properly identified plants before harvesting for food. Alaska has no plants poisonous to the touch such as poison ivy and poison oak, found in almost all other states.

Populations and Zip Codes

The populations for cities and communities in the following list are taken from two sources: the U.S. Department of Commerce 1980 *Census of Population,* and the Alaska Department of Labor 1982 *Alaska Population Overview.*

For population figures by census area, based on U.S. census figures, see page 162.

Community	Year Incorporated	Population	Zip
Akhiok (AH-key-ok)	1972	103	99615
Akiachak (ACK-ee-a-chack)	1974	451	99551
Akiak (ACK-ee-ack)	1970	229	99552
Akolmiut (a-KOL-mee-ut)	1969	353	NA
Akutan (ACK-a-tan)	1979	188	99553
Alakanuk (a-LACK-a-nuk)	1969	546	99554
Aleknagik (a-LACK-na-gik)	1973	232	99555
Allakaket (alla-KAK-it)	1975	169	99720
Ambler	1971	202	99786
Anaktuvuk Pass (an-ak-TU-vuk)	1957	250	99721
Anchorage (Municipality)	1920	200,503	995 - -
Eastchester Station			99501
Fort Richardson			99505
Elmendorf AFB			99506
Mountain View			99508
Spenard Station			99509
Downtown Station			99510
South Station			99511
Alyeska Pipeline Co.			99512
Federal Building			99513
Anchor Point	NA	226	99556
Anderson	1962	522	99790
Angoon	1963	562	99820
Aniak (AN-ee-ack)	1972	351	99557
Annette	NA	139	99926
Anvik	1969	115	99558
Arctic Village	NA	111	99722
Atka	NA	93	99502
Atmautluak (an-MAUT-loo-ack)	1976	236	99559
Auke Bay	NA	NA	99821
Barrow	1959	2,882	99723
Beaver	NA	66	99724

Community	Year Incorporated	Population	Zip
Belkofski (bel-KOF-ski)	NA	NA	99695
Bethel	1957	3,683	99559
Bettles Field	NA	NA	99726
Big Lake	NA	410	99687
Border	NA	NA	99780
Brevig Mission	1969	134	99785
Buckland	1966	217	99727
Cantwell	NA	89	99729
Cape Yakataga	NA	NA	99574
Central	NA	36	99730
Chalkyitsik (chal-KEET-sik)	NA	100	99788
Chatanika (chat-a-NEEK-a)	NA	NA	99701
Chefornak (cha-FOR-nack)	1974	244	99561
Chevak	1967	513	99563
Chicken	NA	37	99732
Chignik	NA	178	99564
Chignik Lagoon	NA	48	99565
Chignik Lake	NA	138	99564
Chitina (CHIT-nah)	NA	42	99566
Chuathbaluk (chew-ATH-ba-luck)	NA	124	99557
Chugiak (CHOO-gee-ack)	NA	NA	99567
Circle	NA	81	99733
Clam Gulch	NA	50	99568
Clarks Point	1971	80	99569
Clear	NA	NA	99704
Cold Bay	1982	250	99571
Cooper Landing	NA	116	99572
Copper Center	NA	213	99573
Cordova	1909	2,244	99574
Craig	1922	604	99921
Crooked Creek	NA	108	99575
Curry's Corner	NA	NA	99710
Deadhorse	NA	64	99734
Deering	1970	158	99736
Delta Junction	1960	1,047	99737
Denali Park	NA	32	99755
Dillingham	1963	1,791	99576
Diomede (DY-o-mede)	1970	134	NA
Dot Lake	NA	67	99737
Douglas	1902	NA	99824

Community	Year Incorporated	Population	Zip
Dutch Harbor	NA	NA	99692
Eagle	1901	142	99738
Eagle River	NA	NA	99577
Eek	1970	235	99578
Egegik (IG-a-gik)	NA	75	99579
Ekwok (ECK-wok)	1974	78	99580
Elfin Cove	NA	28	99825
Elim (EE-lum)	1970	205	99739
Emmonak (ee-MON-ak)	1964	581	99581
Ester	NA	149	99725
Fairbanks	1903	25,967	9970-
Main Office			99701
Eielson AFB			99702
Fort Wainwright			99703
Main Office Boxes			99706
Downtown Station			99707
College Branch			99708
Salcha			99714
False Pass	NA	70	99583
Flat	NA	NA	99584
Fortuna Ledge	1970	260	99585
Fort Yukon	1959	625	99740
Gakona (ga-KOH-na)	NA	87	99586
Galena (ga-LEE-na)	1971	847	99741
Gambell	1963	432	99742
Girdwood	NA	NA	99587
Glennallen	NA	511	99588
Golovin (GULL-uh-vin)	1971	112	99762
Goodnews Bay	1970	173	99589
Grayling	1969	211	99590
Gustavus (ga-STAY-vus)	NA	98	99826
Haines	1910	1,078	99827
Healy	NA	334	99743
Holy Cross	1968	243	99602
Homer	1964	2,900	99603
Hoonah	1946	864	99829
Hooper Bay	1966	651	99604
Hope	NA	103	99605
Houston	1966	826	99694
Hughes	1973	74	99745
Huslia (HOOS-lee-a)	NA	241	99746
Hydaburg	NA	412	99922

Community	Year Incorporated	Population	Zip
Hyder	NA	77	99923
Iliamna (ill-ee-AM-na)	NA	94	99606
Juneau	1900	22,030	9980-
Main office			99801
Main office boxes			99802
Mendenhall Station			99803
state government offices			99811
Kachemak (CATCH-a-mack)	1961	288	NA
Kake	1952	631	99830
Kaktovik (kack-TOE-vik)	1971	214	99747
Kalskag	NA	NA	99607
Kaltag	1969	246	99748
Karluk	NA	96	99608
Kasaan (Ka-SAN)	1976	70	NA
Kasigluk (ka-SEEG-luk)	1982	328	99609
Kasilof (ka-SEE-loff)	NA	201	99610
Kenai (KEEN-eye)	1960	5,261	99611
Ketchikan	1900	7,778	99901
Kiana (Ky-AN-a)	1964	364	99749
King Cove	1947	523	99612
King Salmon	NA	545	99613
Kipnuk (KIP-nuck)	NA	371	99614
Kivalina	1969	253	99750
Klawock (kla-WOCK)	1929	433	99925
Kobuk	1973	64	99751
Kodiak	1940	5,873	99615
U.S. Coast Guard Station			99619
Koghanok (KO-ghan-ock)	NA	83	99606
Koliganek (ko-LIG-a-neck)	NA	117	99576
Kongiganak (kon-GIG-a-nack)	NA	239	99559
Kotlik	1970	347	99620
Kotzebue (KOT-sa-bue)	1958	2,470	99752
Koyuk	1970	183	99753
Koyukuk (KOY-u-kuck)	1973	99	99754
Kupreanof (ku-pree-AN-off)	1975	54	NA
Kwethluk (KWEETH-luck)	1975	467	99621
Kwigillingok (kwi-GILL-in-gock)	NA	354	99622
Lake Minchumina (min-CHOO-min-a)	NA	NA	99757
Larsen Bay	1974	180	99624
Levelock	NA	79	99625

Community	Year Incorporated	Population	Zip
Levelock	NA	79	99625
Lower Kalskag	1969	260	99626
Manley Hot Springs	NA	61	99756
Manokotak (man-a-KO-tack)	1970	299	99628
McGrath	1975	498	99627
Medfra	NA	NA	99629
Mekoryuk (ma-KOR-ee-uk)	1969	178	99630
Metlakatla	NA	1,056	99926
Meyers Chuck	NA	50	99903
Minto	NA	153	99758
Moose Pass	NA	76	99631
Mountain Village	NA	601	99632
Naknek (NACK-neck)	NA	318	99633
Napakiak (na-PA-kee-ack)	1970	286	99634
Napaskiak (na-PASS-kee-ack)	1971	251	99559
Nenana (nee-NA-na)	1921	475	99760
Newhalen	1971	140	NA
New Stuyahok (STU-ya-hock)	1972	337	99636
Newtok	1976	175	99681
Nightmute	1974	141	99690
Nikishka	NA	1,109	99611
Nikolai	1970	110	99691
Nikolski	NA	50	99638
Ninilchik	NA	341	99639
Noatak	NA	273	99761
Nome	1901	3,430	99762
Nondalton	1971	176	99640
Noorvik	1964	518	99763
North Pole	1953	942	99705
Northway	NA	73	99764
Nuiqsut (noo-IK-sut)	1975	287	99723
Nulato	1963	353	99765
Nunapitchuk (see Akolmiut)			99641
Nyac (NY-ack)	NA	NA	99642
Old Harbor	1966	355	99643
Ouzinkie (u-ZINK-ee)	1967	233	99644
Palmer	1951	2,542	99645
Paxson	NA	30	99737
Pedro Bay	NA	33	99647

Community	Year Incorporated	Population	Zip
Pelican	1943	185	99832
Perryville	NA	111	99648
Petersburg	1910	3,040	99833
Pilot Point	NA	66	99649
Pilot Station	1969	337	99650
Pitkas Point	NA	88	99658
Platinum	1975	57	99651
Point Baker	NA	90	99927
Point Hope	1966	544	99766
Port Alexander	1974	98	99836
Port Alsworth	NA	NA	99653
Port Graham	NA	161	99603
Port Heiden	1972	94	99549
Port Lions	1966	291	99550
Quinhagak (QUIN-a-hock)	1975	427	99655
Rampart	NA	50	99767
Red Devil	NA	39	99656
Ruby	1973	214	99768
Russian Mission	1970	175	99657
Saint George	NA	158	99660
Saint Marys	1967	442	99658
Saint Michael	1969	295	99659
Saint Paul	1971	595	99660
Sand Point	1978	797	99661
Savoonga	1969	477	99769
Saxman	1930	273	NA
Scammon Bay	1967	251	99662
Selawik (SELL-a-wick)	1977	602	99770
Seldovia	1945	733	99663
Seward	1912	1,839	99664
Shageluk (SHAG-a-look)	1970	132	99665
Shaktoolik (shack-TOO-lick)	1969	159	99771
Sheldon Point	1974	107	99666
Shishmaref	1969	425	99772
Shungnak (SHOONG-nack)	1967	214	99773
Sitka (City and Borough)	NA	8,223	99835
Skagway	1900	790	99840
Skwentna	NA	NA	99667
Slana	NA	49	99586
Sleetmute	NA	107	99668

Community	Year Incorporated	Population	Zip
Soldotna	1967	3,025	99669
South Naknek	NA	145	99670
Stebbins	1969	321	99671
Sterling	NA	919	99672
Stevens Village	NA	96	99774
Stony River	NA	62	99557
Sutton	NA	182	99674
Takotna	NA	48	99675
Talkeetna (Tal-KEET-na)	NA	264	99676
Tanacross	NA	117	99776
Tanana (TAN-a-nah)	1961	486	99777
Tatitlek	NA	68	99677
Teller	1963	206	99778
Tenakee Springs	1971	141	99841
Tetlin	NA	107	99779
Thorne Bay	1982	316	NA
Togiak (TOE-gee-ack)	1969	507	99678
Tok (TOKE)	NA	589	99780
Toksook Bay	1972	357	99637
Trapper Creek	NA	NA	99688
Tuluksak (tu-LOOK-sack)	1970	243	99679
Tuntutuliak (tun-too-TOO-li-ack)	NA	216	99680
Tununak	1975	302	99681
Twin Hills	NA	70	99576
Tyonek (ty-O-neck)	NA	239	99682
Unalakleet (YOU-na-la-kleet)	1974	604	99684
Unalaska (UN-a-LAS-ka)	1942	1,922	99685
Upper Kalskag	1975	133	NA
Usibelli	NA	53	99787
Valdez (val-DEEZ)	1901	3,698	99686
Venetie (VEEN-a-tie)	NA	132	99781
Wainwright	1962	436	99782
Wales	1964	129	99783
Ward Cove	NA	NA	99928
Wasilla (WA-sil-la)	1974	2,403	99687
White Mountain	1969	121	99784
Whittier	1969	224	99693
Willow	NA	139	99688
Wrangell	1903	2,376	99929
Yakutat (YAK-a-tat)	1948	462	99689

Alaska Population by Census Area

Census Area Code	Census Area	Population 1982	Population 1980	1970
	Alaska	460,837	401,851	302,583
01	North Slope Borough	4,849	4,199	—
02	Kobuk	5,090	4,831	4,434
03	Nome	7,459	6,537	5,749
04	Yukon-Koyukuk	7,942	7,873	—
05	Fairbanks-North Star Borough	59,222	53,983	45,864
06	Southeast Fairbanks	6,056	5,676	—
07	Wade Hampton	4,832	4,665	3,917
08	Bethel	11,323	10,999	—
09	Dillingham	4,697	4,616	—
10	Bristol Bay Borough	1,271	1,094	1,147
11	Aleutian Islands	8,525	7,768	—
12	Matanuska-Susitna Borough	25,212	17,816	6,509
13	Municipality of Anchorage	200,503	174,431	126,385
14	Kenai Peninsula Borough	32,486	25,282	—
15	Kodiak Island Borough	12,714	9,939	9,409
16	Valdez-Cordova	9,455	8,348	—
17	Skagway-Yakutat-Angoon	3,578	3,478	—
18	Haines Borough	1,854	1,680	—
19	City & Borough of Juneau	22,030	19,528	13,556
20	Sitka-City & Borough	8,223	7,803	3,370
21	Wrangell-Petersburg	6,698	6,167	—
22	Prince of Wales-Outer Ketchikan	4,386	3,822	—
23	Ketchikan Gateway Borough	12,432	11,316	10,041

Source: 1982 *Alaska Population Overview*, Alaska Department of Labor.

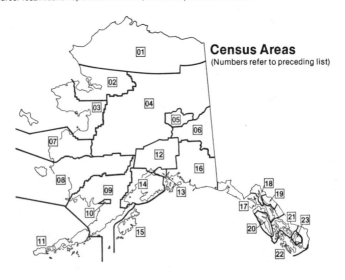

Census Areas
(Numbers refer to preceding list)

Population of Alaska's Major Towns and Cities 1900-1980

Community	1900	1920	1940	1950	1960	1970	1980
Anchorage	—	1,856	4,229	11,254	44,237	48,081	174,431
Barrow	—	—	—	—	—	2,104	2,207
Bethel	—	—	—	—	—	2,416	3,576
Cordova	—	955	938	1,165	1,125	1,164	1,879
Fairbanks	—	1,155	3,455	5,771	13,311	14,771	22,645
Juneau	1,864	3,058	5,729	5,956	6,797	6,050	19,528
Kenai	290	332	303	321	778	3,533	4,324
Ketchikan	459	2,458	4,695	5,305	6,483	6,994	7,198
Kodiak	341	374	864	1,710	2,628	3,798	4,756
Kotzebue	—	—	—	—	—	1,696	2,054
Nome	12,488	852	1,559	1,876	2,316	2,357	2,301
Petersburg	—	879	1,323	1,619	1,502	2,042	2,821
Seward	—	652	949	2,114	1,891	1,587	1,843
Sitka	1,396	1,175	1,987	1,985	3,237	3,370	7,803
Valdez	315	466	529	554	555	1,005	3,079
Wrangell	868	821	1,162	1,263	1,315	2,029	2,184

— Population figures unavailable
Source: Alaska Department of Labor

Potlatch

These Native gatherings, primarily an Indian custom, are held to commemorate just about any kind of event. Traditional Native foods are served and gifts are distributed to everyone who attends. A funeral potlatch might result in the giving away of the deceased's possessions to relatives or to persons who had done favors for the deceased during his or her lifetime. Before the federal government imposed legal constraints in the nineteenth century, potlatches could take years of preparation. The host family might give away all its possessions in an attempt to demonstrate its wealth to the guests. Each guest in turn would feel an obligation to hold an even bigger potlatch.

Radio Stations

Alaska's radio stations broadcast a wide variety of music, talk shows, religious and educational programs. Several radio stations in Alaska also broadcast personal messages, long a popular and necessary form of communication in Alaska —especially in the Bush. It was in consideration of these messages — and the importance of radio stations in providing the sole source of vital weather information to fishermen and hunters — that the United States and Canada agreed to grant 16 Alaska radio stations international communication status. The "clear channel" status, scheduled to be effective during the summer of 1984, provides protection against interference from foreign broadcasters. Personal message broadcasts are heard on KCAM's Caribou Clatter, Glennallen; KJNP's Trapline Chatter, North Pole; KIAK's Pipeline of the North,

Fairbanks; and KSKO's Messages, McGrath. One of the longest running personal message programs was KFAR's Tundra Topics, Fairbanks, which aired for 37 years.

Anchorage, **KBYR** 700 kHz; **KNIK-FM** 105.5 MHz; 1007 West 32d Avenue, 99503.
Anchorage, **KCMG-FM** 100.5 MHz; 2550 Denali, Suite 1305, 99503.
Anchorage, **KENI** 550 kHz; Box 1160, 99510.
Anchorage, **KFQD** 750 kHz; **KWHL-FM** 106.5 MHz; 9200 Lake Otis Parkway, 99507.
Anchorage, **KHAR** 590 kHz; **KKLV-FM** 104.1 MHz; 3900 Old Seward Highway, 99503.
Anchorage, **KRKN-FM** 102.1 MHz; 338 Denali Street, 99501.
Anchorage, **KSKA-FM** 91.4 MHz; 5101 University Drive, 99508.
Anchorage, **KTNX** 1080 kHz; 1549 East Tudor Road, 99507.
Anchorage, **KYAK** 650 kHz; **KGOT-FM** 101.3 MHz; 2800 East Dowling Road, 99507.
Barrow, **KBRW** 680 kHz; Box 109, 99723.
Bethel, **KYUK** 580 kHz; Box 468, 99559.
Big Lake, **KABN** 830 kHz; Box 17000 D, 99687.
Cordova, **KLAM** 1450 kHz; Box 278, 99574.
Dillingham, **KDLG** 670 kHz; Box 670, 99576.
Fairbanks, **KAYY-FM** 101.1 MHz; Box 80268, 99701.
Fairbanks, **KCBF** 900 kHz; Box 950, 99701.
Fairbanks, **KFAR** 660 kHz; Box 910, 99701.
Fairbanks, **KIAK** 970 kHz; **KQRZ-FM** 102.5 MHz; Box 73410, 99707.
Fairbanks, **KSUA-FM** 103.9 MHz; Constitution Hall, University of Alaska, 99701.
Fairbanks, **KUAC-FM** 104.7 MHz; 208 Theatre Building, University of Alaska, 99701.
Glennallen, **KCAM** 790 kHz; Box 249, 99588.
Haines, **KHNS-FM** 101.3 MHz; Box 0, 99827.
Homer, **KBBI** 1250 kHz; Box 1085, 99603.
Homer, **KGTL** 620 kHz; **KGTL-FM,** 103.5 MHz; Box 103, 99603.
Juneau, **KJNO** 630 kHz; Box 929, 99802.
Juneau, **KJUD** 800 kHz; 1107 Eighth Street, Suite 2, 99801.
Juneau, **KTOO-FM** 104.3 MHz; 224 Fourth Street, 99801.
Kenai, **KSRM** 920 kHz; **KQOK-FM** 100.1 MHz; Box 1000, 99611.
Ketchikan, **KETH** 1290 kHz; Box 299, Sitka 99835.
Ketchikan, **KRBD-FM** 105.9 MHz; 716 Totem Way, 99901.
Ketchikan, **KTKN** 930 kHz; Box 7700, 99901.
Kodiak, **KMXT-FM** 100.1 MHz; Box 484, 99615.
Kodiak, **KVOK** 560 kHz; Box 53, 99615.
Kotzebue, **KOTZ** 720 kHz; Box 78, 99752.
McGrath, **KSKO** 870 kHz; Box 4, 99627.
Nome, **KICY** 850 kHz; **KICY-FM,** 100.3 MHz; Box 820, 99762.
Nome, **KNOM** 780 kHz; Box 988, 99762.
North Pole, **KJNP** 1170 kHz; **KJNP-FM,** 100.3 MHz; Box 0, 99705.
Petersburg, **KFSK-FM** 100.9 MHz; Box 149, 99833.
Petersburg, **KRSA** 580 kHz; Box 650, 99833.
Sand Point, **KDSP** 840 kHz; Box 16, 99661.
Seward, **KRXA** 950 kHz; Box 276, 99664.
Sitka, **KCAW-FM** 104.7 MHz; Box 1766, 99835.
Sitka, **KIFW** 1230 kHz; Box 299, 99835.
Valdez, **KVAK** 1230 kHz; Box 367, 99686.

Valdez, **KVLD** 1400 kHz; Prince William Sound Broadcasting, 99686.
Wrangell, **KSTK-FM** 101.7 MHz; Box 282, 99929.
Yakutat, **KJFP-FM** 103.9 MHz; Box 55, 99686.

In addition to the preceding commercial and public radio stations, the Air Force Arctic Broadcasting Squadron at Elmendorf Air Force Base (Elmendorf AFB 99506) operates the Alaskan Forces Radio Network. AFRN is the oldest broadcast network in the U.S. military. It began in January 1942 on Kodiak Island with a volunteer crew that pieced together a low-power station from second-hand parts, borrowed records and local talent. Eventually the servicemen generated enough interest in Hollywood and Washington, D.C., to receive "official" status. Those early efforts resulted in what is now the Armed Forces Radio and Television Service, a far-flung system of broadcast outlets serving U.S. forces around the world.

Nearly all the programming heard at AFRN locations in Alaska originates at Elmendorf AFB. (In addition to network programming, both Eielson AFB and Fort Greely originate about six hours of programming a day at their locations.) Following is a list of AFRN outlets.

Black Rapids, **AFRN** 1550 kHz
Campion Air Force Station, **AFRN** 1490 kHz
Cape Lisburne Air Force Station, **AFRN** 1400 kHz
Cape Newenham Air Force Station, **AFRN** 1450 kHz
Cape Romanzof Air Force Station, **AFRN** 1240 kHz
Clear Air Force Station, **AFRN** 1490 kHz
Cold Bay Air Force Station, **AFRN** 1490 kHz
Eielson Air Force Base, **AFRN** 1490 kHz
Fort Greely, **AFRN** 1360 kHz, **AFRN-FM** 90.5 MHz
Fort Yukon Air Force Station, **AFRN** 1340 kHz
Galena Airport, **AFRN** 1400 kHz
Indian Mountain Air Force Station, **AFRN** 1240 kHz
King Salmon Airport, **AFRN** 970 kHz
Kodiak Coast Guard Station, **AFRN** 960 kHz
Kotzebue Air Force Station, **AFRN** 1340 kHz
Shemya Air Force Base, **AFRN** 90.5 kHz, **AFRN-FM** 101.1 MHz
Sparrevohn Air Force Station, **AFRN** 1550 kHz
Tatalina Air Force Station, **AFRN** 1450 kHz
Tin City Air Force Station, **AFRN** 1490 kHz
Tok Coast Guard Station, **AFRN** 1400 kHz

Railroads

The Alaska Railroad is the only operating railroad in Alaska today. In 1982, the White Pass and Yukon Route suspended service indefinitely.

The Alaska Railroad is the northernmost railroad in North America and the only one owned by the United States government, although efforts are under way to transfer ownership to the state of Alaska. The ARR rolls on 470 miles of mainline track from the ports of Seward and Whittier, to Anchorage on Cook Inlet, and Fairbanks in the Interior.

The Alaska Railroad began in 1912 with the appointment by Congress of a commission to study transportation problems in Alaska. In March 1914 the president authorized railroad lines in the territory of Alaska to connect open harbors on the southern coast of Alaska with the Interior.

The Alaska Engineering Commission surveyed possible railroad routes in 1914 and, in April 1915, Pres. Woodrow Wilson announced the selection of a route from Seward north 412 miles to the Tanana River (where Nenana is now located), with branch lines to Matanuska coal fields. The main line was later extended to Fairbanks. Construction of the railroad began in 1915. On July 15, 1923, Pres. Warren G. Harding drove the golden spike—signifying completion of the railroad — at Nenana.

Run by the Department of Transportation, the railroad offers year-round passenger, freight, and vehicle service. The ARR features flag-stop service along the Anchorage-to-Fairbanks corridor, as well as summer express trains to Denali National Park and Preserve. Passenger service is daily between mid-May and mid-September, and in winter, once-weekly service is available between Anchorage and Fairbanks. For information contact The Alaska Railroad, Pouch 7-2111, Anchorage 99510.

The privately owned White Pass and Yukon Route provided a narrow-gauge link between Skagway, Alaska, and Whitehorse, Yukon Territory. At the time it was built — 1898 to 1900 — it was the farthest north any railroad had operated in North America. The railway maintained one of the steepest railroad grades in North America, climbing to 2,885 feet at White Pass in only 20 miles of track. The White Pass and Yukon Route provided both passenger and freight service. Although no longer operating, the line is maintaining its rolling stock in storage until such time as the local economy improves.

Regions
Southeast
Southeast, Alaska's panhandle, stretches approximately 500 miles from Icy Bay, northwest of Yakutat, to Dixon Entrance at the United States-Canada border beyond the southern tip of Prince of Wales Island. Massive ice fields, glacier-scoured peaks and steep valleys, more than a thousand named islands, and numerous unnamed islets and reefs characterize this vertical world where few flat expanses break the steepness. Spruce, hemlock, and cedar, basis for the region's timber industry, cover many of the mountain sides.

Average temperatures range from 50°F to 60°F in July and from 20°F to 40°F in January. Average annual precipitation varies from 80 to more than 200 inches. The area receives from 30 to 200 inches of snow in the lowlands and more than 400 inches in the high mountains.

The region's economy revolves around fishing and fish processing, timber, and tourism. Mining is taking on increasing importance with development of a world-class molybdenum mine near Ketchikan and a base metals mine on Admiralty Island.

Airplanes and boats provide the principal means of transportation. Only three communities in Southeast are connected to the road system: Haines via the Haines Highway to the Alaska Highway at Haines Junction; Skagway, via Klondike Highway 2 to the Alaska Highway; and Hyder, to the continental road system via the Cassiar Highway in British Columbia. Juneau, on the Southeast mainland, is the state capital; Sitka, on Baranof Island, was the capital of Russian America.

Southcentral

The Southcentral/gulf coast region curves 650 miles north and west of Southeast to Kodiak Island. About two-thirds of the state's residents live in the arc between the Gulf of Alaska on the south and the Alaska Range on the north, the region commonly called Southcentral. On the region's eastern boundary, only the Copper River valley breaches the mountainous barrier of the Chugach and Saint Elias mountains. On the west rise lofty peaks of the Aleutian Range. Within this mountainous perimeter course the Susitna and Matanuska rivers.

The irregular plain of the Copper River lowland has a colder climate than the other major valley areas, with January temperatures hitting -16°F compared with average lows of 0°F in the Susitna Valley. July temperatures average 50°F to 60°F in the region.

Precipitation in the region ranges from a scant 17 inches annually in drier areas to more than 76 inches a year at Thompson Pass in the coastal mountains.

Vegetation varies from the spruce-hemlock forests of Prince William Sound to mixed spruce and birch forests in the Susitna Valley to tundra in the highlands of the Copper River-Nelchina Basin.

Alaska agriculture historically has been most thoroughly developed in the Matanuska Valley. The state's dairy industry is centered there and at a new project at Point MacKenzie across Knik Arm from Anchorage.

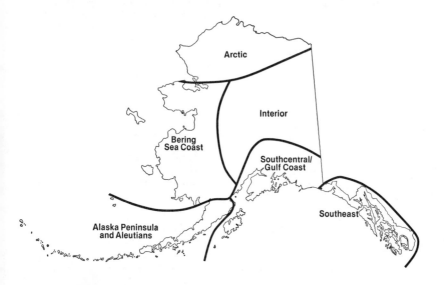

Vegetables thrive in the area, and Matanuska Valley is well known for its giant cabbages.

Hub of the state's commerce, transportation, and communications is Anchorage, on a narrow plain at the foot of the Chugach Mountains and bounded by Knik Arm and Turnagain Arm, offshoots of Cook Inlet. Population of this, Alaska's largest city, is closely tied to shifts in the state's economy.

Alaska's major banks and oil companies have their headquarters in Anchorage, as does The Alaska Railroad. The city's port handles much of the shipping in and out of the state. Anchorage International Airport handled over 4 million passengers and 3.4 million pounds of freight in 1982. Valdez to the east of Anchorage on Prince William Sound is the southern terminal of the trans-Alaska pipeline, which brings oil from Prudhoe Bay on the North Slope.

Interior

Great rivers have forged a broad lowland, known as the Interior, in the central part of the state between the Alaska Range on the south and the Brooks Range on the north. The Yukon River carves a swath across the entire state. In the Interior the Tanana, Porcupine, Koyukuk, and several other rivers join with the Yukon to create summer and winter highways. South of the Yukon, the Kuskokwim River rises in the hills of western Interior before beginning its meandering course across the Bering Sea coast region.

Winter temperatures in the Interior commonly drop to -50°F and -60°F. Ice fog sometimes hovers over Fairbanks and other low-lying communities when the temperature falls below zero. Controlled by the extremes of a continental climate, summers usually are warmer than in any other region; high temperatures are in the 80s and 90s. The climate is semiarid, with about 12 inches of precipitation recorded annually.

Immense forests of birch and aspen bring vibrant green and gold to the Interior's landscape. Spruce cover many of the slopes and cottonwood thrive near river lowlands. But in northern and western reaches of the Interior, the North American taiga gives way to tundra. In highlands above tree line and in marshy lowlands, grasses and shrubs replace trees.

Gold lured the first large influx of non-Natives to Alaska's Interior. Fairbanks, largest community in the region, was once a booming gold-mining camp. Now the city on the banks of Chena Slough is a transportation and supply center for eastern and northern Alaska. The main campus of the University of Alaska overlooks the city.

About 100 miles east of Fairbanks, farmers at the Delta project hope to build a foundation for agriculture based on barley. With barley for feed, Alaska farmers look for development of a beef cattle industry. At Healy, southwest of Fairbanks, the state's only operating coal mine produces coal used to generate electricity for the Interior. The rest of the Interior relies primarily on a subsistence economy, sometimes combined with a cash economy where fishing or seasonable government jobs are available.

Arctic

Beyond the Brooks Range, more than 80,000 square miles of tundra interlaced with meandering rivers and countless ponds spread out along the North Slope. In far northwestern Alaska, the Arctic curves south to take in Kotzebue and other villages of the Kobuk and Noatak river drainages.

Short, cool summers with temperatures usually between 30°F and 40°F allow the permanently frozen soil to thaw only a few inches. Winter temperatures range well below zero, but the Arctic Ocean moderates temperatures in coastal areas. Severe winds sweep along the coast and through mountain passes. The combination of cold and wind often drops the chill-factor temperature far below the actual temperature. Most areas receive less than 10 inches of precipitation a year, but the terrain is wet in summer because of little evaporation and frozen ground.

Traditionally the home of Inupiat Eskimos, the Arctic was inhabited by few non-Natives until oil was discovered at Prudhoe Bay in the 1960s. Today the region's economy is focused on Prudhoe Bay and neighboring Kuparuk oil fields. Petroleum-related jobs support most of the region's residents either directly or indirectly. Subsistence hunting and fishing fill any economic holes left by the oil industry.

Largest Inupiat Eskimo community in the world, Barrow is the center of commerce and government activity for the region. Airplanes, the major means of transportation, fan out from there to the region's far-flung villages. The 416-mile Dalton Highway, formerly the North Slope Haul Road, connects the Arctic with the Interior. The road is open to the public only to Disaster Creek near Dietrich Camp, about 200 miles north from the junction with the Elliott Highway in the Interior. Only permit holders can travel the road north of Disaster Creek.

Western

Western Alaska extends along the Bering Sea coast from the Arctic Circle south to where the Alaska Panhandle joins the mainland near Naknek on Bristol Bay. Home of Inupiat and Yup'ik Eskimos, the region centers around the immense Yukon-Kuskokwim river delta, the Seward Peninsula to the north, and Bristol Bay to the south.

Summer temperatures range from the 30s to low 60s. Winter readings generally range from just above zero to the low 30s. Wind chill lowers temperatures considerably. Total annual precipitation is about 20 inches with northern regions drier than those to the south.

Much of the region is covered with tundra, although a band of forests covers the hills on the eastern end of the Seward Peninsula and Norton Sound. In the south near Bristol Bay the tundra once again gives way to forests. In between, the marshy flatland of the great Yukon-Kuskokwim delta spreads out for more than 200 miles.

Gold first attracted non-Natives to the hills and creeks of the Seward Peninsula. To the south, only a few biologists studying wildlife and anthropologists entered the world of the Yup'ik Eskimos of the delta. At the extreme south, fish, including the world's largest sockeye salmon run, drew fishermen to the riches of Bristol Bay.

The villages of western Alaska are linked by air and water, dog sled and snow machine. Commerce on the delta radiates out from Bethel, largest community in western Alaska. To the north, Nome dominates commerce on the Seward Peninsula, while several fishing communities take their livelihood from the riches of Bristol Bay.

Southwestern

Southwestern Alaska includes the Alaska Peninsula and Aleutian Islands. From Naknek Lake, the peninsula curves southwest about 500 miles to the first of the Aleutian Islands; the Aleutians continue south and west more than 1,000 miles. Primarily a mountainous region with about 50 volcanic peaks, only on the Bering Sea side of the peninsula does the terrain flatten out.

The Aleutian climate is cool, with summer temperatures up to the 50s and winter readings in the 20s and lower. Winds are almost constant and fog is common. Precipitation ranges from 21 to more than 80 inches annually. The peninsula's climate is somewhat warmer in summer and cooler in winter.

More than 200 islands, roughly 5,500 square miles in area, form the narrow arc of the Aleutians, which separate the North Pacific from the Bering Sea. Nearly the entire chain is in the Alaska Maritime National Wildlife Refuge. Unimak Island, closest to the Alaska Peninsula mainland, is 1,000 miles from Attu, the most distant island. Five major island groups make up the Aleutians, all of which are treeless except for a few scattered stands that have been transplanted on the islands.

Aleuts, original inhabitants of the chain, still live at Atka, Atka Island; Nikolski, Umnak Island; Unalaska, Unalaska Island; Akutan, Akutan Island; and False Pass, Unimak Island.

The quest for furs first drew Russians to the islands and peninsula in the 1700s. The traders conquered the Aleuts and forced them to hunt marine mammals. After the United States purchased Alaska, fur traders switched their efforts to fox farming. Many foxes were turned loose on the islands, where they flourished and destroyed native wildlife. With collapse of the fur market in the 1920s and 1930s, the islands were left to themselves. This relative isolation was broken during World War II when Japanese military forces bombed Dutch Harbor and landed on Attu and Kiska islands. The United States military retook the islands, but after the war the government resettled Aleuts living in the western Aleutians to villages in the eastern Aleutians that are closer to the mainland and thus easier to defned.

Today fishing provides the main economic base for the islands and the peninsula. Many Aleuts go to Bristol Bay to fish commercially in summer.

Religion

Nearly every major religion practiced in American society is found in Alaska. Following is a list of addresses for some of the major ones:

Alaska Moravian Church, Bethel 99559
Assemblies of God, 1048 West International Airport Road, Anchorage 99502
Baha'i Faith, Star Route 500-E, Anchorage 99507
Chancery Orthodox Diocese of Alaska, P.O. Box 55, Kodiak 99615
Christian Science Church, 1347 L Street, Anchorage 99501
Church of God, 1348 Bennington Drive, Anchorage 99504
Church of Jesus Christ of Latter Day Saints, 6871 Old Seward Highway, Anchorage 99502
Congregation Beth Sholom, 1000 West 20th Avenue, Anchorage 99503
Episcopal Diocese of Alaska, 1205 Denali Way, Fairbanks 99701
Presbyterian Churches United, 501 West Northern Lights Boulevard, Anchorage 99503
Roman Catholic Archdiocese of Anchorage, Box 2239, Anchorage 99510
The Salvation Army, P.O. Box 1459, Anchorage 99510
Southern Baptist Church, Star Route A, Box 1791, Anchorage 99507
United Methodist Church, 2300 Oak Drive, Anchorage 99508
Universal Life Church, Inc., P.O. Box 4-2669, Anchorage 99509

Reptiles

For all practical purposes, reptiles are not found in Alaska outside of captivity. The northern limits of North American reptilian species may be the latitude at which their embryos fail to develop during the summer. Three sightings of a species of garter snake, *Thamnophis sirtalis*, have been reported on the banks of the Taku River and Stikine River.

Related reading: *Amphibians & Reptiles in Alaska, the Yukon & Northwest Territories,* by Robert Parker Hodge. Life histories, color photos, charts and maps. 89 pages, $4.95. See page 208.

Rivers

There are more than 3,000 rivers in Alaska. The major navigable Alaska inland waterways are as follows:

Chilkat — Navigable by shallow-draft vessels to village of Klukwan, 25 miles above mouth.

Kobuk — Controlling channel depth is about 5 feet through Hotham Inlet, 3 feet to Ambler, and 2 feet to Kobuk Village, about 210 river miles.

Koyukuk — Navigable to Allakaket by vessels drawing up to 3 feet during normally high river flow and to Bettles during occasional higher flows.

Kuskokwim — Navigable (June 1-September 30) by 18-foot draft ocean-going vessels from mouth upriver 65 miles to Bethel. Shallow-draft (4-foot) vessels can ascend river to mile 465. McGrath is at mile 400.

Kvichak — The river is navigable for vessels of 10-foot draft to Alaganak River, 22 miles above the mouth of Kvichak River. Remainder of this river (28 miles) navigable by craft drawing 2 to 4 feet, depending on stage of river. Drains Lake Iliamna, which is navigable an additional 70 miles.

Naknek — Navigable for vessels of 12-foot draft for 12 miles with adequate tide. Vessels with 3-foot draft can continue an additional 7.5 miles.

Noatak — Navigable (late May-mid-June) for shallow-draft barges to a point about 18 miles below Noatak village. Shallow-draft vessels can continue on to Noatak.

Nushagak — Navigable (June 1-August 31) by small vessels of 2½-foot draft to Nunachuak about 100 miles above the mouth. Shallow-draft, ocean-going vessels can navigate to mouth of Wood River at mile 84.

Porcupine — Navigable to Old Crow, Yukon Territory, by vessels drawing 3 feet during spring runoff and fall rain floods.

Stikine — Navigable (May 1-October 15) from mouth 165 miles to Telegraph Creek, British Columbia, by shallow-draft, flat-bottom river boats.

Susitna — Navigable by sternwheelers and shallow-draft, flat-bottom river boats to confluence of Talkeetna River, 75 miles upstream, but cannot cross bars at mouth of river. Not navigable by ocean-going vessels.

Tanana — Navigable by shallow-draft (4-foot), flat-bottom vessels and barges from the mouth to Nenana and by smaller river craft to the Chena River 201 miles above the mouth. Craft of 4-foot draft can navigate to Chena River on high water to University Avenue Bridge in Fairbanks.

Yukon — Navigable (June 1-September 30) by shallow-draft, flat-bottom river boats from the mouth to near the head of Lake Bennett. It cannot be entered or navigated by ocean-going vessels. Controlling depths are 7 feet to Stevens Village and 3 to 5 feet thereon to Fort Yukon.

Following are the 10 longest rivers in Alaska:

Map Key	Miles	Map Key	Miles
1 Yukon*	1,875	6 Innoko	463
2 Porcupine**	555	7 Colville	428
3 Koyukuk	554	8 Noatak	396
4 Kuskokwim	540	9 Kobuk	347
5 Tanana	531	10 Birch Creek	314

*The Yukon flows about 1,400 miles in Alaska; the remainder is in Canada. It ranks fourth in North America in length, fifth in drainage area (327,600 square miles).
**About two-thirds of the Porcupine's length is in Canada.

The Longest Rivers
(Numbers refer to preceding list)

Roadhouses

An important part of Alaska history, roadhouses were modest quarters that offered bed and board to travelers along early-day Alaska trails. The majority provided accommodations for sled dog teams, as most travel occurred in winter. By 1920, there were roadhouses along every major transportation route in Alaska. Several roadhouses are included in the National Register of Historic Places (see *National Historic Places*). Some of these historic roadhouses house modern businesses.

School Districts

Alaska's 53 public school districts serve approximately 93,000 kindergarten through 12th grade students. There are two types of school districts: city and borough school districts and Regional Educational Attendance Areas. The 32 city and borough school districts are located in municipalities, each contributing funds for the operation of their local schools. The 21 REAAs are located in the unorganized borough, and as such have no local government to contribute funds to their schools. The REAAs are almost solely dependent upon state funds for school support. City and borough school districts are supported by about 75 percent state, 20 percent local and 5 percent federal funding.

Following are the names and addresses of Alaska's 53 public school districts:

Adak Region Schools
Adak Naval Station
Box 34
FPO Seattle 98791
(IntraAK)

Alaska Gateway Schools
Box 226
Tok 99780

Aleutian Region School District
Technical Center
640 West 36th Avenue
Anchorage 99503

Anchorage Schools
4600 DeBarr Road
Pouch 6-614
Anchorage 99502

Annette Island Schools
Box 7
Metlakatla 99926

Bering Strait Schools
Box 225
Unalakleet 99684

Bristol Bay Borough Schools
Box 169
Naknek 99633

Chatham Schools
Box 109
Angoon 99820

Chugach Schools
Box 638
Whittier 99639

Copper River Schools
Box 103
Glennallen 99588

Cordova City Schools
Box 140
Cordova 99574

Craig City Schools
Box 71
Craig 99921

Delta/Greely Schools
Box 527
Delta Junction 99737

Dillingham City Schools
Box 202
Dillingham 99576

Fairbanks N. Star Borough Schools
Box 1250
Fairbanks 99701

Galena City Schools
Box 299
Galena 99741

Haines Borough Schools
Box 636
Haines 99827

Hoonah City Schools
Box 157
Hoonah 99829

Hydaburg City Schools
Box 109
Hydaburg 99922

Iditarod Area Schools
Box 105
McGrath 99627

Juneau Borough Schools
Box 808
Douglas 99824

Kake City Schools
Box 450
Kake 99830

Kenai Peninsula Borough Schools
Box 1200
Soldotna 99669

Ketchikan Gateway Borough Schools
Pouch Z
Ketchikan 99901

King Cove City Schools
Box 6
King Cove 99612

Klawock City Schools
Box 9
Klawock 99925

Kodiak Island Borough Schools
Box 886
Kodiak 99615

Kuspuk Schools
Box 108
Aniak 99557

173

Lake & Peninsula
Schools
Box 498
King Salmon 99613

Lower Kuskokwim
Schools
Box 305
Bethel 99559

Lower Yukon Schools
Box 200
Mountain Village
99632

Mat-Su Borough
Schools
Box AB
Palmer 99645

Nenana City Schools
Box 10
Nenana 99760

Nome City Schools
Box 131
Nome 99762

North Slope Borough
Schools
Box 169
Barrow 99723

Northwest Arctic
Schools
Box 51
Kotzebue 99752

Pelican City Schools
Box 603
Pelican 99832

Petersburg City
Schools
Box 289
Petersburg 99833

Pribilof Schools
Saint Paul Island
99660

Railbelt School
District
Drawer 129
Healy 99743

Saint Marys
Public Schools
Box 71
Saint Marys
99658

Sand Point School
District
Box 158
Sand Point 99661

Sitka Borough
Schools
Box 179
Sitka 99835

Skagway City
Schools
Box 497
Skagway 99840

Southeast Island
Schools
Box 8340
Ketchikan 99901

Southwest Region
Schools
Box 196
Dillingham 99576

Tanana City
Schools
Box 89
Tanana 99777

Unalaska City
Schools
Pouch 260
Unalaska 99685

Valdez City Schools
Box 398
Valdez 99686

Wrangell City
Schools
Box 651
Wrangell 99929

Yakutat City Schools
Box 427
Yakutat 99689

Yukon Flat Schools
Box 359
Fort Yukon 99740

Yukon/Koyukuk
Schools
Box 309
Nenana 99760

Shipping

With only a few major highways, and waterways that are navigable seasonally at best, Alaska's shipping situation is truly unique unto itself. Throughout much of the state, cargo-carrying planes provide the only year-round supply lines for bush cities and villages. However, numerous truck, air and moving van lines serve Alaska from the Lower 49 and within the state. Truck and van lines offer an all-highway service through Canada and, the method more often used, service via ship or barge from Puget Sound.

The following water carriers provide interstate ship and barge line service from Seattle to Alaska:

Alaska Marine Lines (formerly Southeast Alaska Barge Lines), 7100 Second Avenue S.W., Seattle, Washington 98106 — provides scheduled barge service from Seattle to Juneau and seasonal service to central and western Alaska, the Aleutian Islands and the North Slope.

Boyer Alaska Barge Lines, Inc., 7318 Fourth Avenue South, Seattle, Washington 98108 — provides weekly barge service betweeen Seattle and the southeastern Alaska ports of Ketchikan, Wrangell and Petersburg.

Bureau of Indian Affairs, 4735 East Marginal Way South, Seattle, Washington 98134 — operates the diesel ship *North Star III,* delivering food and supplies to remote Alaska villages during the ice-free summer months.

Coastal Alaska Lines, Inc., 1031 West Ewing Street, Seattle, Washington 98119 — provides direct barge service from Seattle to Anchorage.

Crowley Maritime Corporation, Fourth & Battery Building, Seattle, Washington 98111 — operating *Alaska Hydro-Train,* a barge line moving railcars between Seattle and Whittier, Alaska; *Pacific Alaska Lines,* scheduled barge service to Anchorage from Seattle and Portland; and *Pacific Alaska Lines — West,* a seasonal barge line serving western Alaska.

Foss Alaska Lines, Inc., Terminal 115, P.O. Box 80587, Seattle, Washington 98108 — operates barges between Seattle, southeastern Alaska and the Gulf of Alaska; provides seasonal service to western Alaska.

Northland Services, Inc., 6425 N.E. 175th Street, Seattle, Washington 98155 — provides direct year-round barge service to southcentral Alaska and direct seasonal service to the Aleutian Chain, Bristol Bay, Yukon and Kuskokwim rivers, Norton Sound and Kotzebue Sound.

Pacific Western Lines, Inc., 5225 East Marginal Way South, Seattle, Washington 98134 — provides direct barge service from Seattle to Anchorage.

Samson Tug and Barge, Inc., 337 N.W. 40th Street, Seattle, Washington 98107 — provides barge service to Sitka, Wrangell, various Southeast logging ports, Valdez, Cordova, and Kodiak Island.

Sea-Land Service, Inc., 2805 26th Avenue S.W., Seattle, Washington 98114 — provides direct container ship service between Seattle and Anchorage.

Totem Ocean Trailer Express, Inc., 130 Sitcum Waterway, Alaska Terminal, Tacoma, Washington 98421 — provides direct trailership service between Tacoma and Anchorage.

Except for southeastern Alaska, intra-Alaska water service is limited to the spring and summer months when the rivers and bays are free of ice. A few carriers providing intra-Alaska water service are:

Black Navigation Company, Inc., P.O. Box 238, Nenana 99760; Saint Michael 99695; 9750 Third Avenue N.E., Suite 403, Seattle, Washington 98115 — offers barge service during ice-free months to villages along the lower Yukon River and Norton Sound.

Kuskokwim Transportation Company, P.O. Box 285, Bethel 99559 — provides barge service during ice-free months from Bethel to villages along the Kuskokwim River and along the coast from Kuskokwim Bay to Hooper Bay.

Smith Lighterage Company, P.O. Box 106, Dillingham 99576 — provides barge service during ice-free months from Dillingham to points along the Nushagak River and Manokotak.

Valentine Transportation Company, P.O. Box 5600, Ketchikan 99901 — provides weekly freight-boat service from Ketchikan to outlying villages in southeastern Alaska.

Yutana Barge Lines, Inc., P.O. Box 238, Nenana 99760; Saint Michael 99695; 9750 Third Avenue N.E., Suite 403, Seattle, Washington 98115 — provides barge service during ice-free months from Nenana to points along the Yukon River in northcentral Alaska to Marshall on the Yukon River Delta.

Sitka Slippers

Heavy-duty rubber boots, also known as Wrangell sneakers and Petersburg sneakers, worn by residents of rainy southeastern Alaska.

Skiing

Both cross-country and downhill skiing are popular forms of outdoor recreation in Alaska from November through May. There are developed ski facilities in several Alaska communities, back-country powder skiing is available by charter helicopter or ski-equipped aircraft, and cross-country skiing opportunities are virtually limitless throughout the state. It is also possible to ski during the summer months by chartering a plane to reach glacier skiing spots.

Anchorage

There are two major downhill ski areas in the Anchorage area: Alyeska Resort and Arctic Valley. Alyeska Resort, 40 miles southeast of Anchorage, has all the amenities expected of a large ski area. Alyeska, the state's largest ski resort, offers four chairlifts with runs up to a mile long, and chair no. 3 is equipped for night skiing. A fifth chairlift is reserved for racer training. The resort also has two rope tows and a Poma lift. Alyeska is open year-round, with skiing from November through April. Hours of operation depend on daylight, except for chair no. 3.

Arctic Valley, a few miles from Anchorage, is owned and operated by the Anchorage Ski Club, a nonprofit corporation. Arctic Valley is open on winter weekends and holidays. Facilities include two double chairlifts, a T-bar/Poma lift combination, and three rope tows on beginner slopes.

Several smaller alpine slopes are maintained by the municipality of Anchorage, including: Centennial Park, Russian Jack Springs Park, with rope tows; and a new area at Hilltop, south of town, featuring the closest chairlift in the Anchorage area.

Popular cross-country ski trails in the Anchorage area include trails in Anchorage city parks maintained by the municipality of Anchorage: Russian Jack Springs, with nearly 5 miles of trails, 3 miles lighted; Kincaid Park, which was the site of the first World Cup and U.S. National men's and women's championship races in Alaska and the U.S. in March 1983, has about 15 miles of trails with 2 miles lighted; Centennial Park with 3 miles of trails and about ½ mile lighted; Hillside Park with 5 miles of trails, 1½ miles lighted; and Chester Creek Greenbelt with 10 kilometers of trails, none lighted; ski trails in Chugach State Park; and ski trails in the Turnagain Pass area in Chugach National Forest, about 57 miles south of Anchorage.

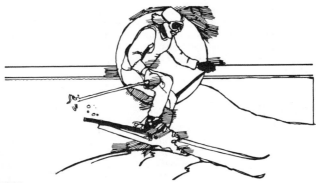

Palmer

Hatcher Pass, site of the Independence Mine State Park, north of Palmer, is an excellent cross-country ski area with several maintained trails. The lodge has a coffee shop and warm-up area. The ski area is open from October through May.

Fairbanks

Fairbanks has a few small downhill ski areas, but none as large as Alyeska resort. Cleary Summit and Skiland, about 20 miles from town on the Steese Highway, both privately owned and operated, have rope tows and a chairlift at Cleary Summit; Ski Boot Hill at 4.2 mile Farmer's Loop Road has a rope tow; Birch Hill, located on Fort Wainwright, is mainly for military use; the University of Alaska has a small slope and rope tow; and Chena Hot Springs Resort at mile 57 on the Chena Hot Springs Road has a small alpine ski area which uses a tractor to transport skiers to the top of the hill.

Popular cross-country ski trails in the Fairbanks area include: Birch Hill recreation area, about 3 miles north of town on the Steese Expressway to a well-marked turnoff, then 2 miles in; the University of Alaska, Fairbanks, has 26 miles of trails, which lead out to Ester Dome; Creamers Field trail is near downtown; Salcha cross-country ski area, bout 40 miles south of town on the Richardson Highway, has a fairly large trail system which is also used for ski races; Two Rivers trail area is near the elementary school at mile 10 Chena Hot Springs Road; and Chena Hot Springs Resort has cross-country ski trails available for both novice and more experienced skiers.

Juneau

Eaglecrest Ski Area on Douglas Island, 12 miles from Juneau, has a 4,800-foot-long chairlift, a Platter Pull lift, a 3,000-foot-long chairlift, and a day lodge. Cross-country ski trails are also available. Open from November to May. A few smaller alpine ski areas are located at Cordova, Valdez, Ketchikan, and Homer. All have rope tows.

Several cross-country ski races are held each year, with the largest being the Alaska Nordic Ski Cup Series, which determines contestants for the Arctic Winter Games and Junior Olympic competitions. The series of five races is held in Anchorage, Homer, Salcha, and Fairbanks.

Several alpine ski races are held each year to assist competition skiers in their quest to earn points for the national ski team. The largest of these events are held at Alyeska Resort and Eaglecrest. The ARCO Alaska Division Championships, the 25th World Airlines Ski Championship (a new event for Alaska), and the Pepsi Alyeska Spring Carnival are scheduled at Alyeska in 1984, and Eaglecrest will host the Southeast Championship.

Several Alaskans are scheduled to participate in ski trials in the upcoming Olympic games: Judy Rabinowitz-Endestad and her husband, Auden Endestad, of Fairbanks; and Jim Galanes and Lynn Spencer-Galanes of Anchorage.

Skookum

Native word meaning strong or serviceable. It originated with the Chehalis Indians of western Washington and was incorporated into the Chinook jargon, a trade language dating from the early 1800s. A skookum chuck is a narrow passage between a saltwater lagoon and the open sea. In many areas of Alaska, because of extreme tides, skookum chucks may resemble fast-flowing river rapids during changes of the tide.

Soapstone

This soft, easily worked stone is often carved into art objects by Alaskans. Most of the stone, however, is imported. Alaska soapstone is mined in the Matanuska Valley by blasting, which gives the stone a tendency to fracture when being worked, and, therefore, it is not as desirable as imported soapstone.

Sourdough

This versatile, yeasty mixture was carried by many early-day pioneers and used to make bread and hot cakes. Sourdough cookery remains popular in Alaska today. Because the sourdough supply is replenished after each use, it can remain active and fresh indefinitely. A popular claim of sourdough cooks is that their batches trace back to pioneers at the turn of the century. The name also came to be applied to any Alaska or Yukon old-timer.

Related reading: *Alaska Sourdough: The Real Stuff by a Real Alaskan,* by Ruth Allman. Sourdough cookery. 190 pages, $6.95. *Cooking Alaskan,* by the editors of *ALASKA®* magazine. Hundreds of time-tested recipes including a section on sourdough. 500 pages, $14.95. See pages 207-10.

Speed Limits

The basic speed law in Alaska states the speed limit is "no speed more than is prudent and reasonable."

The maximum speeds are 15 miles per hour in an alley, 20 miles per hour in a business district or school zone, 25 miles per hour in a residential area, and 55 miles per hour on any other roadway.

Locally, municipalities and the state may, and often do, reduce or alter maximums as long as no maximum exceeds 55 miles per hour.

Squaw Candy

Salmon dried or smoked for a long time until it's very chewy. It's a staple food in winter for rural Alaskans and their dogs.

State Park System

The Alaska state park system began in July 1959 with the transfer of federally-managed campgrounds and recreation sites from the Bureau of Land Management to the new state of Alaska. These sites were managed by the state Division of Lands until 1970; under the Forestry, Parks and Recreation Section until 1966; then under the Parks and Recreation Section. The Division of Parks was created in October 1970.

The Alaska state park system consists of approximately 100 individual units divided into 7 park management districts. There are 56 recreation sites, 11 recreation areas, 4 historic parks, 3 historic sites, 3 state trails, 5 state parks (Chugach, Denali, Chilkat, Kachemak Bay, and Wood-Tikchik), and 1 state preserve, the 49,000-acre Alaska Chilkat Bald Eagle Preserve. In addition there are the following state-owned park facilities under non-state management: Chilkoot Trail, 13 acres, Skagway, managed by the National Park Service; Totem Square, 0.5 acre, Sitka, managed by the Pioneers' Home; and Valdez Glacier Wayside, 226 acres, Valdez, managed by the city of Valdez.

Campsites are available on a first-come, first-served basis. In addition to camping and picnicking, many units offer hiking trails and boat launching ramps; most developed campgrounds have picnic tables and toilets. General information on the state park system is available from the Division of Parks, 619 Warehouse Avenue, Suite 210, Anchorage 99501.

The state park units are listed by park management district below and on the following pages. Designations for units of the Alaska state park system are abbreviated as follows: SP-State Park, SHP-State Historic Park, SHS-State Historic Site, SRA-State Recreation Area, SRS-State Recreation Site, ST-State Trail, MPS-Marine Park Site. Park units designated "undeveloped" may have camping, hiking trails, and limited facilities. Parks which indicate no developed campsites or picnic sites may offer fishing or river access, hiking and other activities. Numbers in the list refer to the map on pages 182-83. Marine park sites were acquired by the state park system shortly before press time and are not keyed to the map.

Map Key	Acreage	Camp- sites	Picnic Sites	Nearest Town
Southeast District Pouch M Juneau 99811				
1 Baranof Hill SHS	1			Sitka
Chilkat Islands MPS	503			Haines

Map Key		Acreage	Camp-sites	Picnic Sites	Nearest Town
2	Chilkat SP	6,045	32	15	Haines
3	Chilkoot Lake SRS	80	32		Haines
4	Halibut Point SRS	40		9	Sitka
5	Juneau ST	15			Juneau
6	Mosquito Lake SRS	5	13		Haines
7	Old Sitka SHS	51			Sitka
	Oliver Inlet MPS	365			Juneau
	Pioneer Park MPS	3.4		6	Sitka
8	Portage Cove SRS	7	9	3	Haines
9	Refuge Cove SRS	13		14	Ketchikan
	Saint James Bay MPS	3,683			Juneau
	Settler's Cove MPS	275	9	6	Ketchikan
	Shelter Island MPS	889		8	Juneau
	Sullivan Island MPS	639			Haines
10	Totem Bight SHP	11			Ketchikan

Copper Basin District
P.O. Box 286
Glennallen 99588

Map Key		Acreage	Camp-sites	Picnic Sites	Nearest Town
	Bettles Bay MPS	555			Whittier
11	Blueberry Lake SRS	192	9	10	Valdez
12	Dry Creek SRS	320	58	4	Glennallen
	Horseshoe Bay MPS	286			Whittier
13	Lake Louise SRA	90	25	4	Glennallen
14	Little Nelchina SRS	22	9		Glennallen
15	Little Tonsina SRS	102	8		Copper Center
16	Porcupine Creek SRS	240	12		Tok
	Sawmill Bay MPS	1,430			Valdez
	Shoup Bay	2,925			Valdez
	South Esther Island	2,285			Whittier
17	Squirrel Creek SRS	325	14		Copper Center
	Surprise Cove	1,425			Whittier
18	Tolsona Creek SRS	600	11		Glennallen
19	Worthington Glacier SRS	113		3	Valdez
	Zeigler Cove	305			Whittier

Mat-Su District
P.O. Box 182
Palmer 99645

Map Key		Acreage	Camp-sites	Picnic Sites	Nearest Town
20	Big Lake (East) SRS	19	15	2	Wasilla
21	Big Lake (South) SRS	16	13	6	Wasilla
22	Bonnie Lake SRS	129	8		Palmer
23	Denali SP	421,120			Cantwell

Map Key		Acreage	Camp-sites	Picnic Sites	Nearest Town
	Byers Lake		61	15	Cantwell
	Troublesome Creek				Cantwell
24	Finger Lake SRS	47	41		Palmer
25	Iditarod ST				
26	Independence Mine SHP	271			Palmer
27	Kepler Bradley SRA	111	undeveloped		Palmer
28	King Mountain SRS	20	22	2	Palmer
29	Long Lake SRS	480	8		Palmer
30	Matanuska Glacier SRS	229	12	5	Palmer
31	Moose Creek SRS	40	14	1	Palmer
32	Nancy Lake SRA	22,685			Willow
	South Rolly Lake		106	20	Willow
33	Nancy Lake SRS	35	30	30	Willow
34	Rocky Lake SRS	48	10		Wasilla
35	Willow Creek SRS	240	17		Willow

Chugach District
2601 Commercial Drive
Anchorage 99501

Map Key		Acreage	Camp-sites	Picnic Sites	Nearest Town
36	California Creek ST	58	undeveloped		Girdwood
37	Chugach SP	495,204			Anchorage
	Bird Creek		25	14	Anchorage
	Eagle River		36	12	Eagle River
	Eklutna Lake		17	4	Eagle River
	Upper Huffman			8	Anchorage
	McHugh Creek			30	Anchorage
38	Mirror Lake SRS	90		30	Peters Creek
39	Peters Creek SRS	52	closed		Peters Creek
40	Thunderbird Falls ST	3			Eagle River

Interior District
4420 Airport Way
Fairbanks 99701

Map Key		Acreage	Camp-sites	Picnic Sites	Nearest Town
41	Chatanika River (lower) SRS	570	undeveloped		Fairbanks
42	Chatanika River (upper) SRS	73	15		Fairbanks
43	Chena River SRA	254,080	unlimited		Fairbanks
44	Chena River SRS	27		101	Fairbanks
45	Clearwater SRS	27	12		Delta Junction
46	Deadman Lake SRS	20	16		Tok
47	Donnelly Creek SRS	42	12		Delta Junction
48	Eagle Trail SRS	640	40	4	Tok
49	Gardiner Creek SRS	10	6		Tok

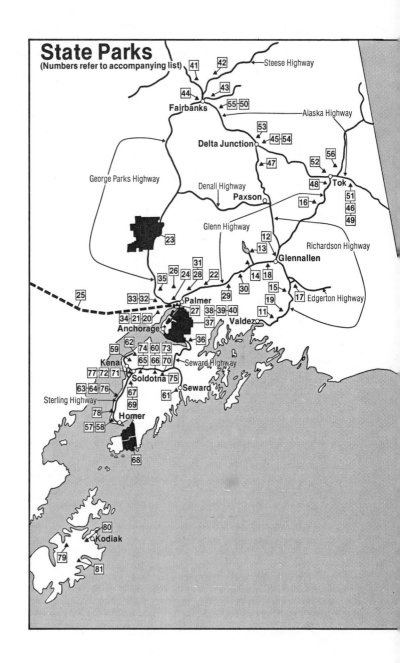

State Parks
(Numbers refer to accompanying list)

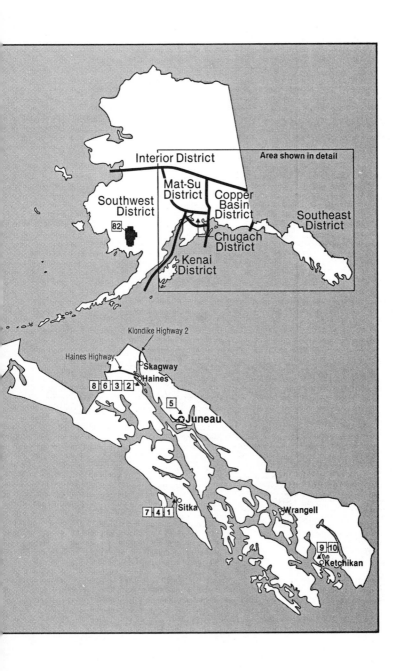

Interior District

Area shown in detail

Mat-Su District

Southwest District

Copper Basin District

Chugach District

Southeast District

82

Kenai District

Klondike Highway 2

Haines Highway

Skagway

Haines

8 6 3 2

5

Juneau

7 4 1 Sitka

Wrangell

9 10

Ketchikan

Map Key		Acreage	Camp-sites	Picnic Sites	Nearest Town
50	Harding Lake SRA	169	89	52	North Pole
51	Lakeview SRS	25	8		Tok
52	Moon Lake SRS	22	15		Tok
53	Quartz Lake SRS	380	13		Delta Junction
54	Rika's Landing SHS	10	undeveloped		Delta Junction
55	Salcha River SRS	61		20	North Pole
56	Tok River SRS	4	10		Tok

Kenai District
Box 1247
Soldotna 99669

Map Key		Acreage	Camp-sites	Picnic Sites	Nearest Town
57	Anchor River SRS	53	10		Homer
58	Anchor River SRA	208	409		Anchor Point
59	Bernice Lake SRS	152	17		Kenai
60	Bings Landing SRS	92	undeveloped		Sterling
61	Caines Head SRA	5,961	undeveloped		Seward
62	Captain Cook SRA	3,257			Kenai
	Bishop Creek		12		Kenai
	Discovery		57	30	Kenai
	Stormy Lake		10	40	Kenai
	Swanson River Canoe Landing				Kenai
63	Clam Gulch SRA	122	343	20	Soldotna
64	Deep Creek SRA	130	548	10	Ninilchik
65	Funny River SRS	292	3		Soldotna
66	Izaak Walton SRS	8	76		Soldotna
67	Johnson Lake SRA	325	46	24	Soldotna
68	Kachemak Bay SP	400,290	undeveloped		Homer
69	Kasilof River SRS	50	42	5	Kasilof
70	Kenai Keys SRA	193	undeveloped		Soldotna
71	Kenai River Island SRS	60	undeveloped		Soldotna
72	Kenai River (lower) SRS	20	undeveloped		Soldotna
73	Kenai River (upper) SRS	193	undeveloped		Sterling
74	Morgans Landing SRA	262		3	Sterling
75	Nilnunga SHP	42	undeveloped		Soldotna
76	Ninilchik SRA	97		137	Ninilchik
77	Slikok Creek SRS ·	40	undeveloped		Soldotna
78	Stariski SRS	30	13		Anchor Point

Southwest District
619 Warehouse Avenue
Suite 210
Anchorage 99501

Map Key		Acreage	Camp-sites	Picnic Sites	Nearest Town
79	Buskin River SRS	40	18		Kodiak
80	Fort Abercrombie SHP	183	14	15	Kodiak
81	Pasagshak River SRS	13			Kodiak
82	Wood-Tikchik SP	1,428,320	undeveloped		Dillingham

State Symbols

Flag

Alaska's state flag was designed in 1926 by Benny Benson, who entered his design in a territorial flag contest for students in grades 7 through 12. The Alaska legislature adopted his design as the official flag of the territory of Alaska on May 2, 1927. The flag consists of eight gold stars on a field of blue — the Big Dipper and the North Star. In Benson's words: "The blue field is for the Alaska sky and the forget-me-not, an Alaska flower. The North Star is for the future state of Alaska, the most northerly of the Union. The dipper is for the Great Bear — symbolizing strength."

Benny Benson was born October 12, 1913, at Chignik, Alaska. His mother was of Aleut-Russian descent and his father was a Swedish fisherman who came to the Alaska Territory in 1904. Benson's mother died of pneumonia when Benny was four, and he entered the Jesse Lee Memorial Home (then located at Unalaska).

Benny, then a seventh grade student at the Jesse Lee Home, was one of 142 students whose designs were selected for the final judging by a committee chosen by the Alaska Department of the American Legion.

Benny was awarded a $1,000 scholarship and was presented an engraved watch for winning the contest. He used the scholarship to attend the Hemphill Engineering School in Seattle in 1937. In 1963, the Alaska legislature awarded Benson an additional $2,500 as a way "of paying a small tribute to a fellow Alaskan." In November of the same year, Benson presented his award watch to the Alaska State Museum.

Benny's prophetic words, "The North Star is for the future state of Alaska, the most northerly of the Union," were realized on January 3, 1959, when Alaska was proclaimed the 49th state of the Union. The drafters of the Constitution for Alaska stipulated that the flag of the territory would be the official flag of the state of Alaska, and when the flag was first flown over the capital city on July 4, 1959, Benny proudly led the parade that preceded the ceremony, carrying the flag of "eight stars on a field of blue," which he had designed 33 years before.

Benson settled in Kodiak in 1949 where he worked as a mechanic for Kodiak Airways. He was active in a movement to integrate the Elks, a white-only national organization which now has a number of Native members in Alaska. Benson had a leg amputated in 1969 and his health declined; he died of a heart attack on July 2, 1972, in Kodiak.

In 1981, the Alaska legislature appropriated $25,000 for a monument to Benson, which is being erected at the intersection of Benson Boulevard and Minnesota Drive in Anchorage. The bowl-shaped aluminum sculpture (six feet by four feet, on a nine-foot concrete base) by artist Gerald Conoway of Anchorage features spokes representing the stars of the Alaska flag. A plaque on the base will have Benson's profile and appropriate text.

There is a also memorial to Benny Benson on the Seward Highway just outside Seward.

Seal

The first governor of Alaska designed a seal for the then District of Alaska in 1884. In 1910, Gov. Walter E. Clark redesigned the original seal, which became a symbol for the new territory of Alaska in 1912. The constitution of Alaska adopted the territorial seal as the Seal for the State of Alaska in 1959.

Represented in the state seal are icebergs, northern lights, and Native people, along with symbols for mining, agriculture, fisheries, fur seal rookeries, and a railroad.

Song

Alaska's Flag

Eight stars of gold on a field of blue —
Alaska's flag. May it mean to you
The blue of the sea, the evening sky,
The mountain lakes, and the flow'rs nearby;
The gold of the early sourdough's dreams,
The precious gold of the hills and streams;
The brilliant stars in the northern sky,
The "Bear" — the "Dipper" — and,
shining high,
The great North Star with its steady light,
Over land and sea a beacon bright.
Alaska's flag — to Alaskans dear,
The simple flag of a last frontier.

The song was written by Marie Drake as a poem that first appeared on the cover of the October 1935 *School Bulletin,* a territorial Department of

Education publication which she edited while assistant commissioner of education.

The music was written by Mrs. Elinor Dusenbury, whose husband, Col. Ralph Wayne Dusenbury, was commander of Chilkoot Barracks at Haines from 1933 to 1936. Mrs. Dusenbury wrote the music several years after leaving Alaska because, she was later quoted as saying, "I got so homesick for Alaska I couldn't stand it." She died October 17, 1980, in Carlsbad, California.

Other Symbols

Bird: Willow ptarmigan, *Lagopus lagopus,* a small arctic grouse that lives among willows and on open tundra and muskeg. Its plumage changes from brown in summer to white in winter, the feathers covering the entire lower leg and foot. Common from southwestern Alaska into the Arctic.

Fish: King salmon, *Oncorhynchus tshawytscha,* an important part of the Native subsistence fisheries and a significant species to the state's commercial salmon fishery. This anadromous fish ranges from beyond the southern extremes of Alaska to as far north as Point Hope.

Gem: Jade (see *Jade*)

Mineral: Gold (see *Gold*)

Motto: North to the Future, adopted in 1967

Sport: Dog mushing (see *Dog Mushing*)

Tree: Sitka spruce, *Picea sitchensis,* the largest and one of the most valuable trees in Alaska. Sitka spruce grows to 160 feet in height and 3 to 5 feet in diameter. Its long, dark green needles surround twigs that bear cones. It is found throughout Southeast and Kenai Peninsula, along the gulf coast, and the west coast of Cook Inlet.

Subsistence

Alaska is unique among states in that it has established the subsistence use of fish and game as the highest priority consumptive use of the resource. Alaska's legislature passed a subsistence priority law in

1978. In addition, Congress passed a priority subsistence law in 1980 for federal lands in Alaska.

Still a controversial issue and a difficult concept to define, subsistence is defined as "the customary and traditional uses in Alaska of wild, renewable resources for direct personal or family consumption as food, shelter, fuel, clothing, tools, or transportation, for the making and selling of handicraft articles out of nonedible by-products of fish and wildlife resources taken for personal or family consumption, and for the customary trade, barter, or sharing for personal or family consumption."

Under the 1983 state regulations, only rural residents can be considered subsistence users. In addition to the rural requirement, subsistence users can be identified by a variety of other criteria, such as use patterns and availability of alternative resources. Subsistence also depends upon the biological status of fish and game resources.

Subsistence fishing regulations are available as a separate pamphlet from the Alaska Department of Fish and Game. Subsistence hunting regulations are included with the annually published state hunting regulations, also available from the ADF&G.

Sundog

"Mock suns" (parhelia) usually seen as bright spots on opposite sides of the winter sun. This optical phenomenon is created by the refraction of sunlight through tiny ice crystals suspended in the air. The ice crystals are commonly called "diamond dust."

Taiga

Taken from a Russian word that means "land of little sticks," this name is applied to the spindly white spruce and black spruce forests found in much of southcentral and interior Alaska.

Telecommunications

History

Alaska's first telecommunications project, begun in the 1860s, was designed to serve New York, San Francisco and the capitals of Europe, not particularly the residents of Nome or Fairbanks. It was part of Western Union's ambitious plan to link California to Russian America (Alaska) with an intercontinental cable that would continue under the Bering Strait to Siberia and on to Europe. Men and material were brought together on both sides of the Bering Sea, but with the first successful Atlantic cable crossing in 1867, the trans-Siberian intercontinental line was abandoned.

The first operational telegraph link in Alaska was laid in September 1900 when 25 miles of line were stretched from military headquarters in Nome to an outpost at Port Safety. It was one part of a $450,000 plan by the Army Signal Corps to connect scattered military posts in the territory with the United States. By the end of 1903, land lines linked western Alaska, Prince William Sound, the Interior, and southeastern Alaska (where underwater cable was used).

Plagued by blocks of ice that repeatedly tore loose underwater cables laid across Norton Sound, the military developed in 1903 "wireless telegraphy" to span the icy water. It was the world's first application of radio-telegraph technology and marked the completion of a fragile network connecting all military stations in Alaska with the United States and each other. Sitka, Juneau, Haines, and Valdez were connected by a line to Whitehorse, Yukon Territory. Nome, Fort Saint Michael, Fort Gibbon (Tanana), and Fort Egbert (Eagle) were linked with Dawson, Yukon Territory. A line from Dawson to Whitehorse continued on to Vancouver, British Columbia, and Seattle.

In 1905 the 1,500 miles of land lines, 2,000 miles of submarine cables, and the 107-mile wireless link became the Washington-Alaska Military Cable and Telegraph System. This, in turn, became the Alaska Communications System in 1935, reflecting a shift to greater civilian use and a system relying more heavily on wireless stations than land lines. The

Typical Long-Distance
Telephone Call Within Alaska

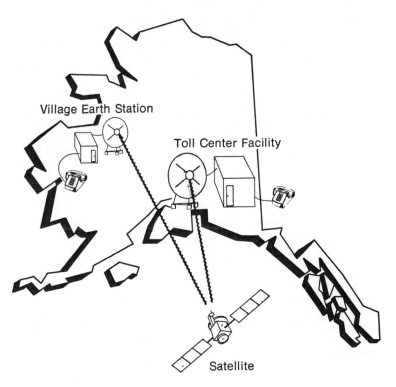

Village Earth Station

Toll Center Facility

Satellite

Courtesy of Alascom, Inc.

Alaska Communications System operated under the Department of Defense until RCA Corporation, through its division RCA Alascom, took control in 1971.

Alascom

Alascom, Inc., is the certified long lines carrier for the state and provides a full range of modern long-distance telecommunications services to all Alaska. When Alascom purchased Alaska Communications Systems about 5 million calls were being handled each year. Today, with more than 160 communication sites in operation, Alascom handles more than 45 million toll calls each year.

Alascom maintains a sophisticated satellite communications system and has established an extensive network of satellite earth stations, manned and unmanned, throughout the state that provide communication with the entire world.

On October 27, 1982, Alascom launched its own telecommunications satellite, *Aurora,* into orbit from Cape Canaveral, Florida. The launching marked several firsts for Alaska: it was the first completely solid-state satellite to be placed in orbit; it was the first telecommunications satellite dedicated to a single state; and it was the first satellite to be named by a youngster in a contest. Sponsored by Alascom and the State Chamber of Commerce, the contest drew some 5,000 entries from schoolchildren across Alaska. The winner was eight-year-old Nick Francis of Eagle River, who chose *Aurora* "because it's our light in the sky to tell us we are special people."

Improvements over the past 10 years have made long-distance telephone service available to every community in Alaska of 25 persons or more, and live or same-day television is now available to 90 percent of the state's population. In addition to message toll service and television transmissions, Alascom also provides telex, computer data transmission and access, Wide Area Telecommunications Service (WATS), Zenith toll-free numbers, telegram and mailgram, dedicated line service, marine radio, radio transmissions, foreign exchange, and transportable earth stations to the more than 400,000 residents of the state. Alascom is one of the largest private employers in the state with more than 1,000 employees.

General Communications

A relative newcomer in providing Alaska telephone service, General Communications, Inc., provides long-distance telephone service to points outside the state. GCI transmits signals via a Canadian communications satellite tying in with the AT&T national phone network in Seattle.

Telephone Numbers in the Bush

A number of bush villages have only one telephone. The following telephone numbers are published by Alascom Inc. Area code for all of Alaska is 907. For villages not listed, call the information number 555-1212.

Village	Telephone Number	Village	Telephone Number
Cape Pole	879-8001	Meshik (Port Heiden)	976-8001
Chuathbaluk	675-4342	Meyers Chuck	Call LD Operator
Clarks Point	842-5943	Minchumina	939-0000
Council	665-8001		
		New Stuyahok	693-8001
Eek	543-2004	Nightmute	597-8001
Egegik	246-3430	Nondalton	571-1270
Ekuk	842-5937		
Ekwok	464-8001	Oscarville	543-2066
Igiugig	533-8001	Pilot Point	797-8001
Ivanof Bay	669-8001	Point Baker	559-8001
		Portage Creek	842-5966
Kasaan	542-8001	Port Alsworth	781-8001
Kobuk	948-8001	Port Protection	489-8001
Kokhanok	571-1260		
Koliganek	596-8001	Red Devil	447-8001
Kongiganak	696-8001		
Koyukuk	927-8001	Sheldon Point	323-8001
Kwigillingok	769-8001	Sleetmute	449-8001
		Squaw Harbor	383-3322
Levelock	246-3420	Stony River	439-8001
Lime Village	648-8001		
Little Diomede	686-8001	Tetlin	883-2791
		Tuntutuliak	543-2101
Manokotak	842-5978	Twin Hills	972-8001
Mentasta	883-4401		

Television Stations

Television in Alaska's larger communities, such as Anchorage and Fairbanks, was available years before satellites. The first satellite broadcast to the state was Neil Armstrong's moon walk in July 1969. Television reached the Bush in the late 1970s with the construction of telephone earth stations which could receive television programming via satellite transmissions. Same day broadcasts, arriving via satellite, of news and sports events are subsidized in part by state revenues. The state also funds Satellite Television Project and LEARN/Alaska Television Network in nearly 250 rural communities with general and educational programming.

Regular network programming (ABC, CBS, NBC, and PBS) from the Lower 48 reaches Alaska on a time delayed basis. Most of the stations listed here carry a mixture of network programming, with local broadcasters specifying programming. Some stations, such as KJNP, carry locally produced programming. Cable television is available in Fairbanks, Nome, and several other communities, with the cable companies offering dozens of channels. At least one cable system offers a complete satellite earth station and 24-hour programming. The state's Instructional Telecommunications Network (ITV) LEARN/Alaska is aired statewide.

Local television viewing in Bethel, for example, includes channel 4 (KYUK) which carries ITV programming such as PBS's "NOVA" series and "Sesame Street," and local news; cable channel 8, which carries regular network programming; and a half-dozen other channels carrying cable programming such as movies, sports, and specials.

The following list shows the 12 commercial and public television stations in Alaska:

Anchorage, **KAKM** Channel 7 (public television); 2651 Providence Drive, 99504.
Anchorage, **KTUU** Channel 2; Box 1160, 99510.
Anchorage, **KIMO** Channel 13; 2700 East Tudor Road, 99507.
Anchorage **KTVA** Channel 11; 1007 West 32d Avenue, 99503.
Bethel, **KYUK** Channel 4; P.O. Box 468, 99559.
Fairbanks, **KTTU** Channel 2; 516 Second Avenue, 99701.
Fairbanks, **KTVF** Channel 11; P.O. Box 950, 99707.
Fairbanks, **KUAC** Channel 9 (public television); University of Alaska, 99701.
Juneau, **KJUD** Channel 8; 1107 Eighth Street, Suite 2, 99801.
Juneau, **KTOO** Channel 3; 224 Fourth, 99801.
North Pole, **KJNP** Channel 4; Box O, 99705.
Sitka, **KIFW** Channel 13; P.O. Box 299, 99835.

Tides

(See also *Bore Tide*)
In southeastern Alaska, Prince William Sound, Cook Inlet and Bristol Bay, salt water undergoes extreme daily fluctuations, creating powerful tidal currents. Some bays may go totally dry at low tide. The second greatest tide range in North America occurs in upper Cook Inlet near Anchorage, where the maximum diurnal range during spring tides is 38.9 feet. (The greatest tide range in North America is Nova Scotia's Bay of Fundy with spring tides to 43 feet.)
Here are diurnal ranges for some coastal communities:

	Feet		Feet
Bethel	4.0	Nushagak	19.6
Cold Bay	7.1	Point Barrow	0.4
Cordova	12.4	Port Heiden	12.3
Haines	16.8	Port Moller	10.8
Herschel Island	0.7	Sand Point	7.3
Ketchikan	15.4	Sitka	9.9
Kodiak	8.5	Valdez	12.0
Naknek River entrance	22.6	Whittier	12.3
Nikiski	20.7	Wrangell	15.7
Nome	1.6	Yakutat	10.1

Timber

According to the USDA Forest Service, 119 million acres of Alaska's 366 million acres of land surface are forested (28 million acres of which are classified as commercial forests).
Alaska has two distinct forest ecosystems: the coastal rain forest and the interior forest. The vast interior forest covers 106 million acres, extending from the south slope of the Brooks Range to the Kenai Peninsula, and from Canada to Norton Sound. Over 22 million acres of white

spruce, paper birch, quaking aspen and balsam poplar stands are considered commercial forest land, comparing favorably in size and growth productivity with the forests of the lake states (Minnesota, Michigan and Wisconsin). The Interior's remoteness from markets and land management policies have limited timber use to approximately 50 small local sawmills with limited export of cants and chips.

The coastal rain forests extend from Cook Inlet to the Alaska-Canada border south of Ketchikan and provide the bulk of commercial timber in Alaska today. Of the 13,247,000 acres of forested land, 5,749,000 acres contain commercial stands. Western hemlock, 70 percent of the total, and Sitka spruce, 25 percent of the total, provide the bulk of the timber harvest for domestic and export lumber and pulp markets. Western red cedar and Alaska (yellow) cedar make up the balance, with pine and other species also present.

The Alaska forest products industry reflected the depressed national industry in 1982. Preliminary estimates of the 1982 timber harvest on the Chugach and Tongass national forests was 346 million board feet, down from 525 million board feet in 1981 for all Alaska lands.

Time Zones

On September 15, 1983, transportation secretary Elizabeth Dole signed a plan to reduce the number of time zones in Alaska from four to two. The plan, which became effective October 30 when daylight saving time reverted to standard time, places 90 percent of Alaska residents on Yukon time, only one hour behind the West Coast. The far reaches of the Aleutian Islands and Saint Lawrence Island enter Alaska standard time.

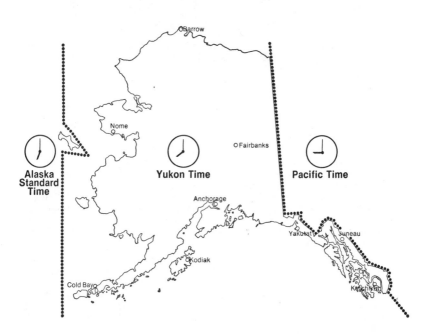

Before the change, Alaska's time zones were Pacific time (southeastern Alaska), Yukon time (Yakutat), Alaska time (from just east of Cold Bay and west of Yakutat northward, including Barrow) and Bering time (Cold Bay and the Aleutian Islands northward, including Nome). The shift was accomplished to facilitate doing business in Alaska, improve communications, and unify residents. It had the support of the governor, the state legislature, and the majority of Alaskans.

Totems

In the early days of southeastern Alaska and British Columbia, the way of life of the Indian people living there was based on the rich natural resources of the land, on respect for all living things, and on a unique and complex social structure. The totemic art of the Indians reflects this rich culture. Totems are bold statements making public records of the lives and history of the people who had them carved, and represent pride in clans and ancestors.

Totems, carved from yellow cedar, are a traditional art form among the Indians of British Columbia and southeastern Alaska. Although most well-known totems are tall and free standing, totemic art also was applied to houseposts and short entrance poles. The carved monuments were erected by the leading clans in each tribe in memory of their chiefs who had died. The poles also symbolized power and prestige.

Animals of the region are most often represented on the poles. Of all the crests, the frog appears most frequently, then the bear, eagle, raven, thunderbird, wolf, owl, grouse, starfish, finback whale, and halibut. Also represented are figures from Indian mythology: monsters with animal features, humanlike spirits, and semihistorical ancestors. Occasionally depicted are objects, devices, masks, and charms, and most rarely, art illustrating plants and sky phenomena.

The poles are traditionally painted with pigments made from soil of yellow, brown, and red hues, coal, cinnabar, berry juice, and spruce sap. Fungus found on hemlock produces various colors: yellow when decayed, red when roasted, and black when charred. Before modern paints became available, salmon eggs chewed with cedar bark formed the case, or glue, for the paint.

Totem art reached its peak after 1830, with the introduction of steel European tools acquired through fur trade, and endured to about 1890.

Carving activity has not been as plentiful since. Leading families competed with others, building larger and more elaborate totem poles to show their wealth and prestige.

The pole was left to stand as long as nature would permit, usually no more than 50 to 60 years. Once a pole became so rotten that it fell, it was pushed aside, left to decay naturally or used for firewood. Most totem poles still standing in parks today are 40 to 50 years old. Heavy precipitation and acid muskeg soils hasten decomposition.

Collections of totem poles may be seen in several Alaska communities, including Ketchikan, Wrangell, and Sitka. Carvers may be seen practicing their art in Haines and Sitka.

A good source of more information is *Carved History, The Totem Poles and House Posts of Sitka National Historical Park,* published in cooperation with the National Park Service by the Alaska Natural History Association, Sitka Chapter, and is available from them for $2.75 postage paid at P.O. Box 738, Sitka, Alaska 99835.

Tourism

Although Alaska has been attracting tourists for nearly one hundred years, many people are surprised to learn that tourism has become the state's third largest industry. In terms of gross sales or employment, tourism is exceeded only by the petroleum and commercial fishing industries. Historically, visitor volume has grown annually by 6 to 15 percent. In excess of 1,500 businesses in Alaska derive most of their income from sales to visitors.

State government has long recognized the value of visitor industry growth and supports this segment of the state's economy through the programs of the Alaska Division of Tourism. In fiscal year 1983-84, the division will spend $6.25 million in support of the visitor industry; primarily for print and broadcast advertising and the production and distribution of Alaska travel promotion literature.

Approximately 90 percent of Alaska's visitors come from the continental United States. Western Europe, Canada and Japan provide the majority of foreign arrivals. Nearly 80 percent travel on independent itineraries, with the remainder purchasing package tour programs. By transportation mode, approximately 70 percent of visitor arrivals are by air, 13 percent by cruise ship, 5 percent by ferry, and 12 percent by auto and camper.

Alaska's scenic beauty, abundant wildlife and colorful history remain its biggest attractions. The recent, rapid growth in the adventure travel market is also evident in Alaska with increasing numbers of visitors participating in river rafting, back-country trekking and a variety of wilderness experiences.

Nonresident Visitor Volume and Impact

Year	Visitor Volume	In-State Sales* (in millions)	Primary Employment
1978	430,000	$194.7	6,140
1979	505,400	251.7	7,220
1980	566,100	310.1	8,090
1981	640,000	388.8	9,140
1982	690,000	457.3	9,860

*Excludes transportation costs to and from Alaska.
Source: State of Alaska, Division of Tourism.

Trans-Alaska Pipeline

The pipeline designer, builder, and operator is the Alyeska Pipeline Service Company, a consortium of the following eight oil companies:

Sohio Pipe Line Company	33.34%
ARCO Pipe Line Company	21.35%
Exxon Pipeline Company	20.34%
BP Pipelines Inc.	16.67%
Mobil Alaska Pipeline Company	4.08%
Union Alaska Pipeline Company	1.36%
Phillips Alaska Pipeline Corporation	1.36%
Amerada Hess Pipeline Corporation	1.50%

Pipeline length: 800 miles, slightly less than half that length is buried, the remainder is on 78,000 aboveground supports, located 60 feet apart, built in a flexible zigzag pattern. More than 800 river and stream crossings. Normal burial of pipe was used in stable soils and rock; aboveground pipe — insulated and jacketed — was used in permafrost areas. Thermal devices prevent thawing around vertical supports. 151 stop flow valves.

Pipe: Specially manufactured coated pipe with zinc anodes installed to prevent corrosion. Size is 48 inches in diameter, with thickness from 0.462 to 0.562 inch. Pipe sections before construction in lengths of 40 to 60 feet.

Cost: $8 billion, which includes terminal at Valdez, but does not include interest on money raised for construction.

Amount of oil pumped through pipeline: As of July 1983, 3 billion barrels of crude oil.

Operations: Control center at Valdez terminal and 10 operating pump stations along line monitor and control pipeline.

Pipeline capacity: By July 1983, 1.6 million barrels per day; can be increased to design capacity of 2 million barrels per day by construction of two more pump stations or by adding pumps at existing stations.

Estimated crude oil reserves recoverable on the North Slope: 6.4 billion barrels.

Terminal: 1,000-acre site at Port Valdez, northernmost ice-free harbor in the U.S., with 18 tanks providing storage capacity of 9,180,000 barrels of oil.

Valdez ship-loading capacity: 110,000 barrels per hour for each of three berths; 80,000 barrels per hour for one berth.

Length and cost of pipeline haul road built by Alyeska: 360 miles, from the Yukon River to Prudhoe Bay, $150 million.

Yukon River bridge: First bridge (2,290 feet long) spanning the Yukon in Alaska.

Important dates: July 1968, Prudhoe Bay oil field discovery confirmed; **1970,** suits filed to halt construction, Alyeska Pipeline Service Company formed; **November 16, 1973,** presidential approval of pipeline legislation; **April 29, 1974,** construction begins on North Slope Haul Road (now the Dalton Highway) and is completed 154 days later; **March 27, 1975,** first pipe installed at Tonsina River; **June 20, 1977,** first oil leaves Prudhoe Bay, reaches Valdez terminal July 28; **August 1, 1977,** first tanker load of oil shipped aboard the SS *ARCO Juneau;* **June 13, 1979,** tanker number 1,000 (SS *ARCO Heritage*) sails; **July 15, 1983,** 3-billionth barrel of oil leaves pump station.

Trees and Shrubs

According to the U.S. Department of Agriculture, the number of native tree species in Alaska is less than in any other state. Species of trees and shrubs in Alaska fall under the following families: yew, pine, cypress, willow, bayberry, birch, mistletoe, gooseberry, rose, maple, elaeagnus, ginseng, dogwood, crowberry, pyrola, heath, dispensia, honeysuckle, and composite.

Commercial timber species include white spruce, Sitka spruce, western hemlock, mountain hemlock, western red cedar, Alaska cedar, balsam poplar, black cottonwood, quaking aspen, and paper birch.

Rare tree species include the Pacific yew, Pacific silver fir, subalpine fir, silver willow and Hooker willow.

Tundra

Areas with cool temperatures, frequent winds and moisture-retaining soils. Tundra climates are harsh on plant species attempting to grow there. Mechanical stress is incurred as soils freeze around root systems and winds wear away portions exposed above rocks and snow. Consequently, the three distinct types of Alaska tundra — wet, moist and alpine — support low-growing vegetation that includes a variety of delicate flowers, mosses and lichens.

According to a report in *Alaska Science Nuggets,* every acre of arctic tundra contains more than two tons of live fungi which survives by feeding on, thus decomposing, dead organic matter. Since the recession of North Slope ice-age glaciers 12,000 years ago, a vegetative residue has accumulated a layer of peat three to six feet thick overlying the tundra.

Ulu

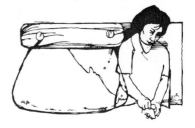

A traditional Eskimo woman's knife designed for scraping and chopping. This fan-shaped tool was originally made of stone with a bone handle, but today it is often shaped from an old saw blade and a wood handle is attached.

Umiak

A traditional Eskimo skin-covered boat, whose design has changed little over the centuries. Although mostly powered by outboard motors today, paddles are still used when stalking game and when ice might damage the propeller. Because the *umiaks* must often be pulled for long distances over the ice, the boats are designed to be lightweight and easily repairable. The frames are wood, often driftwood found on the beaches, and the covering can be sewn should it be punctured. The bottom is flat and the keel is bone, which prevents the skin from wearing out as it is pulled over the ice.

Female walrus skins are the preferred covering because they are the proper thickness when split (bull hides are too thick), and because it only takes two to cover a boat. However, sometimes female walrus skins are unavailable, so the Eskimos substitute skins of the bearded seal, or *oogruk*. But *oogruks* are smaller, and it takes six or seven skins to cover an *umiak*.

Once the skins are stretched over the frame and lashed into place, the outside is painted with marine paint for waterproofing. Historically, the skin would have been anointed with seal oil or other fats, but the modern waterproofing is now universally accepted because it does not have to be renewed after each trip.

Umiak is the Inupiat word for skin boat and is commonly used by the coastal Eskimos throughout Alaska. The Saint Lawrence Islanders, however, speak the Yup'ik dialect, and their word for skin boat is *angyaq*.

Universities and Colleges

Higher education in Alaska is provided by two private institutions and a statewide university system composed of three senior colleges, 11 community colleges and 12 rural education and extension centers.

The private colleges are Alaska Pacific University and Sheldon Jackson College. Alaska Pacific is a four-year liberal arts and science college with a graduate program. It also maintains an associate degree program. Sheldon Jackson College began more than 100 years ago as a Presbyterian mission school for Tlingit Indians. Today, it offers a two-year coeducational college with a four-year program leading to a bachelor of arts degree. It also offers a certificate in teacher education.

The three senior colleges in the statewide university system are located at Anchorage, Fairbanks, and Juneau. The 2,250-acre Fairbanks campus — research center for the statewide university system — is the state's largest campus and only residential campus. The 11 community colleges are degree-granting institutions. The rural education centers offer both credit and community service courses. Rural education centers are located at Adak, Cold Bay, Delta Junction, Dillingham, Fort Yukon, Galena, King Cove, McGrath, Nenana, Sand Point, Tok, and Unalaska. For more information on rural education centers write the University of Alaska, Community Colleges, Rural Educational and Extension Affairs, 3601 C Street, Suite 400, Anchorage 99503. For information on state colleges and universities and private institutions of higher education, contact the following:

Alaska Pacific University
3500 University Drive
Anchorage 99508

Anchorage Community College
2533 Providence Drive
Anchorage 99508

Chukchi Community College
P.O. Box 748
Kotzebue 99752

Islands Community College
Box 490, Sitka 99835

Kenai Peninsula
Community College
Box 848, Soldotna 99669

Ketchikan Community College
Box 358, Ketchikan 99901

Kodiak Community College
Box 946, Kodiak 99615

Kuskokwim Community College
Box 368, Bethel 99559

Matanuska-Susitna
Community College
Box 899, Palmer 99645

Northwest Community College
Box 400, Nome 99762

Prince William Sound
Community College
Box 590, Valdez 99686

Sheldon Jackson College
Box 479, Sitka 99835

Tanana Valley Community College
201 Constitution Hall
504 Tok Lane
University of Alaska
Fairbanks 99701

University of Alaska, Anchorage
3211 Providence Drive
Anchorage 99504

University of Alaska, Fairbanks
Fairbanks 99701

University of Alaska, Juneau
11120 Glacier Highway
Juneau 99802

Many additional schools and institutes in Alaska offer religious, vocational, and technical study. For a complete listing of these and other schools, write for the *Directory of Postsecondary Educational Institutions in Alaska,* Alaska Commission on Postsecondary Education, Pouch FP, Juneau 99811.

Volcanoes

The state's 10 tallest active volcanic peaks, based on information from the Smithsonian Insitution, are as follows:*

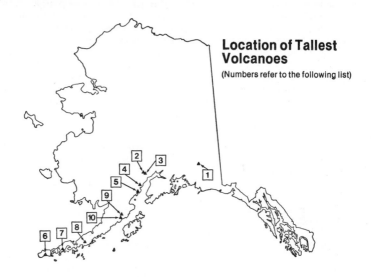

Location of Tallest Volcanoes
(Numbers refer to the following list)

Map Key	Elevation	Map Key	Elevation
1 Mount Wrangell	14,163	6 Pavlof Volcano	8,259
2 Mount Spurr	11,067	7 Mount Veniaminof	8,223
3 Redoubt Volcano	10,194	8 Isanolski Peaks	8,023
4 Iliamna Volcano	10,014	9 Denison	603
5 Shishaldin Volcano	9,371	10 Mount Griggs	7,429

*Active volcanoes are considered those which have erupted during the last 10,000 years.

The Aleutian Islands and the Alaska Peninsula are part of the "rim of fire" that surrounds the Pacific basin. The majority of the region's 57 volcanic mountains have been active since 1760. The major eruption in modern times was the Mount Katmai eruption of 1912. On November 11, 1980, Pavlof Volcano, on the lower Alaska Peninsula 35 miles northeast of Cold Bay, erupted for the first time since 1976, sending plumes of steam and ash 20,000 feet in the air. Pavlof has had a long history of eruptions: more than 25 separate eruptions since 1700. Mount Veniaminof has shown the most recent activity, erupting on June 4, 1983, and continuing in July. Dense ash clouds have been observed as high as three and one-half miles. Lava flow activity was observed in June and July, sending bombs more than 300 feet above the cone. Mount Veniaminof's last recorded eruption occurred in 1944; however, U.S. Geological Survey personnel suspect a later eruption occurred sometime between 1954 and 1973.

Whales and Whaling

The Species

Fifteen species of large whales inhabit Alaska waters. Baleen, or whalebone, whales found in Alaska waters are: blue, bowhead, northern right, fin or finback, humpback, sei, minke or little piked, and gray. Toothed whales inhabiting Alaska waters are: sperm, beluga, killer, pilot, and beaked (three species: giant bottlenose, goose-beaked, and Bering Sea beaked whales). Although rarely encountered in Alaskan waters, the narwhal is a full-time resident of the Arctic. Saint Lawrence Islanders call it *bousucktugutalik,* or "beluga with tusk" because a spiraled, yard-long, tusk juts from the left side of its upper jaw.

The nine species seen frequently off Alaska are identified by their surfacing, blowing and diving characteristics in the accompanying chart.

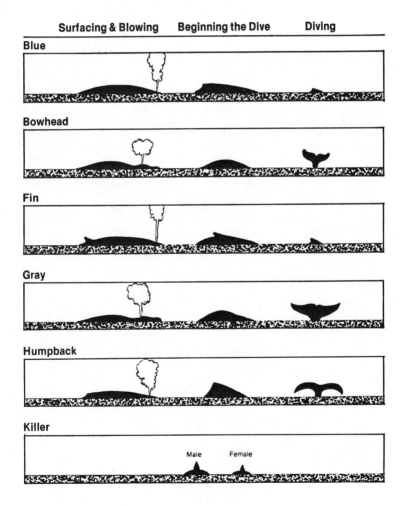

201

	Surfacing & Blowing	Beginning the Dive	Diving

Minke

Spout almost invisible

Sei

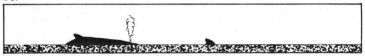

Sperm

Whaling

Bowhead whales have been protected from commercial whaling by the Convention for the Regulation of Whaling of 1931, the International Convention for the Regulation of Whaling of 1947, the Marine Mammal Protection Act of 1972, the Endangered Species Act of 1973, and the Convention of International Trade in Endangered Species of Wild Fauna and Flora. Commercial whaling for gray whales has been banned by the International Convention for the Regulation of Whaling since 1947. These conventions and acts have, however, allowed for a subsistence harvest by Alaska Indians, Aleuts, and Eskimos.

Since 1978 the International Whaling Commission has regulated the take of bowheads by establishing an annual catch limit for Alaska Eskimos. Also in 1978 the IWC reclassified the eastern stock of gray whales from a protected speces to a sustained management stock with an annual catch limit of about 179 whales, based on the average known removals during the period 1968-77. The entire catch limit has been reserved for taking by Natives or by member governments on behalf of Natives. Other species of large baleen whales, such as minke and fin whales, are occasionally taken by Alaska Eskimos for food. The only toothed whale taken by Eskimos is the beluga, and its harvest is managed by the state.

According to the National Marine Fisheries Service and the Alaska Department of Fish and Game, harvest figures for the years 1978-82 are as follows:

Year	Whale Species		
	Beluga	Gray	Minke
1978	177	NR	NR
1979	138	3	2
1980	NA	3	1
1981	210*	NR	1
1982	325*	4	3

*Approximate figures   NA = not available   NR = none reported

Related reading: *Alaska Whales and Whaling.* Color photos and maps. 144 pages, $12.95. See page 207.

Wild Berries

Wild Berries abound in Alaska with the circumboreal lowbush cranberry (*Vaccinium vitis-idaea*) being the most widespread. Blueberries of one species or another inhabit most of the state, also. Some 50 other species of wild fruits are found in the state and include strawberries, raspberries, cloudberries, salmonberries, crowberries, nagoonberries, and crab apples.

Highbush cranberries (which are not really cranberries) can be found on bushes even in the dead of winter, and the frozen berries provide a refreshing treat to the hiker.

Lingonberry/ Lowbush Cranberry, Vaccinium vitis-idaea *(Reprinted from* Alaska Wild Berry Guide and Cookbook*)*

The fruit of the wild rose, or rose hip, is not strictly a berry but is used in similar fashion and is an ideal source of vitamin C for bush dweller and city resident alike. A few hips will provide as much of the vitamin as a medium-sized orange. The farther north the hips are found, the richer they are in vitamin C.

Related reading: *Alaska Wild Berry Guide and Cookbook,* by the editors of *ALASKA®* magazine. How to find, identify and prepare Alaska's wild edible berries. 216 pages, $13.95. See page 207.

Wild Flowers

Wild flowers in Alaska are seldom gaudy but commonly are rather small and delicate. More than 1,500 plant species occur in the state including trees, shrubs, ferns, grasses, and sedges, as well as flowering plants.

Alpine regions are particularly rich in flora and some of the species are rare. Anywhere there is tundra there is apt to be a bountiful population of flowers. The Steese Highway (Eagle Summit), Richardson Highway (Thompson Pass), Denali Highway (Maclaren Summit), Denali National Park and Preserve (Polychrome Pass), Seward Highway (Turnagain Pass), Glenn Highway just north of Anchorage (Eklutna Flats) and a locale near Wasilla (Hatcher Pass) are wonderful wild flower-viewing spots. These are all readily accessible by car. Less easily accessible floral Edens are certain of the Aleutian Islands, Point Hope, Anvil Mountain and the Nome-Teller Road (both near Nome), Pribilof Islands and other remote areas.

Alaska's official state flower, the forget-me-not *(Myosotis alpestris),* is a delicate little beauty found throughout much of the state in alpine meadows and along streams. Growing to 18 inches tall, forget-me-nots are recognized by their bright blue petals surrounding a yellow "eye." A northern "cousin," the arctic forget-me-not *(Eritrichium aretioides),* grows in sandy soil on the tundra or in the mountains, and reaches only 4 inches in height.

Related reading: *The Alaska-Yukon Wild Flowers Guide,* edited by Helen A. White and Maxcine Williams; original drawings by Virginia Howie. 218 pages, $12.95. See page 208.

Wild Land Fires

The 1982 fire season was the first year for the newly organized Alaska Fire Service, the only Department of the Interior fire suppression organization in Alaska. AFS responsibility is for the initial attack on all lands, excluding the state initial attack zone, which is primarily in the southeastern portion of the state. The development of the AFS has allowed the Bureau of Land Management, in cooperation with the National Park Service, Fish and Wildlife Service, Bureau of Indian Affairs, Native corporations and the state, to develop fire protection goals and guidelines for public lands in Alaska. The AFS protection boundary is approximately 209 million acres. Each can provide initial attack or assume responsibility on a fire at the request of the other protecting body, even if the fire is within the other's protection zone.

The AFS has approximately 2,000 emergency fire fighters and 470 fire management personnel in Alaska, of which 95 are smoke jumpers. Most of emergency fire fighters are village volunteers who are trained by AFS personnel and paid when providing fire suppression assistance. As of July, AFS forces for 1983 have included an additional 184 smoke jumpers and 175 fire specialists on detail from the Lower 48 and southeastern Alaska. (Typically, an additional 25 U.S. Forest Service smoke jumpers, plus other fire specialists, are brought up from the Lower 48.)

Lightning is the leading cause of wild land fires in Alaska, accounting for 66.8 percent of reported fires in 1982. Man-caused fires followed second at 21.2 percent. False alarms accounted for 12 percent of the reports. As of July 11 there were 393 fires for a total of 116,193 acres burned in 1983, an increase of 45,395 acres over all of 1982. (A three- to four-week late spring breakup in 1982 retarded the drying of wild lands, and unusual amounts of moisture remained in the fire fuels throughout the season.)

The largest single fire ever recorded in Alaska burned 1,161,200 acres 74 miles northwest of Galena in 1957, according to BLM figures. In 1977, the Bear Creek fire, largest in the United States that year, consumed 361,000 acres near the Farewell airstrip. During that same fire season, the BLM logged 24,000 flying hours and smoke jumpers made a record 1,795 jumps.

The chart following shows the number of fires and acres burned from 1955 through 1982.

Calendar Year	No. of Fires	Acres Burned	Calendar Year	No. of Fires	Acres Burned
1955	190	23,582	1964	164	3,430
1956	226	476,593	1965	148	7,093
1957	391	5,049,661	1966	256	672,765
1958	278	317,215	1967	207	109,005
1959	320	596,574	1968	442	1,013,301
1960	238	87,180	1969	511	4,231,820
1961	117	5,100	1970	487	113,486
1962	102	38,975	1971	472	1,069,108
1963	194	16,290	1972	641	963,686

Calendar Year	No. of Fires	Acres Burned	Calendar Year	No. of Fires	Acres Burned
1973	336	59,816	1978	356	7,757
1974	782	662,960	1979	620	432,425
1975	344	127,845	1980	417	188,778
1976	622	69,119	1981	556	758,335
1977	681	2,209,408	1982	283	70,798

Winds

Winds abound in Alaska, from the eastern fringes of Southeast to the western islands of the Aleutian Chain where some of the state's windiest weather has been recorded. Overall, the causes are the same as elsewhere, incorporating planet rotation and the tendency of the atmosphere to equalize the difference between high and low pressure fronts (see also *Climate*). A few winds occur often and significantly enough to be given names: chinook, taku and williwaw.

Chinook

Old-timers describe chinook winds as unseasonably warm winds that can cause thaw in the middle of winter. What they also cause are power outages and property damage, especially in the Anchorage bowl, where in recent years hundreds of homes have sprung up on the Chugach Mountain hillsides over which the chinook winds howl. One such wind occurred on April Fool's Day, 1980, causing $25 million property damage and nominating the city as a disaster area. Parts of Anchorage were without power for 60 hours.

Until recently it was not possible to predict the coming of a chinook wind. Today, however, Anchorage meteorologists can tell if the winds are gathering, when they will arrive, and their relative strength. It was discerned that such a warm wind could only originate in Prince William Sound and that its strength had to be at least 55 miles per hour or faster just to cross the 3,500-foot Chugach Mountains. Other factors that need to be present are a storm near Bethel and relatively stable air over Anchorage. Meteorologists predict the coming of chinook winds 55 percent of the time.

Taku

Taku winds are the sudden, fierce gales that sweep down from the icecap behind Juneau and Douglas and plague residents there. Takus are shivering cold winds capable of reaching 100 miles per hour. They have been known to send a two-by-four timber flying through the wall of a frame house.

Williwaws

Williwaws are sudden gusts of wind that can reach 100 knots after the wind "builds up" on one side of a mountain and suddenly spills over into what may appear to be a relatively protected area. Williwaws are considered the bane of Alaska mariners. The term was originally applied to a strong wind in the Strait of Magellan.

World Eskimo-Indian Olympics

An audience of thousands watches the annual spectacle of several hundred Native athletes from Alaska and Canada competing in the World Eskimo-Indian Olympics in Fairbanks. Held the last weekend in July, the self-supporting games draw participants from all of Alaska's Native populations (Eskimo, Aleut, Athabascan, Tlingit, Haida, and Tsimshian), as well as from Canada's Eskimos.

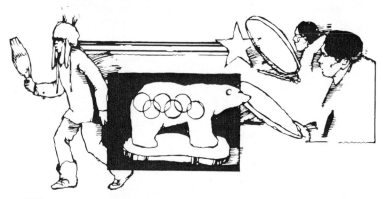

While the bloody but popular ear-pull contest has been dropped from the games, spectators still can thrill to the sight of such feats as the knuckle hop and the ear-weight competition. Other traditional Native sports and competitions include the greased pole walk, seal and muskrat skinning, fish cutting, stick pull, Indian leg wrestling, Indian-Eskimo dancing, men's and women's blanket toss and the spectacular two-foot and one-foot high kicks. Each year the judges choose a Native queen to reign over the three-day olympics, pick the prettiest baby, and select the most outstanding Native-made garments. Some of the more boisterous games include the lively white men/Native women tug of war and the muktuk eating contest.

The games are held on Thursday, Friday, and Saturday evenings at the Patty Gymnasium on the University of Alaska campus. Advance tickets may be purchased from the World Eskimo-Indian Olympics Committee, P.O. Box 2433, Fairbanks, Alaska 99707.

BOOKS ABOUT ALASKA AND THE NORTH

Alaska Northwest Publishing Company is the U.S.'s largest and most active publisher of Alaskana, and many of its North Country books are suggested as related reading throughout The ALASKA ALMANAC®.

Following is Alaska Northwest Publishing Company's whole Alaska library — North Country books that are available in bookstores or direct from ANWP (Box 4-EEE, Anchorage, Alaska 99509). Mail orders require a postage and handling fee of $1.00 fourth class or $3.00 first class per book. Or write for our free book catalog.

Admiralty . . . Island in Contention — Admiralty's many faces emerge in crisp text and color photos. 78 pp., 11 x 8½, $5.00

Adventure Roads North — Tracing the history of Alaska's highways. 224 pp., 11 x 8½, $14.95

The Alaska Adventures of a Norwegian Cheechako: A Greenhorn with a Gold Pan — Warm, witty and incredible story of a charming gold seeker. 128 pp., 5⅜ x 8⅜, $5.95

The Alaska Airlines Story — A book of adventure and aviation history. 224 pp., 8½ x 11, $12.95

The ALASKA ALMANAC® — Facts About Alaska — Annual collection of facts about Alaska, from agriculture to williwaws, with illustrations. 186 pp., 5⅜ x 8⅜, $5.95

ALASKA: A Pictorial Geography — A full-color photographic tour of the last frontier. 64 pp., 8½ x 11, $4.95

Alaska Blues: A Fisherman's Journal — True account of commercial fishing in southeastern Alaska waters with 198 black-and-white photos. 236 pp., 8⅜ x 10⅞, cloth, $14.95

Alaska Bear Tales — Encounters between bears and humans. 318 pp., 5⅜ x 8⅜, $9.95

Alaska Game Trails With a Master Guide — Hunt with Master Guide Hal Waugh. 310 pp., 5⅜ x 8⅜, $6.95

Alaska Mammals includes more than 80 species and subspecies and excellent color photographs and maps. 184 pp., 11 x 8½, $12.95

Alaska National Interest Lands — A detailed look at the complex and controversial d(2) lands issue; color photos and maps. 240 pp., 11 x 8½, $14.95

Alaska Sourdough — Handwritten recipes "by a real Alaskan." 190 pp., 7⅜ x 9, $6.95

Alaska Whales and Whaling — Authoritative look at the wonders of whales in Alaska. Beautiful color photos and superb maps. 144 pp., 11 x 8½, $12.95

Alaska Wild Berry Guide and Cookbook, — How to find and identify edible wild berries, and how to cook them. Line drawings and color photos. 216 pp., 6 x 9, $13.95

The Alaskan Bird Sketches of Olaus Murie, with excerpts from his field notes, compiled and edited by Margaret E. Murie. 64 pp., 11 x 9, $11.95

The Alaskan Camp Cook — Mouth-watering recipes for wild foods. 88 pp., 6 x 9, $4.95

Alaskan Igloo Tales — Eskimo stories, rich in humor; illustrated by a noted Eskimo artist. 139 pp., 9⅞ x 6¾, $6.95

The Alaskan Mushroom Hunter's Guide — No-mistake text and precise color illustrations. 286 pp., 6 x 9, $13.95

Alaska's Glaciers — More than 200 color/b&w photos, 3 maps plus full-color, fold-out map. 144 pp., 11 x 8½, $9.95

Alaska's Great Interior — The heartland of Alaska, including such highlights as Mount McKinley and Fairbanks. 128 pp., 11 x 8½, $9.95

Alaska's Native People — A look at the lives of Alaska's Natives, from the Yup'ik and Inupiat to the Indians and Aleuts. 304 pp., 11 x 8½, $24.95

Alaska's Oil/Gas & Minerals Industry — A complete and understandable book on the subject. 216 pp., 11 x 8½, $12.95

Alaska's Salmon Fisheries — The ideal book on the subject for experts and the lay public. 128 pp., 11 x 8½, $12.95

The Alaska-Yukon Wild Flowers Guide — Large color photos and detailed drawings of 160 species. 218 pp., 5⅜ x 8⅜, $12.95

The Aleutians — The rugged island chain, its people, its history and its future. 224 pp., 11 x 8½, $14.95

Along Alaska's Great River — Danger and excitement along the Yukon River. 88 pp., 8½ x 11, $7.95

Amphibians & Reptiles in Alaska, The Yukon & Northwest Territories — Natural history, identification keys, color photos, maps. 89 pp., 5⅜ x 8⅜, $4.95

Anchorage — A beautiful guidebook to Alaska's largest city, including detailed area and walking tour maps. 64 pp., 8⅜ x 10⅞, $2.95

Anchorage and the Cook Inlet Basin — A completely revised and updated look at this remarkable piece of Alaska. 168 pp., 11 x 8½, $14.95

Aurora Borealis: The Amazing Northern Lights — A complete words and picture story of this amazing natural light show. 96 pp., 11 x 8½, $7.95

E.T. Barnette: The Strange Story of the Man Who Founded Fairbanks — Colorful history from gold rush days. 176 pp., 5½ x 8½, $7.95

Bits and Pieces of Alaskan History Published Over The Years in From Ketchikan to Barrow® — A Department in *The ALASKA SPORTSMAN®* and *ALASKA® magazine, Volume I, 1935-1959,* 208 pp., and *Volume II, 1960-1974,* 216 pp., 11 x 14, $14.95 each volume

Chilkoot Pass: The Most Famous Trail in the North — Updated in 1983; a popular guide for hikers and history buffs. 214 pp., 5⅜ x 8⅜, $7.95

Cooking Alaskan — Hundreds of time-tested recipes including a section on sourdough. 500 pp., 8½ x 11, $14.95

The Copper Spike — An epic adventure. The whole truth of heroes and scoundrels who punched a railroad through "impossible" terrain to mine the riches of Kennicott. 175 pp., 8⅜ x 10⅞, $9.95

Dale De Armond: A First Book Collection of Her Prints — Special color sampler featuring 63 of the Juneau artist's work. 80 pp., 8½ x 11, $14.95

Early Visitors to Southeastern Alaska: Nine Accounts — Detailed accounts of early-day visitors, beginning with the story of Capt. James Cook's voyage, all illustrated by original Dale De Armond woodcuts. 214 pp., 5⅜ x 8⅜, $5.95

Fair Chase With Alaskan Guides — Tales of the hunt for sportsmen. 205 pp., 5⅜ x 8⅜, $5.95

Fisheries of the North Pacific — Completely revised edition of the 1974 classic, with the latest on gear, processing and vessels. 432 pp., 8⅜ x 10⅜, $24.95

The Freshwater Fishes of Alaska — A complete species by species index of the fish found in Alaska's rivers and lakes. 248 pp., 8⅜ x 10⅞, $24.95

Glacier Bay — Beautiful color photos, clear text, large-scale map. 132 pp., 11 x 8½, $11.95

Gold Hunting in Alaska — A grand and glorious tale of hunting gold in the 1890s. 80 pp., 8½ x 11, $7.95

The Gold Hustlers — Wheeling and dealing in the Klondike gold fields. 340 pp., 5⅜ x 8⅜, $7.95

A Guide to the Birds of Alaska — Newly updated and expanded; the perfect field guide to every species found in the 49th state. 320 pp., 6 x 9, $16.95

A Guide to the Queen Charlotte Islands — This 1984 revised edition provides all the maps and information needed when visiting these rugged islands. 90 pp., 5⅜ x 8⅜, $3.95

Handloggers — Love story of a couple's 43 years as "one-man" loggers in southeastern Alaska. 251 pp., 5⅜ x 8⅜, $4.95

How to Build An Oil Barrel Stove — Practical instructions; illustrated. 24 pp., 8½ x 11, $1.95

How to Have Your Cake & Eat It Too! Revised Edition — Recipes for diabetic, hypoglycemic, low-cholesterol/low-fat, low-salt, and low-calorie diets. 308 pp., 7⅜ x 9, $8.95

I Am Eskimo — Eskimo legends told by an Eskimo, illustrated by an Eskimo artist. 86 pp., 7¾ x 9¼, $3.95

I Beat the Arctic — 132 days mushing across the top of Alaska. 64 pp., 8½ x 11, $4.95

Icebound in the Siberian Arctic — For ship, wireless and aircraft buffs. 164 pp., 5⅜ x 8⅜, $4.95

In Search of Gold — A stampeder follows the gold from the Yukon to Nome in 1898-99. 314 pp., 5⅜ x 8⅜, $9.95

Introduction To Alaska — Color photos, facts and figures. 64 pp., 8½ x 11, $4.95

Islands of the Seals: The Pribilofs — Home of the Aleut people and a haven for wildlife. 128 pp., 11 x 8½, $9.95

Juneau: A Book of Woodcuts — Handsome prints by Dale De Armond; a whimsical history of Juneau. 50 pp., 8 x 10, slipcased, $12.95

Kahtahah — Tales of a Tlingit girl, illustrated by Rie Munoz. 109 pp., 8⅜ x 10⅜, $7.95

Klondike Lost: A Decade of Photographs by Kinsey & Kinsey — Text on a long-forgotten segment of gold rush history, illustrated with a collection of rare photographs. 138 pp., 11 x 8½, $12.95

Kotzebue Basin — Native culture, village life, hunting and fishing. 184 pp., 11 x 8½, $12.95

The Lost Patrol — First book to unravel the tragedy of the Mounted Police patrol that perished in the winter of 1910-11 in the Northwest Territories. 138 pp., 5⅜ x 8⅜, $4.95

Lowbush Moose (And Other Alaskan Recipes) — A former Alaska State Trooper adds special flavor to mouthwatering family recipes by telling the stories behind them. 198 pp., 7⅜ x 9, $5.95

The MILEPOST® All-the-North Travel Guide® 1984 edition — All travel routes in western Canada and Alaska with photos and detailed maps. 500 pp., 8⅜ x 10⅞, $11.95

Mudhole Smith, Alaska Flier — Great tales of bush flying. 160 pages, 5½ x 8½, $6.95

My Ninety Years — Autobiography of the indomitable Martha Black, who climbed Chilkoot Pass to the Klondike in 1898. 166 pp., 5⅜ x 8⅜, $7.95

One Man's Wilderness — A classic wilderness experience illustrated by beautiful color photos. 116 pp., 11 x 8½, $9.95

One Survived — One of the great survival stories of our time, reprinted from the pages of *ALASKA®* magazine. 41 pp., 5⅜ x 8⅜, $2.95

Pacific Halibut: The Resource and The Fishery — An impressive book on the history of this fish and fishery. 288 pp., 8½ x 11; paper $19.95, cloth $24.95

Pacific Troller: Life on the Northwest Fishing Grounds — A close-up of the fisherman's life, the frustrations, the humor, the excitement. 143 pp., 5⅜ x 8⅜, $5.95

A Photographic Geography of Alaska — Revised in 1983, a words-and-picture look at the six Alaskas, each a distinct region within the state. 192 pp., 11 x 8½, $15.95

Racing Alaskan Sled Dogs — Expert mushers, racers and breeders give inside advice. Includes 30 years of racing records. 133 pp., 8⅜ x 10⅞, $7.95

Raven: A Collection of Woodcuts — De Armond woodcuts, Tlingit tales of Raven; signed, numbered, limited edition. 132 pp., 12 x 12, $100

Richard Harrington's Antarctic — A voyage through the Antarctic. 104 pp., 11 x 8½, $8.95

The Roots of Ticasuk, An Eskimo Woman's Family Story — Native history at its best. 120 pp., 5½ x 8½, $4.95

Secrets of Eskimo Skin Sewing — Guide to fashioning with fur and skin; patterns and color photos. 125 pp., 5⅜ x 8⅜, $6.95

Selected Alaska Hunting & Fishing Tales — Adventure-packed stories for hunters and fishermen. Volume 4, 140 pp., 8½ x 11, $4.95

Sitka And Its Ocean/Island World — The heart of old Russian Alaska. Native culture, fishing, furs, wildlife. 128 pp., 11 x 8½, $9.95

The Skagway Story — Bright look at historical Skagway; many old photos. 165 pp., 8⅜ x 5⅜, $5.95

Smokehouse Bear — Great stories and recipes from Alaska. 180 pp., 7⅜ x 9, $5.95

Southeast: Alaska's Panhandle — Beautiful and informative look at southeastern Alaska's wilderness, communities, history and people. Color photos. 192 pp., 11 x 8½, $12.95

The Stikine River — Visual tour of the 400 miles of Stikine wilderness from the headwaters in British Columbia to the mouth at Wrangell, Alaska. 96 pp., 11 x 8½, $9.95

13 Years of Travel & Exploration In Alaska — By an early-day prospector. 105 pp., 5⅜ x 8⅜, $3.95

This Old House: The Story of Clara Rust — A house, a family and a town (Fairbanks) that grew. 262 pp., 5⅜ x 8⅜, $6.95

A Tourist Guide to Mount McKinley Revised Edition — By climber-scientist Bradford Washburn. Magnificent color and black-and-white photos. 80 pp., 8⅜ x 10⅞, $5.95

Two in the Far North — Margaret Murie's classic adventure is back in print with 3 new chapters on Alaska today and 40 drawings. 385 pp., 5⅜ x 8⅜, $7.95

Under Alaskan Seas, The Shallow Water Marine Invertebrates — A handy guide and an excellent reference book. 224 pp., 5⅜ x 8⅜, $14.95

We Live in the Alaskan Bush — True account of a young couple and their infant daughter. 135 pp., 8⅜ x 9, $7.95

A Whaler and Trader in the Arctic: 1895 to 1944 — Whale hunting and fur trading in the Far North and the characters the author ecountered. 213 pp., 5⅜ x 8⅜, $5.95

Wolves, Bears and Bighorns — Sensitive wilderness observations and an unusual insight into the life-and-death struggle of animals in the wild. 192 pp., 8⅜ x 10⅞; paper, $19.00, cloth, $25.00

Wood Stoves: How to Make and Use Them — Even how to tame a stubborn stove and build a barrel stove. Photos, diagrams. 194 pp., 5⅜ x 8⅜, $5.95

Wrangell-Saint Elias: International Mountain Wilderness — A colorful and in-depth look at this vast area that encompasses both Canadian and U.S. territory. 144 pp., 11 x 8½, $9.95